Identity and Repartnering after Separation

Also by Richard Lampard

PRACTICAL SOCIAL INVESTIGATION: Qualitative and Quantitative Methods in Social Research (*with Christopher J. Pole*)

Identity and Repartnering after Separation

Richard Lampard and Kay Peggs

First published 2007 by
PALGRAVE MACMILLAN
Houndmills, Basingstoke, Hampshire RG21 6XS and
175 Fifth Avenue, New York, N.Y. 10010
Companies and representatives throughout the world

PALGRAVE MACMILLAN is the global academic imprint of the Palgrave Macmillan division of St. Martin's Press, LLC and of Palgrave Macmillan Ltd. Macmillan® is a registered trademark in the United States, United Kingdom and other countries. Palgrave is a registered trademark in the European Union and other countries.

ISBN-13: 978–1–4039–3934–0
ISBN-10: 1–4039–3934–9

This book is printed on paper suitable for recycling and made from fully managed and sustained forest sources. Logging, pulping and manufacturing processes are expected to conform to the environmental regulations of the country of origin.

A catalogue record for this book is available from the British Library.

Library of Congress Cataloging-in-Publication Data
Lampard, Richard.
   Identity and repartnering after separation / by Richard Lampard and Kay Peggs.
      p. cm.
   Includes bibliographical references and index.
   ISBN 1–4039–3934–9 (alk. paper)
   1. Man–woman relationships.   2. Interpersonal relations.   3. Couples.
   4. Remarriage.   5. Unmarried couples.   I. Peggs, Kay, 1957–   II. Title.
   HQ801.L278 2007
   306.84—dc22   2007018262

10   9   8   7   6   5   4   3   2   1
16   15   14   13   12   11   10   09   08   07

Printed and bound in Great Britain by
Antony Rowe Ltd, Chippenham and Eastbourne

Contents

List of Tables

Acknowledgements

We thank Social and Community Planning Research (now the National Centre for Social Research) and the Wellcome Trust for allowing us to use data from the National Survey of Sexual Attitudes and Lifestyles 1990 (Field et al. 1995). We also thank the Office for National Statistics for permission to use data from the General Household Survey 2001–2002 (ONS 2006b), and from the ONS Omnibus Survey of April 2002 (ONS 2003b).

We also thank the UK Data Archive for providing us with access to the above data. None of the above bodies bears any responsibility for the further analyses and interpretations of these data in this book.

We would also like to thank everyone who has played a role in our research or in the production of this book, our transcriber, and most especially the women and men who agreed to be interviewed.

Acknowledgements

1
Introduction

In contemporary Britain, high rates of marital dissolution mean that many individuals spend one or more periods of their lives as separated or divorced people. Furthermore, the rising incidence of cohabitation means that at any given time, in addition to formerly married people, there is a substantial number of former cohabitees in the population. Until now, research has tended to focus on the formerly married rather than on formerly partnered people more generally, and has also concentrated on formerly married parents. Our book, however, is oriented towards formerly partnered people in general. Our main aim is to examine the experiences, identities, attitudes to repartnering and repartnering behaviour of formerly partnered people in a society in which profound changes have been, and are, taking place (or, at least, are argued to have been taking place) in relation to intimate couple relationships. Of course, continuities in ideals relating to 'marriage' also form part of the context in which formerly partnered people's identities and orientations towards relationships are, or are not, revised after separation, as do their own relationship histories.

In our research we have addressed the topics of identity and repartnering among the formerly partnered in an appropriately wide-ranging way, drawing on existing substantive and theoretical literature, and carrying out our own qualitative and quantitative analyses. This is reflected in the structure of this book, the content of which is outlined in this introductory chapter. A short description of the research project which ultimately led to this book is given in Chapter 2. We explain why we think it is important to study formerly partnered people and repartnering using both qualitative and quantitative methods, and outline the characteristics of the sample of formerly married people and former cohabitees who took part in in-depth, qualitative interviews. (The data used for quantitative analyses of repartnering behaviour and orientations are described in Chapter 4.) Chapter 2 continues by discussing how our interviewees were recruited, and by providing more detail of the content and nature of the interviews. We then reflect on the interview process, on the implications of the nature of interview data for what we can learn from it about our research topic, and on issues arising from the 'therapeutic' role that some interviewees ascribed to the interviews. The chapter concludes by commenting on the ways in which we approached the qualitative analyses of our interview data.

In Chapter 3 we set out a historical and theoretical context for the analysis of our data by highlighting significant changes relating to intimacy and couple relationships in the late twentieth century and by examining the theoretical literature on changing couple relationships. Unsurprisingly, given the decline in marriage and marital stability and a greater diversity among contemporary relationships, theoretical accounts emphasize change. In 'high modernity', societies such as Britain are said to be characterized by a greater level of individualism, which has contributed to a detraditionalization of intimacy. A key feature of contemporary relationships is said to be choice, more specifically the freedom to leave an unsatisfactory relationship. In Chapter 3 we discuss the work of Giddens, Bauman, Beck and Beck-Gernsheim, and Gross (among others), highlighting the relevance of concepts such as love, self-identity, commitment and insecurity. The views of such authors on the origins, extent and universality of the changes vary, and some regard the changes less positively than others do, but there appears to be a consensus within their work that contemporary couple relationships are less permanent and less clearly (or narrowly) defined; hence formerly partnered people are repartnering in a rather unpredictable (and hence perhaps 'risky') context.

The substantive focus of Chapter 4 is more limited, as we concentrate on the formerly partnered and repartnering, documenting in the first section of the chapter what is known about these topics from earlier research. For the most part we restrict our attention to Britain, but we also draw on key North American studies that contain important findings and valuable conceptual material. The studies examined exhibit some recurring (and overlapping) themes: the heterogeneity of formerly partnered people and their lives, ambiguity within the lives of particular individuals, various forms of marginality that are common but not universal, changes relating to identity and the self, issues of independence and control, and experiences of constraints. Often linked to these themes and of significance in its own right is the impact of past relationships. The first section of the chapter concludes with a summary of existing knowledge about repartnering orientations and behaviour. The second section consists of new quantitative analyses of social survey data that update or extend beyond earlier research on the formerly partnered and repartnering; the analyses pay greater attention to former cohabitees, and cohabitation in general, than most other studies, and include an examination of non-resident couple or sexual relationships and an examination of repartnering orientations.

We then move on to analyses based on our interviews with formerly partnered people. Chapter 5 provides an overview of the repartnering orientations of our interviewees and includes material relating to aspects of their lives that they perceive as being relevant (or potentially relevant) to their current or future repartnering behaviour. To a large extent the themes covered in this chapter reflect the broad content of the interviewees' own accounts: whether and why repartnering is currently on/off their agenda, its relevance (if any) in the period immediately following separation, the (heterogeneous) legacies of past relationships, the practicalities and acceptability of actively searching for a new partner, and preferred features of any new relationship and partner. However, the material echoes many of the theoretical ideas, concepts and substantive issues discussed in earlier chapters, with some of these being of explicit relevance (e.g. commitment, independence and non-resident relationships) and others implicit but clearly evident (e.g. identity and heterogeneity). At the end of the chapter there is a discussion of a typology of repartnering orientations derived from our interviewees' reported orientations and behaviour.

Chapter 6 takes a different approach to the analysis of our interview data by linking it to some concepts that have been argued to be of relevance to people's lives in contemporary Britain and elsewhere – namely, 'risk', emotions and choice. Past relationship experiences can undermine the sense of security of formerly partnered people and heighten their perceptions of the inherent risks of new relationships. Furthermore, since 'pure relationships', as described by Giddens (see Chapter 3), which end when a partner ceases to find the relationship satisfactory, have been argued to be a growing feature of contemporary Western societies, new relationships are said to be, and felt by many to be, inherently more risky. In addition to 'risk', the chapter considers emotions, rationality and control in relation to decision-making about new couple relationships, and reflects on the possibility that images of ideal relationships informed by traditional ideas such as romantic love and lifelong marriage are still important in this context.

Like the preceding chapter, Chapter 7 makes connections between our interview data and two linked concepts that are regarded as being of particular salience in contemporary societies: identity and the self. The end of a relationship often leads to marked changes in self-identity, self-esteem and lifestyle, and can change the ways in which individuals perceive themselves to be viewed by others, as well as the ways in which they view themselves. Identities are complex and multifaceted, as well as subject to change, hence the development (or rediscovery) of an independent, 'authentic' self-identity after separation can lead to a hesitancy to repartner, but being loved by another may be felt to be necessary for a positive sense of self, thus encouraging an individual to repartner. Pressure to repartner to regain a 'legitimate' identity may also come from a sense of being outside the norm in a society organized around couples. Thus we examine attitudes to self-advertising as a repartnering strategy, and the effects that such strategies have on an individual's sense of self. We also examine how gender, bodily appearance and ageing are connected to formerly partnered people's identities and views of repartnering.

In Chapter 8 we draw together the ideas and results from the earlier chapters, linking them to key themes. This final chapter is part-summary and part-synthesis, and aims to convey an impression of how our results and interpretations both differ from and also echo other theoretical work and earlier substantive studies. However, the chapter also has the straightforward objective of highlighting key features of formerly partnered people's lives, of their perspectives on repartnering and of their repartnering behaviour.

It is not our intention to offer advice to formerly partnered people about repartnering or their lives more generally. Nevertheless, we hope that our results are of interest to formerly partnered readers, since we are very grateful for the time and insights that our formerly partnered interviewees gave to this research.[1]

2
Methods and Methodology

This chapter starts with a brief overview of the research project that led to this book, then moves on to a discussion of its use of quantitative and qualitative methods. The rest of the chapter focuses on issues relating to the processes of data collection and data analysis, with a particular emphasis on key aspects of the qualitative component of the research, specifically the selection and composition of the sample, the interviews and issues relating to the analysis of the interview data.

The research study on the formerly partnered and repartnering

Our involvement in a research study focusing on the experiences and perspectives of formerly partnered women and men reflects in part our view that it is an interesting area to research, both academically and more generally. The origins of our research study lay in an awareness of the relative paucity of research on repartnering in contemporary Britain, coupled with an existing research interest in marital formation and dissolution more generally (Lampard 1992, 1993, 1994), and the potential availability of funding from an Economic and Social Research Council (ESRC) research programme on contemporary demographic change in the United Kingdom (see McRae 1999). As it turned out, funding for a research project was eventually received under the auspices of the ESRC's generic research grants scheme.[1]

The project's aims were to examine the socio-demographic composition of the formerly partnered population, to identify factors relevant to the decision to repartner and to investigate the perspectives of individuals within the formerly partnered population, on both repartnering and their socio-economic circumstances and position in society. The methods to be used were secondary analyses of a variety of existing quantitative data sources, in combination with qualitative research consisting of in-depth, focused (but open-ended) interviews. Furthermore, the integration of quantitative and qualitative approaches was a stated aim.

In addition to reflecting a recognition of the value of using qualitative and quantitative methods in a complementary way in social research in general (Bryman 1988; Pole and Lampard 2001), the mixed-methods nature of the project reflected an acknowledgement of the limitations of quantitative research as a way of gaining an understanding of couple relationship-related behaviour and processes, and the consequent value of combining qualitative and quantitative approaches when researching 'marital' histories (Lampard 1996). One of us had previous experience of working across the quantitative/qualitative divide (Peggs 1995, 2000), and both of us have ended up appreciating the merits – and limitations – of all aspects of our research in methodological terms.

Reflections on the use of quantitative and qualitative methods in our research

The broad aims of the research project necessitated the use of both quantitative and qualitative methods. More specifically, two of the project's objectives – documenting the socio-demographic composition of the formerly partnered population and identifying factors of demonstrable empirical relevance, in a statistical sense, to repartnering behaviour – required analyses of quantitative data. However, the third objective – gaining an understanding of the experiences of formerly partnered people, and of their attitudes and perspectives regarding their situation and regarding repartnering – required the generation of qualitative data.

The research design of the project was influenced by the idea that quantitative approaches to studying couple formation often neglect the perspectives of the people being studied, and was also influenced by the fact that the ranges of variables available in data from existing social surveys do not usually allow the consideration of important forms of heterogeneity in people's orientations towards the formation of couple relationships (Rajulton and Burch 1992). In contrast, qualitative research can facilitate a fuller understanding of the reasons why some people repartner by highlighting the perspectives of formerly partnered people as social actors (Bryman 2004: 279). To illustrate this, in addition to ascertaining the attitudes of formerly partnered individuals to the formation of new relationships, the qualitative aspect of our research sheds light on the actual incentives or disincentives to repartner perceived by formerly partnered people, as opposed to those that we, or earlier researchers, may have presumed to exist.

Various other issues illuminated by our qualitative interviews would have been difficult to study using quantitative methods: for example, the opportunities perceived by a formerly partnered individual to be available to them in terms of 'suitable' prospective partners, or the extent to which finding a partner is currently the primary concern of a formerly partnered individual. Our research shows that finding a partner often comes a poor second to issues such as employment, childcare or personal well-being. However, while a formerly partnered person's marital status (or, more precisely, relationship status) may or may not be central to their self-identity at a given point, contemporary Britain is still, notwithstanding substantial social and cultural changes, a society where couple relationships and 'families' are of profound personal, ideological and policy significance (Giddens 1992; Smart and Neale 1999; Allan and Crow 2001: 148–9). In this context, our project's qualitative dimension has provided us with insight into the ways in which our interviewees make (or made) sense of their status as formerly partnered people.

The advantages and merits of the qualitative side of our research should not be viewed as undermining the importance of our quantitative findings. Analyses of survey data from large, nationally representative random samples allow generalizations to be made about the characteristics and repartnering behaviour of the formerly partnered. However, in theory at least, there is something specific to be gained by attempting to mix quantitative and qualitative methods, over and above what can be achieved simply by using them alongside each other (Brannen 1992). Demographic analyses of repartnering behaviour, and the results of qualitative fieldwork focusing on the perspectives of formerly partnered people as social actors, can potentially be used in a linked way. For example, the quantitative data can be used to provide a contextual backdrop for results based on the qualitative data, and the qualitative data can facilitate the interpretation of observed quantitative relationships.

As noted above, one of the stated objectives of the research project was to study the repartnering process using quantitative and qualitative methods in a complementary and integrated fashion. Thus in this book (and elsewhere) we have tried to use quantitative and qualitative data in a complementary way. For example, we have constructed a sample of formerly partnered women and men from the General Household Survey which is a good temporal match with our qualitative sample. However, using quantitative and qualitative approaches in an integrated way is more challenging (Huby and Dix 1992), especially if the data do not correspond to the same individuals. The literature on integrating quantitative and qualitative data continues to develop (e.g. Bryman 2006; for a review, see Cresswell et al. 2002).

The qualitative sample

The sample size specified in the research proposal for the project was 80, including the pilot interviews. Since our early interviews appeared successful and sufficiently unproblematic, the pilot interviewees were included in the sample. In total, 81 people were interviewed.[2]

The reasons for recruiting a sample of this size were to facilitate adequate coverage of various subgroups of the formerly partnered population and to allow comparisons to be made between subgroups. However, while it had been estimated that a sample size of 80 would be feasible within the project's funded duration, in retrospect the large sample size put pressure on the research project in terms of time and human resources with respect to the fieldwork and also with respect to the analysis of the data generated.[3]

A numerical bias towards female interviewees in the research proposal had been argued by various people to be unjustified. Our aim in practice was, therefore, to ensure that both sexes were well represented. In the end, 31 of the 81 interviewees (38 per cent) were male. We view this as satisfactory, given that, as we shall show, markedly less than half of the formerly married population (and, we assume, a similar proportion of the formerly partnered population) is male. Clearly, however, it is not just gender that affects the experiences and attitudes of formerly partnered people. Other potentially relevant factors include age, the presence (or absence) of dependent children, employment status and social (occupational) class. Thus the 81 people interviewed cover a suitably wide range of ages, social classes and parental statuses. Focusing specifically on age, the research proposal for the project had specified an upper bound of 45 years, but in retrospect this seemed to provide too narrow a focus, hence we raised it to 60 years, and in fact a few interviewees were older than this.[4] Table 2.1 shows the age distribution and distribution of separation duration (the time elapsed since the end of their last co-residential couple relationship) of our interviewees.

As expected, widowed people, while not excluded from the sample, constitute only a handful (six) of 'case studies'. These interviewees can nevertheless serve to highlight differences and similarities between the experiences and perspectives of the widowed and those of other formerly partnered

Table 2.1   Interviewee characteristics

	Formerly legally married	Former cohabitees	Total
Age (in years)			
Under 30	3 (4%)	8 (57%)	11 (14%)
30–39	13 (19%)	6 (43%)	19 (24%)
40–49	25 (37%)	0	25 (31%)
50–54	22 (33%)	0	22 (27%)
55–59	1 (2%)	0	1 (1%)
60 or more	3 (5%)	0	3 (4%)
Separation duration			
Less than 1 year	12 (18%)	7 (50%)	19 (23%)
1–4 years	30 (45%)	5 (36%)	35 (43%)
5 years or more	25 (37%)	2 (14%)	27 (33%)

people. A more substantial subgroup consists of 14 former cohabitees. Of the remaining interviewees, 15 were separated and 46 divorced.[5]

Our original intention was to become increasingly selective as the field-work progressed, and to engage in something akin to 'theoretical sampling', wherein interviewees are selected according to their perceived relevance to the development of ideas and theory (Glaser and Strauss 1967; Pole and Lampard 2001: 37). However, while we acknowledge the desirability of purposive sampling tailored to the specifics of a project and reflecting ongoing theorizing (Lincoln and Guba 1985), an 'ideal' sampling approach may be neither appropriate nor viable. The idea of turning down volunteers made both of us feel uncomfortable, and being selective in this way would have made achieving the target sample size impossible. In addition, while we tried to recruit a diverse range of interviewees, at no point did we aim to recruit a qualitative sample that was strictly representative of the formerly partnered population since our intention was to complement our qualitative results with results from secondary analyses of more representative samples.

Notwithstanding our lack of concern about strict representativeness, it is still informative to compare our qualitative sample with background inform-ation about the formerly married population.[6] A comparison of the charac-teristics of our sample and relevant microdata from the 1991 Census Samples of Anonymised Records (SARs; Dale and Marsh 1993) indicates that the balance of women and men is about right, but also implies that working-class people are under-represented. We can only speculate about the reasons for this. It might be that the sample reflects a greater inclination among middle-class individuals to engage in a reflexive conversation with a stranger about their marital status and relationship history, and hence to volunteer to participate. However, it seems equally plausible that practical constraints may have contributed to the imbalance, for example in relation to working-class women with young children. Despite their under-representation, our qualitative sample contains a reasonable number in absolute terms of (occu-pationally) working-class people. Additionally, it contains very few people with professional occupations.

A further comparison with Census data, corresponding approximately to the qualitative sample in geographical terms, suggests an under-representation of people from minority ethnic groups. Apart from a few interviewees who identified themselves as belonging to 'white' minority ethnic groups, the sample contains only one other interviewee belonging to a minority ethnic group, rather than the half a dozen or so who should, *pro rata*, have been included. This shortfall does not reflect any form of deliberate exclusion. Although it is in many ways very regrettable, it does avoid the problems that would have accompanied the inclusion of a sketchy and inadequate picture of the specific experiences and attitudes of formerly partnered people from particular minority ethnic groups. Similarly, our qual-itative sample contains only one interviewee who defined him-/herself as homosexual. Again, our recruitment tactics did not intentionally differentiate according to sexual orientation. Hence, while it seems likely that, *pro rata*, we should have recruited more gay, lesbian or bisexual interviewees, a more focused recruitment approach would have been needed for us to have constructed a more diverse sample in terms of sexual orientation.

A comparison of the age distributions in Table 2.1 with data from the General Household Survey (GHS) (shown in Table 4.1, p. 84 below) indicates that our qualitative sample under-represents formerly (legally) married people aged under 40 and over-represents formerly married people aged 50 or more. There is nevertheless a substantial number of formerly married interviewees aged under 40 in absolute terms. A further comparison with the GHS data presented in Chapter 4 indicates that our sample contains disproportionately few interviewees who had been separated for five years or more, though this would seem to reflect to some extent the substantial number of interviewees who had separated in the year prior to their interview, a category who may have been particularly motivated to participate. Again, the absolute number of interviewees who had been separated for more than five years is substantial.

We were also able to make a comparison between data from the British Social Attitudes (BSA) surveys (Jowell et al. 1987, 1990) and data relating to the marriage and family-related attitudes of our qualitative sample, as measured by a short preliminary questionnaire. This comparison indicates that, in most respects, the sample has a similar range of attitudes to the formerly married population in general, though they are more liberal in their attitude to gay marriages and are less likely to view children as a central aspect of marriage.[7]

While it is a non-probability sample, and thus not representative, our interviewees appear fairly unremarkable in demographic and attitudinal terms. Crucially, the sample provides coverage of a range of social groupings, albeit not covering all possibilities. However, as is evident from the discussion of recruitment mechanisms that follows, our sample is very much an opportunistic one. As a sample of volunteers, it almost certainly over-represents formerly partnered people who are motivated to discuss their lives and situations, or who feel that they have something to gain by talking to a willing listener.[8]

Interviewee recruitment

Interviewees were recruited from a major city in the Midlands, and from towns and villages in the surrounding area. Sampling formerly partnered people, who form a relatively small subgroup of the population, and to some extent a transient subgroup, is not straightforward. Some of the planned means of recruitment, such as recruitment via lone-parent organizations and targeting single adult households on the Electoral Register, proved relatively ineffective. By far the most successful approach was the use of the local press. Advertisements and a short article together netted 33 interviewees (41 per cent). The advertisements made a vital contribution to the achievement of our target sample size. In addition, 21 interviewees (26 per cent) were recruited via posters circulated widely in the local area, or via publicizing our research within local organizations. Most of the rest (18 interviewees; 22 per cent) had heard of the research by word of mouth, in some instances from earlier interviewees. The remaining small minority of interviewees were recruited directly by Kay, in the case of six interviewees, or responded to an Electoral Register-based mail-shot, in the case of three interviewees.

At various stages we considered a number of other recruitment mechanisms, such as targeting local workplaces, a strategy used successfully by Smart and Neale, who also recruited separated and divorced parents via solicitors (1999: 41). Another alternative would have been to respond to personal advertisements. This, however, would not only have raised ethical issues regarding appropriate ways of approaching potential interviewees, but would have also generated interviewees who were actively looking for a partner. Our experience of recruiting our qualitative sample suggests that a desire to construct a sample with what is perceived as an 'ideal' composition should be balanced with a pragmatic approach oriented towards achieving an acceptable sample size. An eclectic approach has the benefits of facilitating sample diversity and maximizing the pool of potential interviewees. In contrast, attempting to generate a properly random sample of a population such as the formerly married appears to be an impractical endeavour, as is illustrated by an initial, abortive attempt to construct a random sample in a study of divorced mothers in the United States (Arendell 1986: 161).

The gender balance of our research team ensured that prospective interviewees could be interviewed by someone of a specific sex if they expressed a preference. In practice, this arose as an issue only once.

The interviews

The interviews with members of our qualitative sample were focused, in-depth and open-ended. They investigated the interviewees' views on repartnering, in addition to covering their relationship histories and current situations, and also gave interviewees the freedom to talk about a wider range of topics relating to their day-to-day lives and to couple relationships. A certain amount of structure was needed to achieve a degree of comparability between interviews in relation to key issues. This limited standardization was facilitated by an A4 sheet of topics relating to aspects of the interviewee's past, present and future. This acted as an aide-mémoire in relation to material that might usefully be covered.

In part as a consequence of the use of this list of topics, but as might anyway be expected, the content of the interviews bore some resemblance to the range of issues evident in the existing literature on the formerly partnered and repartnering. However, the content of our interviews was not bounded by this range of issues. As the complexity and sensitivity of issues such as relationship dissolution, widowhood, lone parenthood and searching for a partner necessitated a flexible approach, and since we intended to adopt something akin to a 'grounded theory' approach to analysing our interview data (Glaser and Strauss 1967), the emphasis of the interviews was on listening to what the interviewees wanted to say.

As a preliminary each interviewee completed a short questionnaire (four A4 pages in length), via which we collected some demographic and attitudinal information. The latter was based on questions relating to marriage adapted from the British Social Attitudes surveys (Jowell et al. 1987, 1990). The questionnaire aimed to collect a limited amount of standardized information, in part to allow any idiosyncrasies of our sample relative to the corresponding broader population to be identified.

The interviews took place during the eight-month period January–August 1996. The interviewees chose the interview location, which in the majority of cases, perhaps surprisingly, was one of our offices. Each interview started with a short discussion with the interviewee about the research, and interviews often concluded with a 'debriefing' session, which was sometimes lengthy. In between these 'book-ends', the interviews were taped, with this part varying in length from under one hour to well over four hours.

The original intention had been to employ a local, full-time audio-typist to transcribe the interviews. However, in practice, it would have been impossible to have maintained a steady flow of taped interviews, and in any case we decided that a local person would be inappropriate, for reasons of confidentiality and anonymity. Therefore, the majority of the interviews were transcribed as piecework elsewhere in the country, and we transcribed the rest.

Reflections on the interview process

The level of rapport between interviewee and interviewer varied, as did the emotional intensity of the interview, depending on the specifics of interviewees' past experiences and their feelings about them. However, typically, interviewees seem to have felt able to discuss sensitive issues with either interviewer. Interviewees sometimes provided feedback on their experience of being interviewed during the formal, taped interviews or the less formal conversations that often followed. We also solicited feedback some months after the interviews. Our interviewees typically found talking about their experiences and feelings interesting, enjoyable and/or worthwhile. The interviews were often a positive experience for the interviewer too, although they sometimes left us feeling drained or worn down by 'information overload'.

When asked to reflect on the relevance of the interviewer's gender, inter-viewees seemed to perceive other characteristics as more important, such as being open, able to empathize, visibly interested, non-judgemental and difficult to shock or offend.

Interviewees often commented that the interview had given them a welcome, for some rare, opportunity to talk about things that mattered to them, or even referred to it as 'therapeutic'. One interviewee said, 'I've never really talked about these things before and it's made me think'; another observed, 'The interview has been interesting. I've been focusing on how I felt'. In a later section we reflect on some of the ethical and methodological issues arising from similarities or parallels between interviews and explicitly therapeutic encounters.

The value that many of our interviewees attached to an opportunity to 'tell their stories' in the presence of a willing listener also highlights the pertinence of various points made by Day Sclater when discussing her research on divorcing people. She observed that interview 'narratives' are jointly produced by the interviewee and interviewer. They may also reflect the interviewee's active construction of a self-identity (1999: 116) and their desire to construct a plausible, comprehensible and justifiable account of past events and actions (1999: 160–1). In the next section we reflect on the nature and limitations of our interview data with reference to ideas from published literature relating to the active roles of interviewee and interviewer in the production of knowledge via interviews (Holstein and Gubrium 1997; Mauthner and Doucet 2003; Riessman 2004).

The nature and limitations of our interview data

In narrative interviews (Riessman 2004), the dialogue between interviewee and interviewer generates 'stories' of interviewees' experiences, whether at the level of particular events or of their entire lives (Riessman 2004: 709). In Riessman's research on divorce and gender, which used semi-structured interviews, she found that interviewees linked together different themes and issues in long, coherent, sequential accounts (Riessman 1993: vi, cited in Bryman 2004: 411). A desire to avoid fragmenting these led her to employ narrative analysis techniques focusing on whole stories, rather than a them-atic analysis drawing on material from interviews with different interviewees.

Riessman stresses that narratives are a collaborative product of joint meaning-making by a narrator and a listener/questioner (2004: 709). Simil-arly, Holstein and Gubrium conceptualize interviews as sites of joint knowledge production rather than conduits to convey information from interviewees, viewed as 'vessels of answers' (1997: 113–16). From their perspective, attempts to maintain 'neutrality' as an interviewer, and to develop a questioning approach and interview atmosphere 'conducive to open and undistorted communication' (1997: 116), cannot successfully address problems of interview bias or ineffectiveness. What is instead required is 'self-conscious attention to the interview process and its product' (1997: 114), given that interviews do not generate 'reality reports from a fixed repository' (1997: 127).

According to Riessman, 'narrators' make sense of their experiences and construct their identities in ways that involve their audiences (2004: 708). The narratives generated are interpretations of the past, which also reflect how the narrators want to be known. Holstein and Gubrium note that research subjects mediate the knowledge that they convey (1997: 117), consciously monitoring who they are in relation to their interviewers (1997: 122). In our interviews it was sometimes very evident that interviewees were self-conscious about, or consciously shaping, their presentation of self.

Viewing our interview transcripts from the perspectives of authors such as Riessman, Holstein and Gubrium highlights their constructed, context-specific and holistic nature. However, as Holstein and Gubrium point out, the 'meaning' of information obtained by an interview is 'neither predetermined nor absolutely unique' (1997: 121), and viewing an interview transcript as a situation-specific product does not prevent the researcher from relating its content to interviewees' lives and experiences (1997: 127). Similarly, Mauthner and Doucet (2003: 423) suggest that research encounters can allow the researcher to grasp *something* of interviewees' experiences and subjectivities, although they suggest that the status of subjects' accounts as reflexive products of the interaction between researcher and researched means that the subject is always incompletely known. The reader should also bear in mind the inherent assumptions and limitations of our thematic analyses, as these atomize stories within comparisons across interviewees.

Mauthner and Doucet comment that it is dangerous to assume that interviewees' words provide 'transparent passageways' through which their selves and experiences can be accessed by the researcher (2003: 423). Birch and Miller (2000: 194) suggest that an interviewee's disclosure of emotions and feelings can give the researcher the sense that they have accessed the interviewee's 'authentic self', but query whether more personal necessarily means more authentic (2000: 200). Similarly, Holstein and Gubrium suggest that disclosure of 'deep feelings' may induce a sense of mutual understanding, but does not transcend the situation-specific status of interviewees' accounts (1997: 119–20). Joffe (1999: 111–12) suggests that self-reports cannot provide a complete picture of emotional life, although they can contribute to an understanding of its subjective dimensions. She concludes that theoretically-driven analyses of interview data are required if the researcher is to go beyond conscious representations of emotions (1999: 115).

Mauthner and Doucet suggest that researchers should situate themselves socially, emotionally and intellectually in relation to their interviewees' accounts (2003: 419–24). Mauthner reflects on the impact on her conceptualization of motherhood of her lack of personal experience, reporting that it led to a negative conceptualization, strongly influenced by particular strands of existing literature. Our lack of personal experience of divorce or parenthood at the time of the fieldwork may similarly be pertinent. Doucet suggests that particular feminist perspectives led her to romanticize women's 'voices' and 'subjectivities'. Similarly, familiarity with feminist analyses of marriage and the family may have influenced our responses to our interviewees' subjective accounts. In addition, an awareness of, but ambivalence to, the emphasis on children in much of the existing literature relating to formerly married people may have influenced our views on the likely importance of children to interviewees' identities.

Interviews as 'therapeutic opportunities': issues in research on personal lives

Birch and Miller (2000: 190) suggest that interviews, like therapeutic encounters, can create a space for individuals to reinterpret past experiences in the presence of a listener in a way that may lead to a changed sense of self. They note the 'blurred boundaries' between the activities of researchers and those of other 'experts' (2000: 200). The popularization of a therapeutic culture (Furedi 2004) may increasingly be leading to individuals using research interviews as a context for their 'reflexive projects of self' (Giddens 1991), and an interviewer may thus unwittingly take on the role of mediating a therapeutic process (Birch and Miller 2000: 198). Birch and Miller reflect on what interviewers' responsibilities are in relation to the 'therapeutic opportunities' that arise in interviews, and whether the interviewer can or should avoid being assigned to a therapeutic role by the interviewee (2000: 199). They express concern about interviewers encouraging interviewees to voice their experiences without having the professional skills to deal with the consequences of doing so (2000: 197), and suggest that researchers exploring intimate topics should be prepared to support interviewees in accessing professional help, or to consider providing support themselves (2000: 200).

Some interviewees were motivated to participate in our study simply by the prospect of discussing an interesting topic, but others were explicit that part of their motivation was the opportunity to talk about their past experiences in a way that would be helpful to them. More specifically, they wanted to discuss unresolved issues, or sought some form of catharsis, or wanted to talk about the past in a holistic way to a single listener, or to reflect on past events in a different way, or to talk to an 'outsider' who was 'neutral' or at least uninvolved in their life. However, these interviewees, like many others, sometimes expressed a desire to 'make a contribution', to 'help' the researchers and/or other people in similar situations to themselves. In some instances interviewees conceptualized the interview as an exchange, with the information they were providing being bartered for the opportunity to talk.

Interviewees who had not anticipated that their interviews would be of therapeutic value sometimes reported experiences that echoed the motivations of those who had. They appreciated having had the chance to open up to an interested listener, or to explore issues relating to their past in a fresh way. One interviewee hoped that 'at least some of what I said was of interest [given] the fact I got so much out of unburdening my troubles'. Another could 'see now why so many people go to counselling'. However, while one interviewee observed that it 'made me feel good about myself', they noted that under other circumstances 'it could have had the reverse effect'. Another interviewee wondered, 'Were you prepared to deal with anyone who got really upset ...?' In fact, we anticipated that it was likely that some interviewees would become distressed and thus we offered interviewees the possibility of the tape-recorder being switched off, if at any point they preferred this, we aimed to allow ample time for non-recorded discussion, before, during or after the interviews, and we compiled and provided (where appropriate) a list of contact details relating to individuals and organizations that offered support and information.

Mason (1996: 56–8) highlights ethical issues relating to research on sensitive topics where interviewers gain interviewees' trust. She suggests that interviewers need to monitor whether interviewees are revealing more than it is in their interest to reveal, noting that the researcher may be perceived as a 'friend', leading to the interviewee sharing information that they would not otherwise reveal to someone acting in a professional capacity (1996: 166). Mason points out that a sense of mutual trust and understanding akin to that in a friendship does not absolve the researcher from their professional responsibility to protect their interviewee's interests.

In our study, some interviewees viewed the discussion of sensitive or painful issues as constructive, and hence as a problem to be managed rather than something to be avoided. Even when interviews brought unpleasant and unwelcome memories to the surface, interviewees did not usually regret participating. However, such interviewees often had clear expectations regarding the interviews, occasionally making clear their disinclination to discuss certain issues. Other interviewees were opening up about particular past issues for the first time, or had not been conscious of their 'pent-up feelings', or may not have foreseen that perceiving the interviewer as a 'good listener' would lead them to divulge things that they had not told or would not tell anybody else. The experience of carrying out our study highlighted the fact that some interviewees are markedly more conscious of, and better prepared for, the potential consequences of research participation than others are. Some interviewees were careful to check our credentials or discuss the issue of anonymity.

Frequently, interviewees continued to reflect on issues discussed in the interviews, highlighting the partial and contingent nature of interview data, but also stressing the need for researchers to be prepared to deal with any 'after-effects' of the interviews. Interviewees sometimes contacted us later, wanting to talk further. While this was sometimes, explicitly or implicitly, for their own 'therapeutic' benefit, it did not usually seem necessary to suggest alternative, properly qualified forms of support. Doing so felt like passing the buck. Being prepared to listen seemed an appropriate *quid pro quo* for the interviewees' input to the research. Listening to them could also be an interesting and positive experience; however, for a researcher to be prepared to provide support by listening only if they feel well disposed towards an interviewee might justifiably be viewed as discriminatory. Conversely, providing support in the manner of a 'friend', but primarily out of a sense of obligation as a researcher, seems potentially deceptive, as well as likely to be problematic in the long run.

After the interviews

While ESRC funding was obtained for a cross-sectional, one-off piece of research, the point was made in the research proposal that there might be scope to transform the qualitative sample into a longitudinal panel that could later be interviewed again. This would allow data to be generated on changes in attitudes and perspectives over time, as well as on actual repartnering processes. When the proposal was written this kind of life history-oriented qualitative study, exemplified by Wallerstein and Blakeslee (1989), seemed to be growing in popularity.[9]

At the end of the interview, all but one of our interviewees expressed a willingness to be contacted again. We made an effort to collect a reliable set of contact addresses, with the intention of keeping this up-to-date as far as was practically possible. For a couple of years we attempted to keep in touch with our interviewees via Christmas cards, on the first occasion soliciting any reflections that our interviewees had on the experience of being interviewed. However, while we had superficially kept the option of a longitudinal study open, in practice we simply did not have the time and resources to capitalize on this. Furthermore, an absence of rapid output from the research meant that we had little to offer by way of a progress report, and little chance of obtaining funding for follow-up interviews. In addition, after a few years had passed, a check (using an electronic resource based on the 2001 Electoral Register) suggested that we no longer had reliable addresses for a substantial minority of the interviewees, although some of these appeared to have moved locally.

Qualitative data analysis: strategies and approaches

Chapters 5, 6 and 7 make extensive use of data from our qualitative interviews. Similarities and differences between the approaches to qualitative analysis adopted in the chapters reflect their specific aims. Chapter 5 provides an overview of the interview data in relation to repartnering and to aspects of the lives of formerly partnered people of relevance to repartnering, and incorporates a 'repartnering typology', developed on the basis of inter-viewees' orientations and behaviour. Chapters 6 and 7 relate the interview data to particular theoretical issues of contemporary prominence, namely 'risk', decision-making, emotions and self-identity.

Thus, while in each of these chapters our analyses reflect our interviewees' perspectives as expressed in the interviews, Chapter 5 is more 'data-driven' than the more 'theoretically-driven' Chapters 6 and 7. However, as Bryman (1988: 85) observes, even qualitative research that espouses the principles of 'grounded theory' (Glaser and Strauss 1967) is unlikely to be conducted in a 'theory-neutral' way. Hence the analyses in Chapter 5 can be viewed as reflecting in part, and implicitly, a pre-existing theoretical orientation, which in turn reflects in part theoretical orientations within the existing literature. Conversely, the content of Chapters 6 and 7 is as much determined by what our interviewees had to say about issues of 'risk' and identity as it is by the theoretical ideas of other authors.

Notwithstanding the valuable role that qualitative data analysis software can play in contemporary social research, our experience from this study is that effective and systematic analyses of interview data can be carried out using generic word-processing software, even when the interview transcripts are extensive and numerous. The value of the framework that more specific software provides for a researcher's analyses is, perhaps, open to question.

3
Theorizing Contemporary Intimate Couple Relationships and Relationship Histories

Introduction

To provide a framework for our analyses, in this chapter we examine changes in and theories about contemporary intimate relationships. Thus, as a setting for some of the later chapters that outline our empirical results, here we discuss the theoretical literature on the changing *nature* of intimate couple relationships (e.g. the effects of increased choice that are said to accompany increased individualization), the changing *patterns* of such relationships (e.g. shifts between relationship formations based on marriage and cohabitation) and changes in the *course* that such relationships take (e.g. how relationships move through phases that can lead to relationship dissolution and the search for a new relationship). Thus change is a focus of this chapter and is central to discussion about intimate couple relationships in Western societies. Change is a key feature of existing theoretical material (drawn from both sociology and related disciplines) that is of relevance to an understanding of the past lives, present situations and future plans of formerly partnered people.

In the first half of this chapter we examine changes that have taken place in intimate couple relationships, and we follow this, in Chapter 4, with a more detailed examination of the characteristics, situations and repartnering behaviour of the formerly married and former cohabitees in Britain. In this chapter, in order to contextualize the theoretical positions discussed later, in addition to examining policy initiatives and changes in couple relationship formation and dissolution, we refer briefly to research on adults' experiences of post-partnership life and children's perspectives on post-partnership family life. Although we have come to think of change as 'normal' (Beck and Beck-Gernsheim 1995: 146), it is not necessarily welcomed in all situations or by all those involved. This is clearly the case in relationship dissolution, where often each of the partners involved will have a different perspective on the changes that have been chosen or imposed, and different experiences of the resulting changes in their lives. Moreover, children often have little say in the dissolution of adult relationships,[1] but changes imposed rather than chosen still have significant consequences for their present and future lives. In the second half of the chapter we explore theoretical explanations for the recent changes in partnership formation and dissolution. Here we explore theories about the nature of contemporary relationships that focus on concepts such as Giddens' (1992) notion of the 'pure relationship', Bauman's (2000b) concept of 'liquid love' and the work of Beck and Beck-Gernsheim (1995), who speculate on the role that individualization plays in contemporary intimate couple relationships. Such theories centre on the detraditionalization of intimate relationships and, by way of a critique, we explore Lewis's (2001) multifaceted conceptualization of commitment and Gross's (2005) challenge to the suggestion that detraditionalization wholly explains the conspicuous changes that have occurred in intimate couple relationships in recent decades.

Although we focus on change, and much of the initial discussion focuses on changes in marriage and divorce, it is not our intention to overstate the recent changes, since marriage as an institution has been in constant change. In this respect, marriage can be seen as a 'shell institution' (Giddens 1992), an institution that, according to Giddens, though ever-changing, masquerades as static. Thus thinking about the changes in contemporary intimate couple relationships and relationship histories is an interesting and wide-ranging task. Reflection on this complex area involves consideration of a range of couple relationships, the ways they form, proceed and often dissolve. We begin by exploring intimate couple relationships in Britain today, and in doing so provide a summary of the current situation regarding couple relationship formation and dissolution and new partnership formation.

Changing couple relationships in Britain

In this section we provide an overview of two broad changes relating to couple relationships and new partnership formation: changing trends in couple relationships; and the changing nature of the relationship 'life course' or 'conjugal career' (Furstenberg and Spanier 1984: 47). Evidently, the first impacts on the second; people experience a multifaceted and diverse context in which to search for a partner and a complex set of social circumstances in which to maintain a couple relationship. Thus intimate couple relationships are complex, perhaps especially so for those who have had unsuccessful partnerships in the past. Relationship dissolution is commonplace and the experiences of past partnerships lead to caution and reluctance to enter a new couple relationship (Frazier et al. 1996); however, forming a new partnership is the choice of many and to enter a new couple relationship is a way of recovering from the negative consequences of previous relationship dissolution (Willitts et al. 2004). Thus the situation is dynamic and complex and new partnership formation cannot be viewed outside the lens of wider trends in relationship formation and wider discourses about the consequences of such changes.

Although couple relationships have always been a site of change (Lewis 2001), recent changes – and notably lower marriage rates – have been accompanied by much alarmed interpretation (e.g. Akerloff 1998; Fukuyama 1999). Shifts in rates of marriage (in Britain a legally sanctioned heterosexual couple relationship) have often been conflated with changes in the family (often seen, even in sociology, as a social group comprising adults overseeing the bearing and raising of children). Thus anxieties about lower marriage rates have centred on disquiet about family change and, as Lewis points out, disquiet about family change has itself centred on the implications, especially for children, of men who seem able to saunter away from family responsibilities, and of women who are seen as more interested in their careers than in their families (2001: 3). So concerns about lower marriage rates and higher divorce rates are entrenched within discourses that identify marriage as being the only appropriate context for having and raising children. Although, as Lewis argues, it might be that '[t]he "facts" of family change are real and are hard to exaggerate', whether family change amounts to family breakdown is open to question (2001: 4). The main outcome of family change is the increase in lone motherhood (Lewis 2001: 4), but we do not agree that this amounts to family breakdown since transformed family groupings are not inevitably any less loving or caring. Thus we are inclined to Carrington's view that the family consists of 'people who love and care for one another' (1999: 5). In consequence we do not embrace narrow definitions of the family or confine our discussion of intimate couple relationships to marriage. In our discussion, intimate couple relationship dissolution covers the dissolution of intimate couple relationships that were previously co-resident, including gay, lesbian and heterosexual couples in state or religiously sanctioned partnerships and also partnerships external to such sanctions. Though we recognize the relatively recent emergence of living apart together (LAT) relationships, while no less intimate and important, such relationships fall outside the definition of the living arrangements of those in intimate couple relationships that we used as a condition for inclusion in our sample of interviewees.

Those searching for future couple relationships are doing so in a fluid and changing setting. As has been well documented, studies of relatively recent changes in the nature of couple relationships in Britain reveal more people living alone, fewer marriages, increased marital dissolution, increased lone parenthood and more cohabitation (Murphy and Wang 1999: 100). In 2004 seven million people (29 per cent) in Britain were living alone, a fourfold increase on the 1961 figure (ONS 2005: 2). Though the rise in the proportion of one-person households has slowed since 1991 the proportion of such households has nevertheless more than trebled since the 1960s for paid working-age people (ONS 2005: 2). Regarding first marriage rates, there have been striking changes since the 1960s, when marriage was almost universal (Lewis 2001: 131). In 1961 in England and Wales marriage rates per 1,000 single people were 74.9 for men and 83.0 for women, compared with 25.5 for men and 30.5 for women in 2004, although the 2004 rates represent a very slight increase on those for 2002 (ONS 2006a: Table 9.1). Although married couples remain the main family type in the UK, between 1996 and 2004 the number of married couple-headed families fell by 4 per cent, whereas the number of cohabiting couple families increased by over 50 per cent (ONS 2005: 1). Other indicators of a decline or delays in the occurrence of marriage are also in evidence. For example, between 1961 and 2004 the average mean age at first marriage in England and Wales rose from 25.6 to 31.4 years for men and from 23.1 to 29.1 years for women (ONS 2006a: Table 9.1). In terms of divorce, in 2004 the UK experienced a fourth successive annual increase in its divorce rate, though the increase was modest at 0.2 per cent (National Statistics Online 2005). Although the number of divorces peaked in 1993 (180,018), in 2004 there were still 167,116 divorces, the highest number since 1996, although still 7.2 per cent lower than in 1993 (National Statistics Online 2005).

The declining preference for marriage is explained in part by the increasing acceptance of divorce and cohabitation (Bumpass 1990; Cherlin 1992; Lewis 2001; Jones and Carvel 2005). As marriage is increasingly seen as a voluntary and less permanent arrangement (Furstenberg and Spanier 1984: 53), individuals are now more able to leave a marriage that is unsatisfactory. Maintaining choice is thus an important aspect of relationship formation since the majority of people in Britain expect to be able to divorce if their marriage is unacceptable and changes in divorce laws have endorsed the right of partners in a marriage to decide whether to divorce (Lewis 2001: 113). Thus, though perhaps still based on a 'close and continuing tie to another' (Giddens 1992: 58), in general couple relationships are no longer seen as for life and the idea of a 'till death us do part' commitment perhaps 'looks ever more like a trap that needs to be avoided at all costs' (Bauman 2003: 90).

As indicated above, changes in divorce rates have been explained in terms of the increasing acceptance of divorce (Cherlin 1992; Nakonezny et al. 1995; Scott 1999; Lewis 2001; Jones and Carvel 2005) and above all this has been linked to the acceptance of 'partial no fault divorce'[2] (hereafter termed no fault divorce), which continues to be the hub of divorce law in the UK (Lewis 2001: 117). No fault systems endorse the view that a marriage may be unwanted even though neither partner is at fault (Maclean 1991: 78). Before 1971, one partner in a divorce case was seen as guilty of a matrimonial offence or 'fault' (Hart 1976). Enforced in 1971, the Divorce Reform Act 1969 in England and Wales replaced matrimonial offence with 'irretrievable breakdown' of marriage as the sole ground for divorce. The 1969 Act 'represented a compromise between the legal and religious establishments' (Lewis

2001: 106). The religious establishment had long been concerned about the view of marriage as an individual matter rather than a vocation; the recognition of the importance of the marital *relationship* was seen as threatening the notion of marriage as permanent (Macmillan 1944, cited in Lewis 2001: 107). However, the negative consequences are contested. As we will see, there are many rewards associated with the view that a meaningful loving relationship is a more important goal than marriage (e.g. Giddens 1992). 'The emphasis on marriage as a relationship, and particularly the importance attached to a satisfactory sexual relationship, was blamed for [marriage dissolution] alongside "modern psychology" that stressed the importance of "self-expression"' (Lewis 2001: 108). However, legal reformers acknowledged the importance of the marriage 'relationship', with the attendant view that the legal apportioning of fault in personal relationships was impossible (Lewis 2001: 116). As we will see in the theoretical discussion below, concerns about the implications of this more individualized couple relationship remain (e.g. Bauman 2003). Although there have been attempts to preserve marriage (Lewis 2001) and marriage continues to function as a regulative tradition in moral communities such as the Christian Church (Gross 2005: 297) it seems likely that that no fault will remain the bedrock of divorce law (Lewis 2001) as 'each generation that has entered adulthood is less religious than its predecessors' (Voas and Crockett 2005: 24). The move to no fault divorce has been cited as a partial explanation for the doubling of the number of divorces in the UK one year after the law came into force, to 124,991 in 1972 (National Statistics Online 2005). Although early research in the US suggested that more restrictive or more liberal divorce laws had little impact on the trend in divorce (Abel 1973; Wright and Stetson 1978), recent research in Britain suggests that the switch from fault divorce to no fault divorce has led to an increase in the divorce rate (Nakonezny et al. 1995).

Divorce is now a more common event, affecting a substantial proportion of the population in England and Wales – approximately 14 couples per 1,000 annually (Haskey 1999: 18). Furstenberg and Spanier argue that high divorce rates are not a sign that marriage as an institution is being devalued; rather, such rates are a sign of the reverse (1984: 53). Since, in a cultural system that values individual caution and emotional fulfilment, divorce is now an essential aspect of the marriage system (Furstenberg and Spanier 1984; Phillips 1988; Furstenberg and Cherlin 1991), it represents an optional stage in an increasingly varied 'conjugal career' (Furstenberg and Spanier 1984: 47). Divorce is thus a system by which individuals are permitted a chance to improve their marital situation (Furstenberg and Spanier 1984: 53), but the standards of what constitutes an acceptable and satisfying marriage have risen (Furstenberg and Spanier 1984; Spanier and Thompson 1987). Yet, confluent with the legal acceptance of entitlement to a satisfactory marriage is the personal responsibility to try to repair an unsatisfactory marriage. The reduction of the time bar for a petition for divorce from a discretionary three years to a mandatory one year by the Matrimonial and Family Proceedings Act 1984 was intended to encourage reconciliation (Lewis 2001: 117), and the Family Law Act 1996 emphasizes that each marital partner is responsible for sorting out their affairs, particularly regarding any children, *before* seeking a divorce (Lewis 2001: 115). Thus, with the use of mediation, '[h]usbands and wives are assumed to be able to negotiate and communicate as equals' (Lewis 2001: 115).

The extent of gender equalization in marriage and divorce is disputed. For example, Karney and Bradbury (1995) conclude that gender differences in marriage have been exaggerated, and Yodanis (2005) contends that the possibility of divorce provides women with the leverage to gain more equal status within marriage, with the option of divorce (and thus leverage) being greater for women in paid work. However, other studies suggest that men and women have different expectations and experiences of marriage (see, for example, the pioneering work of Bernard 1976) with wives and husbands, especially those who are mothers and fathers, rarely having an equal relationship within marriage, during the break-up of marriage or during divorce. This is largely due to assumptions about the central role of mothers and of fathers; mothers as carers and fathers as providers.

Two matters exemplify relevant inequalities between partners. The first relates to the unequal division of work, both paid and unpaid, with the allied notion of the male breadwinner. Although the male as sole earner has rarely been realized except in middle-class families (Brannen and Nilsen 2006) there are nevertheless differences between the paid work of mothers, which is frequently discontinuous and part-time (Brannen et al. 2004, cited in Brannen and Nilsen 2006), and that of fathers, which has remained mainly continuous, full-time and connected to the concept of the male as breadwinner (Warin et al. 1999; Lewis 2000 – both cited in Brannen and Nilsen 2006). Even though Yodanis (2005) reports that in countries where divorce is accepted and practised the distribution of work between women and men in marriage is more equal and Cherlin (1992) argues that a woman's work outside the home reduces her economic dependence on her husband thus making it easier for her to end an unhappy marriage, Lewis is sceptical since she finds little evidence that women earn enough to be self-sufficient and economically independent (2001: 5). The Matrimonial and Family Proceedings Act 1984 no longer requires the courts to try to place each divorced spouse in the financial situation that they would have been in had the marriage not broken down. Rather, the courts are required to stress the need for the self-sufficiency of each of the individuals involved. However, divorce has driven many women into poverty (Saul 2003: 10). Although there have been very recent improvements in the situation of divorced women in general (see McKeever and Wolfinger 2001), a high proportion of divorced mothers live below the poverty line. Since mothers are usually given custody of children, as lone parents they 'continue to face the difficulties in the workplace that come from being a primary caregiver' (Saul 2003: 11). In consequence, the worry about financial welfare after divorce can lead women to hesitate about leaving a marriage, even when the marriage has become violent (Okin 1989; Saul 2003).

The assumed role of women as carers means that, after divorce, mothers are more likely than fathers to be granted custody of children. Almost a quarter of families with dependent children are lone-parent families, and, in 2004, nearly nine out of ten lone parents were mothers (ONS 2005: 1). This brings us to our second point about the attendant problems of assuming the equality of partners at the break-up of marriage and during divorce. In this context there have been recent discussions and campaigns, not least by the pressure group Fathers for Justice, about the sense of inequity suffered by fathers regarding access to their children after divorce. The notion of the male breadwinner family has given way to the companionate family (Lewis 1992, 2001); indeed, Gillis (2000) notes a marginalization of fatherhood in Western countries. He talks about a 'crisis of the breadwinner father', suggesting that this, along with the feminization of the home, has weakened men's ties to their children (Gillis 2000). Although research suggests that fathers generally have increasing involvement in their children's lives, it seems that this has been concomitant with an increase in mothers' involvement in childcare (O'Brien and Shemilt 2003). Beyond the directive that separated and divorced fathers take financial responsibility for their children, fatherhood has been little addressed in public policy in Britain (Brannen and Nilsen 2006: 337). While motherhood is ordinarily perceived as caring in essence, fatherhood is a vague concept that has yet to acquire concrete meaning (Hacker 2005). In consequence, conservative family law systems discourage men from assuming an expansive parental role after divorce (Hacker 2005). However, the 'heavy reliance' of lone mothers on state benefits and minimal financial support made by absent fathers have been of central concern to successive governments (Lewis 2001). For example, the Child Support Act 1991 attempted to force fathers to support their biological children financially (Kiernan et al. 1998). Thus, Lewis contends, such new initiatives 'focused, albeit with little success, on securing the male breadwinner role of all fathers, no matter what their marital status' (2001: 115). Consequently many women, and especially mothers, suffer poverty as a result of divorce (Saul 2003). A major factor here is a legal framework that consolidates gendered social expectations about women's and men's parental roles, which in turn makes men disinclined to assume an unreserved parental role after divorce (Hacker 2005).

It is not only divorce that has been referred to as a situation of distress. A bad marriage has also been characterized as a site of possible anguish and suffering for all concerned. For example, though divorce may impact negatively on the well-being of those involved, Hawkins and Booth (2005) show that low-quality marriage also has a significant negative effect on overall well-being and, indeed, contend that there is no evidence that those who remain in unsatisfactory marriages are better off in any facet of overall well-being than those who divorce. In consequence, unhappily married people may have a higher probability of improving their well-being by dissolving their unsatisfactory marriages (Hawkins and Booth 2005). Regarding children, Lewis notes that the British Medical Association took the view in the 1960s that divorce was *not* as harmful to children as a bad marriage (2001: 108). For children and adults divorce can be described, in the terminology of Thomson et al. (2002), as a 'critical moment', or as a 'fateful moment' in Giddens' (1992) lexis. For men and women, 'moments' such as divorce can bring about the start of a new phase (Smart 2005). Notwithstanding the problems mentioned above, for men divorce can mark the establishment of a new relationship with children (Hobson 2002) and for women the moment of returning to their 'old selves' (Smart and Neale 1999). Thus divorce can be positive in its consequences and the justification for the final acceptance of no fault divorce was the effects of adversarial divorce procedures on children (Lewis 2001: 115). The overriding concern with the welfare of children has led Lewis and Maclean (1997), among others, to declare that concomitant with the law becoming increasingly disinterested in the adult partners in a divorce is the regulation of their relations as parents. Thus married parents wishing to divorce must arrange issues concerning their children, with the customary insistence being that they continue with their responsibilities as mothers and as fathers (Lewis and Maclean 1997; Lewis 2001). Although Stacey (1996) suggests that children gain through divorce since their horizons are widened, usually divorce is depicted as detrimental to children's well-being (Cockett and Tripp 1994; Amato and Booth 1997). Smart (2006) notes that children's living standards after divorce are said to drop if they reside with a lone mother (Maclean 1991) and children become distressed if they are introduced to a succession of stepfathers (Flowerdew and Neale 2003). Although other research contends that divorce has no noticeably detrimental effect on a child's well-being (Bengston et al. 2002), the children in post-divorce families interviewed in Smart's study 'articulated a loss and impoverishment which was not just economic but relational' (Smart 2006: 168). Smart (2006) suggests that this might be due to some extent to what Gillis (1996) declares to be the difference between the *actual* families we live with and our *imagined* vision of the idealized conventional family, since the children in her study had a mental picture of the responsibilities of parents and what a 'correct' childhood should be.

Marriage, commitment and cohabitation

Changes in partnership formation reflect and strengthen a fundamental shift in attitudes and expectations (Scott 1999: 69) and expectations of marriage (and other relationship formations) have clearly changed (Lewis 2001: 5). Scott (1999) observes that although individual choices are constrained by gender, age and socio-economic circumstances, the scope of acceptable and feasible relationship and family options seems to have expanded a great deal. Cohabitation has become one of the most common life-course transitions in Western societies (Bumpass and Sweet 1989) and for Kiernan and Estaugh (1993) this is a 'spectacular indicator' of changes in traditional family life. Xu et al. refer to a '1980s cohabitation boom' (2006: 261) and by 2004 the number of cohabiting couple families in the UK was 2.2 million (ONS 2005: 1). Indeed, the actual figure may be higher since, argue Manning and Smock (2005), current measurement strategies probably underestimate cohabitation.

Research on the nature of and commitment in cohabiting relationships is divided. There are many forms of cohabitation, thus interpretations based on an assumed homogeneity are problematic. For example, cohabitation can be partial or full and can be a forerunner of, a successor to or an alternative to marriage (Meuleman 1994, cited in Lewis 2001). Though cohabitation has become, for a minority, an alternative to marriage (Bumpass and Sweet 1989; Rindfuss and Vandenheuvel 1990; Ermisch and Francesconi 1998), Manning and Smock (2005) find that the movement into cohabitation is not akin to marriage and is often not a deliberate decision. Couples do not appear to be deciding between cohabitation and marriage; rather, their decision seems to focus on whether to remain single or to cohabit. However, there are disparities connected to gender. Smart and Stevens' (2000) research indicates that for poorer female cohabitants, cohabitation is seen as a logical alternative to lone motherhood or marriage to an unsuitable man. Other research reports differentials relating to age. King and Scott (2005) report that older cohabiting people are more likely to view their relationship as an alternative to marriage, while younger cohabiting people are more likely to view their relationship as a forerunner to it. Popular cultural representations of marriage have been seen as having an extremely influential effect on the rise of cohabitation as an alternative to marriage. Richard Kane (the founder of National Marriage Week) condemns the 'horror stories' about marriage, which he argues have put people off marriage and have made cohabitation more attractive (Jones and Carvel 2005). He maintains that 'For couples who are living together fairly happily, who are reluctant to get married, it may be because they are scared that it may go wrong' (Kane, quoted in Jones and Carvel 2005). Although recent trends indicate that an increasing percentage of cohabitations are not becoming marriages (Wu and Balakrishnan 1994), cohabitation frequently precedes marriage (McRae 1999: 3) and in Britain, well over half of those who intend to marry cohabit (Haskey 1995). Indeed, living together before marriage is now the norm (Scott 1999: 69).

Gillis (1985) suggests that when cohabitation is used as a forerunner to marriage it is similar to the traditional period of engagement and thus provides some security against entering into a legal bond with an unsuitable person. This trial period, which is usually relatively short (Murphy and Wang 1999: 101), fulfils many of the psychological functions of marriage (Newcomb 1987). For example, cohabitation fulfils the 'need' to be in a union (Becker 1981). However, some theorists view this union as a less committed one since during this trial period the relationship can be ended if either partner is dissatisfied. Cherlin suggests that the 'spread of cohabitation involves the spread of an individualistic outlook on intimate relations' (1992: 16). Certainly, research suggests that, in general, cohabitants are likely to embrace non-traditional attitudes and values (Clarkberg et al. 1995) and are likely to place a high value on independence (Lye and Waldron 1997). However, researchers also point out that conclusions about the associations between cohabitation and commitment are far from clear-cut. The meaning of cohabitation varies (Lewis 2001: 41). Waller and McLanahan advise that if couples view cohabitation as a step towards marriage, cohabiting before the birth of a child may represent a stronger commitment to the relationship than living apart, making early separation less likely (2005: 57). King and Scott (2005) found that there are also age differences. Older cohabiting people report significantly higher levels of relationship quality and stability than younger cohabiting people, although they are less likely to have plans to marry their partners. Few differences are found in the reasons to cohabit, although assessing compatibility is a more important reason for younger cohabiting people (King and Scott 2005). Smock (2000) argues that people who cohabit serially are less family-oriented, more materialistic and more accepting of divorce, and Clarkberg et al. (1995) suggest that those who cohabit are more likely to have poor relationship skills, low levels of commitment and high levels of intolerance (Clarkberg et al. 1995). Though Lewis (2001) observes that the penchant in research is to view the leaning as towards independence in cohabitation and towards relatedness in marriage, she notes that in all forms of couple relationship, including marriage (Askham 1984) and pre-marital cohabitation (de Singly 1996), tension exists between independence and relatedness.

Any attempt to attribute homogeneity of attitudes to cohabitation is problematic since cohabitation has different meanings for different groups (Manting 1996). However, though there are differences between groups (see Lewis 2001), data on cohabitation reveal that cohabitation is more insecure and unstable than marriage (Lewis 2001: 37; Xu et al. 2006) and various reasons for this have been put forward. Wu and Schimmele (2005) argue that because most people enter marriage believing that it is a permanent arrangement, marriage usually lasts substantially longer than cohabitation. It has also been suggested that individuals who choose to cohabit prior to marriage have different needs and attitudes from those who form a marriage without prior cohabitation (Clarkberg et al. 1995). Differences in values have also been suggested (Clarkberg et al. 1995), as has a rise in individualism (discussed below) and less commitment, said to be evidenced by Hall's (1996) study, in which he suggests that cohabiting relationships come nearest to Giddens' (1992) notion of the 'pure relationship' (discussed below). Moreover, research suggests that cohabiting relationships that do convert into marriage are associated with lower marital quality and a higher risk of divorce (Smock 2000). Such research is contested and the effects of relationship dissolution can be as severe for cohabiting people as for married couples. Separation from cohabitation can be an extremely emotionally distressing process and the consequences (financial or otherwise) can be severe. Avellar and Smock (2005) found that formerly cohabiting men's economic standing declines moderately after separation, whereas formerly cohabiting women's declines much more precipitously, leaving a substantial proportion of women in poverty. Thus, they conclude, though the end of a cohabiting relationship reinforces gender stratification, it is also an 'equalizer', since it leaves married and cohabiting women in conspicuously similar economic positions.

A greater number of divorces, rising cohabitation and more living alone do not imply that marriage is obsolete; many marriages today are remarriages rather than first marriages, although cohabitation after divorce may be extending the period between divorce and remarriage (Glick and Spanier 1980; Xu et al. 2006). Indeed, Alcock (1984) observes that the aim in promoting a clean break for adults was in large part to facilitate remarriage. It is to remarriage and repartnering, the focus of our work, that we now turn. Much of the research to be discussed has focused on marriage and remarriage and though repartnering will be discussed (and some of the results from the studies mentioned can be useful for thinking about repartnering generally) the greater part of the discussion is based on divorce and remarriage. In Chapter 4 we discuss in more detail the empirical literature on repartnering behaviour in Britain, but in this chapter we draw on a wider, international literature to provide a backdrop for our discussion of theoretical ideas regarding relationship change.

Remarriage and repartnering

In contrast to North America, where the formerly married and remarriage have long been the focus of research (e.g. Hunt 1966), there has, until recently, been a paucity of comparable research about Britain. Research in recent decades has documented demographic patterns of remarriage and repartnering in Britain (e.g. Haskey 1993; Ermisch and Francesconi 1998) and studies have shown that, although divorced people are less disposed to marriage than the never married (Frazier et al. 1996) and remarriage rates have fallen (Lewis 2001: 40), many still want to marry, even after the dissolution of a previous marriage (Beck and Beck-Gernsheim 1995: 171). Evidence from the US reveals that post-divorce cohabitation, especially with multiple partners, delays remarriage (Xu et al. 2006: 261), so increased post-divorce cohabitation has led to a decline in the remarriage rate (Cherlin 1992; Xu et al. 2006). As in North America, in England and Wales there is an asymmetry between divorced men and women in their likelihood of repartnering (Haskey 1999: 19). Though by definition the numbers of men and women divorcing are equal, subsequently there are differences between divorced men and divorced women in the proportions cohabiting, remarrying and remaining divorced (Haskey 1999: 19). Divorced men, and (as Coleman and Salt 1992 remind us) separated men, are more likely than women on average to repartner either by remarrying or via cohabitation (Haskey 1999: 19). This gender difference in the propensity to repartner is also reflected in the timing of repartnership since men, on average, enter a new couple relationship more rapidly than women (Wu and Schimmele 2005: 34). Duration of first marriage is linked to remarriage propensity and timing (Bumpass et al. 1990; Sweeney 1997). Women whose first marriage lasted longer may be more marriage-oriented and therefore may remarry sooner (Becker et al. 1977). Individuals with a long first marriage have been married for much of their adult life and this may influence their ability to adapt to a single life (Bumpass et al. 1990).

In 1961 in England and Wales the numbers of divorced men and divorced women remarrying were 18.8 thousand and 18.0 thousand respectively (ONS 2006c: Table 9.2). The numbers subsequently increased considerably, as a consequence of the growing population of divorced people and in spite of declining remarriage rates from the early 1970s onwards, but by 1986 the numbers of men (83.4 thousand) and women (80.0 thousand) remarrying had reached a peak. Despite the continuing growth of the divorced population, an ongoing decline in remarriage rates meant that, by 2004, 74,700 divorced men remarried compared with 72,500 divorced women (ONS 2006c: Table 9.2). Repartnering after divorce becomes increasingly less likely with rising age, especially for women (Haskey 1999). In 2004 the mean age at remarriage for divorced men was 44.9 years compared with 41.9 years for divorced women (ONS 2006c: Table 9.2). At younger ages, women's remarriage rates in 2004 were greater than men's, at 109.3 per 1,000 divorced women for women aged 16–24 and 94.0 per 1,000 for women aged 25–29, compared to 67.5 per 1,000 and 86.3 per 1,000 for men of the same ages (ONS 2006c: Table 9.2). However, the gender differentials are inverted from age 30 upwards, with the remarriage rate in 2004 being 87.8 per 1,000 for men aged 30–34 compared with a rate of 81.1 per 1,000 for women of the same age (ONS 2006c: Table 9.2). By age 45 and over the gender differential is dramatic, with the rates for men and women being 30.9 per 1,000 and 17.9 per 1,000 respectively (ONS 2006c: Table 9.2). Of course, this final age range is extremely broad. Repartnering through cohabitation also becomes progressively less likely with increasing age, especially for women (Haskey 1995; Shaw and Haskey 1999). Thus, Haskey predicts, the differential between the likelihood of divorced men and divorced women repartnering will increase since, in the latter decades of the twentieth century, men and women tended to divorce at progressively older ages (1999: 19).

In addition to remarriage being associated with age and gender, remarriage rates are often linked to parental status (Bumpass et al. 1990); however, as shown in Chapter 4, this is made more complicated by age. Moreover, Clarke et al. (1993) highlight the potential relevance of childbearing 'plans' to remarriage patterns. North American research has typically found that the presence of children and/or a greater number of children is linked to a lower rate of remarriage among formerly married women (e.g. Bumpass et al. 1990; Wu and Balakrishnan 1994; see also Lampard and Peggs 1999: 444). Again there is a gender asymmetry. In Britain, demographic research has indicated that a divorced woman's likelihood of remarrying is associated with the number of children she has (Ermisch 1989). However, though Ermisch found that having four or more children reduced the likelihood of a woman remarrying, results were not straightforward for women with fewer than four children. Further research by Clarke et al. (1993) suggests that the likelihood of remarrying is higher for divorced women with no children than for those with one or two children; moreover, 'less socially competent' children can make courtship difficult for divorced mothers (Hetherington, Cox and Cox 1985). Our results reveal that, for women, the presence of young co-resident children reduces the possibilities for repartnering due to the consequential constraints on the time that can be spent searching for and investing in a new couple relationship (Lampard and Peggs 1999). However, results from other studies are inconsistent with some of the above results. Mott and Moore (1983) found that the presence of children is not a significant predictor of remarriage, and Wu and Schimmele found that the presence of young children does not hamper women's possibilities for couple formation (2005: 34).

Although the effect of children on men's repartnering prospects has been less scrutinized and the evidence is inconclusive (de Graaf and Kalmijn 2003), Wu and Schimmele found that, in contrast to women, the presence of young children *increases* men's chances of forming a non-marital couple relationship, which they note is consistent with Stewart et al.'s (2003) observations that being perceived as a 'good father' enhances men's chances of repartnering (2005: 34). As mothers are more likely than fathers to gain custody of a child after divorce or separation (as discussed above), any effects of children on the possibility of remarriage affect women disproportionately. As we have seen, divorce severely disadvantages women, and women and children do much worse financially than men after separating from a partner (Jarvis and Jenkins 1999). Maclean (1991) shows that the main cause of post-divorce poverty in female-headed households is the absence of a male wage-earner and this is particularly the case where dependent children are present. Thus for many divorced women, poverty means that a 'marital search' (Hutchens

1979) is an economic necessity, since remarriage may provide a necessary addition to income from employment (Maclean 1991: 71). As well as causing appalling difficulties, poverty conflicts with a positive self-identity. In her study in Canada, Power (2005) found that lone mothers are constructed as 'Other', as 'welfare bums' and as 'flawed consumers', who do not have the financial resources to participate in the consumer market. Impoverishment is a source of exclusion and embarrassment for many lone parents (e.g. see Richards 1989) to which, Collins (1991) and Shaw (1991) suggest, remarriage may offer a solution.

For women, whether lone parents or not, earlier studies cite the lack of financial resources as a prime motivator in the wish to remarry (e.g. Spanier and Thompson 1987). However, earlier studies have tended to examine the economic situation immediately after divorce (Weitzman 1985) and thus have generated evidence showing dramatic financial losses for women (Maclean 1991: 70). The picture is more complex, e.g. women who are employed full-time have greater economic independence and therefore have a lower probability of remarriage (Mott and Moore 1983). Financial dependence on men has traditionally been assumed to protect women from poverty (Glendinning and Millar 1992: 7), but, since dependence is irreconcilable with individual freedom (Hockey and James 1993), even among women who experience financial difficulties as a result of divorce, many prefer an independent life without the additional domestic responsibilities associated with remarriage (Maclean 1991: 70–1). The feeling of economic independence that creates an incentive for women to leave a bad marriage also reduces the likelihood that she will remarry for financial gain (Mott and Moore 1983). For feminist theorists a woman's economic dependence on her husband is crucial in maintaining her subordinate position in society (Delphy 1984). Hakim's (1996) research shows that financial equality depends on a wife's full-time employment. Despite increases in women's employment, women are still heavily over-represented among those who have a reduced, little or no independent income (Joshi et al. 1995). For women, income dependence is strongly influenced by domestic care and the consequences this has for earning power (Joshi et al. 1995). Since more women than men are secondary earners they are more often financially dependent on another person or on state support (Hakim 1996: 66). So, Lewis (2001) argues, as women's earnings are, on average, lower than men's, women's increased activity in the labour market does not necessarily lead to economic independence; thus perceptions of financial gain could be a motivator for remarriage for some impoverished women.

The break-up of an intimate relationship can have both positive and negative consequences. As we have seen, for women divorce can lead to an 'independent life' (Maclean 1991) and research shows that for widowed women freedom from caring is an advantage of the death of a partner (Lopata 1996; Davidson 2001; van den Hoonaard 2001). Regarding negative consequences, lone mothers can suffer impoverishment (Lewis 2001), and divorced people in general suffer greater physical and mental health problems (Zick and Smith 1991) and greater loneliness (Amato 2000). However, research with women divorcees in midlife shows that the impact on health is different for those who said that they initiated the divorce, those who held that they were victims of divorce and those who said that divorce was a mutual decision (Sakraida 2005). Though remarriage may also introduce new problems, such as conflicts with children (Furstenberg and Cherlin 1991), one way of recovering from the negative impacts of divorce is to enter a new relationship (Holden and Smock 1991; Amato 2000; de Graaf and Kalmijn 2003; Willitts et al. 2004). However, this is not necessarily easy. People who want a new partnership after relationship dissolution may enter a more restricted 'marriage market' than they faced when they were younger (de Graaf and Kalmijn 2003). Rodgers and Conrad (1986) note that, while there are well-defined courtship norms for the young never-married, there is a lack of such norms for formerly married people. In addition, they observe, the past relationship experiences of the formerly married, along with the influence of parents, children and ex-spouses, impact on the courtship patterns of the divorced (Rodgers and Conrad 1986).

Those who want to repartner have diverse relationship histories (Kim and McKenry 2000) and differing degrees of social, cultural and physical capital, and they face people with similar diversity. The type of previous relationship – that is, whether it was a cohabiting relationship, a marriage that ended in divorce or one that ended in the death of a partner – influences the process of repartnering (Wu and Schimmele 2005). Cohabiting unions are frequently short-term arrangements (Nock 1995), involving partners who have low levels of economic consolidation and a more egalitarian division of labour (Lye and Waldron 1997; Batalova and Cohen 2002). Former cohabitees are often younger and have fewer children than divorced people (Wu and Schimmele 2005). They are often looking for cohabitation rather than remarriage and they repartner faster than divorced people (Wu and Schimmele 2005). However, when post-divorce cohabitation takes the form of a short-lived sexual union (Smock 2000) it may be synonymous with a courting relationship (Rindfuss and Vandenheuvel 1990) and thus 'serves as a springboard to remarriage' (Xu et al. 2006: 262). Widows and widowers have greatly reduced chances of repartnering (Wu and Schimmele 2005). The gender/age structure imposes a serious constraint on the repartnering process, especially for women (Smith, Zick and Duncan 1991; Davidson 2002). Moreover, other factors such as inter-family conflict may thwart new relationship formation (Lopata 1980). Wu and Schimmele (2005) conclude that the widowed are slower to repartner than the divorced, and those who were previously cohabiting repartner fastest. Whatever the type of previous relationship, the situation is said to be more difficult for heterosexual women than for heterosexual men. As a man ages there is an increasing pool of women potentially available for a new partnership (Burch 1990). In contrast, as women get older, an obstacle to forming a new partnership is the shrinking pool of men (Johnson and Troll 1996; de Graaf and Kalmijn 2003).

Whether male or female, for repartnering to take place a partner must be found (Mott and Moore 1983). Needs, attractiveness and opportunity have been presented as determinants of partnership formation for the never-married as well as for the formerly married (Becker 1981; Mott and Moore 1983; Goldscheider and Waite 1986; Oppenheimer 1988; de Graaf and Kalmijn 2003). Regarding needs, a partnership might enhance well-being in various ways, including socially, economically and physically (de Graaf and Kalmijn 2003). The chances of repartnering are enhanced if a person is perceived to be attractive (Goldscheider and Waite 1986). Indeed, physical attractiveness is a potent determinant of who is seen as a socially acceptable partner (Sutphin 2006). Other attractiveness 'factors' relating to previous relationships are also important. The conjugal history of prospective partners affects attractiveness to others (Raley and Bratter 2004) as does the presence of children (de Graaf and Kalmijn 2003). Raley and Bratter (2004) assert that, in general, people are less inclined to marry someone who has been previously married and de Graaf and Kalmijn argue that 'potential partners may perceive the experience of divorce itself to be a negative signal' (2003: 1468). Conversely, Berger and Kellner (1964) maintain that people typically approach second marriage with the same idealized image that most couples have in their first marriage, and Furstenberg and Spanier (1984) cite this as one reason why some divorced people prefer to marry someone with previous marriage experience. Strohschein et al. (2005) claim that healthy people are more attractive to others, and since it has been suggested that divorced persons have more psychiatric health problems (Mastekaasa 1995, Thuen 2000) and poorer physical health this may have a negative effect on repartnering. Indeed, Spanier and Furstenberg's (1982) research shows that people who report a high level of psychological well-being are somewhat more likely to remarry. However, Mastekaasa (1995) concludes that, while divorce is generally associated with a low level of psychological well-being, the effect seems wholly temporary.

The third suggestion is that the probability of repartnering depends on opportunity. Marital history affects choice and opportunity (Raley and Bratter 2004). People with prior relationship dissolution often have greater difficulties meeting others due to their changed network and social activities (Kalmijn and Bernasco 2001). This is because, in general, divorce (and to a lesser extent separation after cohabitation) has a negative effect on social integration, although the effects are not as strong as often believed (Kalmijn and van Groenou 2005). New partners are often found through leisure activities or social networks (Kalmijn and Flap 2001). The presence of dependent children may mean that people go out less and thus have fewer opportunities to meet potential partners (Wallerstein and Blakeslee 1989). The effects are, however, not unambiguous. For example, the effects of paid work on women's remarriage prospects are said to be both positive and negative: negative because paid work reduces the need for a partner, but positive because work outside the home increases opportunities to meet people (de Graaf and Kalmijn 2003).

Although women are generally less likely than men to remarry, regardless of financial difficulties or lack of opportunities, it should not be assumed that women desperately want to repartner and that the only reason they do not is because, as some suggest (e.g. Haskey 1991), they are unable to find a partner (Shaw 1991). As we have seen, older women are less likely to remarry than their younger counterparts and than men. Remarriage figures are often interpreted as showing that, in contrast to a man, a woman's chances of remarrying deteriorate rapidly as she ages, particularly after her mid-thirties (Haskey 1991). However, this assumption fails to question whether women actually *want* to remarry (Shaw 1991). Davidson (2001) found that for widows freedom from looking after someone is a major reason for not wanting a new partnership. In interviews with divorced women, Shaw (1991) found that none suggested that they might be too old or unattractive to remarry or would not be able to find a partner; rather, they were often reluctant to remarry because they were cautious, felt a lack of trust of others or were afraid of being hurt again. Extra-marital relationships had often led to the dissolution of the previous marriage, and anger about being hurt and deceived led to wariness of another marriage. However, some women were positive even in the light of previous negative experiences (Shaw 1991). Prominent among reasons given for considering remarriage were pressures to remarry from others, being alone, being lonely, needing someone to discuss things with, wanting someone else to make decisions, longing for someone to laugh with, habit, the need for stability and the desire for physical (although not necessarily sexual) contact (Shaw 1991: 151).

For those who do remarry, remarriage is not the same as first marriage. Berger and Kellner (1964) observe that although all marriages involve the construction of a common worldview or *nomos*, remarriage means that individuals must revise the *nomos* of their first marriage and create a new *nomos* for the subsequent marriage. Thus the long-term process of disappointment and disconnection from a previous marriage is very important in the experience of a subsequent marriage (Berger and Kellner 1964). Furstenberg and Spanier note four reasons for dissimilarity between first and subsequent marriages: the long-lasting effects of the first marriage on the second, with the former marriage acting as a criterion against which to evaluate the latter marriage; continued interaction with the previous spouse, especially if there are dependent children; constraints and expectations resulting from life-course experiences; and the exposure of a remarried individual to different marriage cohorts and consequent cultural standards of how a marriage should operate (1984: 54–5). Remarried people are more likely to get divorced than people in their first marriage, and the levels of marital satisfaction in remarriages are not on the whole as high as they are in first marriages (White and Booth 1985). However, remarriage is associated with greater well-being among men and women (Spanier and Thompson 1987: 232), and men who do not remarry seem to suffer greater social isolation and ill-health than equivalent women (Bumpass et al. 1990). Other studies suggest that there are no differences in mental health following remarriage (e.g. Booth and Amato 1991) though there may be some limited benefits (Simon 2002). Remarriage is quite common among lone parents (Haskey 1983) and research in Europe (Maclean 1991) and the United States (Duncan and Hoffman 1985) suggests that remarriage offers an economic solution for divorced women, including lone parents. The arrival of a stepfather may provide financial support for the whole family (Hetherington 1989). However, the effect of remarriage on the economic situation of female lone parents is by no means straight-forward. For example, although remarriage improves the financial circum-stances of many lone parents (Maclean and Eekelaar 1983; Zick and Smith 1988) in some cases the opposite is true – widows, for example, may lose their pension entitlements. In a small-scale study, Burgoyne and Morison (1997) found that for some women the economic inequalities experienced in first marriage seemed to follow into remarriage, but some women had managed to maintain their financial autonomy. Remarriage can solve the loneliness felt by some lone parents (Colletta 1983; Crosbie-Burnett 1989; Collins 1991). The arrival of a stepfather may provide emotional support for the mother (Hetherington 1989) and remarriage can offer relief from the isol-ation that lone childrearing brings, since remarriage may offer a sharing of the burden of childcare as well as emotional support (Collins 1991). Turning to the effects of remarriage on children, the entry of *a* stepfather (as we have noted, the presence of multiple stepfathers can be a source of distress) has beneficial effects in many instances, since he can provide emotional support (Montgomery et al. 1992: 696). However, Montgomery et al. suggest that cohabiting prior to remarriage has a less negative effect on child–parent rela-tionships than rapid remarriage, because cohabitation can provide a more gentle transition since the rapid switch to remarriage provides little time for children to adjust (1992: 696).

*

The preceding discussion has provided a brief overview of some of the research that has explored the changing nature of couple relationships, and has indicated some of the complexities involved. The next section explores theoretical explanations for the changes that have been discussed.

Theoretical perspectives on the changing nature of couple relationships

Couple relationships are complex. Changes in the legal framework and the broadening of attitudes and norms about the characteristics of 'acceptable' intimate relationships and suitable ways of leaving such relationships have led to much discussion about the associated problems and compensating benefits. Much of the discussion has focused on the notion of a decline in marriage as an institution (Bumpass 1990), a concern noted in numerous studies (e.g. de Graaf and Kalmijn 2003). It is not our intention to engage with this since our focus is not on marriage but on intimate, co-resident couple relationships and repartnering after the end of such relationships. Transformations in couple relationships have occurred, and continue to occur, in the context of more general changes in contemporary Western societies. Thus we turn our attention to theories relating to changes in society and concomitant transformations in couple relationships. Most of the theories of transformations in intimate relationships in high modernity focus on 'intimacy as detraditionalized relative to 50 or 100 years ago' (Gross 2005: 287). However, theoretical positions are varied. In his overview Gross (2005: 287) contends that perspectives have centred on the role of social movements in shaping intimacy (Stacey 1998), how intimacy is structured by late capitalism (Hochschild 2003), how the changes mirror the liberalization of attitudes (Giddens 1992), how the transformations are tied to individualization (Beck and Beck-Gernsheim 1995) and how the changes are bound to the culture of postmodernity (Bauman 2000b). Want of space prevents us from examining all these positions in detail. Here we focus on those most pertinent to our study. It is to the work of Giddens, Beck and Beck-Gernsheim, and Bauman that we now turn. We begin with the somewhat optimistic take on the condition of contemporary intimate couple relationships expounded by Giddens.

Giddens: The transformation of intimacy

Anthony Giddens has much to say about intimate relationships in Western societies. Like the other theoretical positions discussed below, his analysis (1991, 1992) focuses on change. He argues that there has been a positive and democratic process of development in intimate relationships, from passionate love, through romantic love to confluent love. In his discussion of this transformation he introduces concepts such as the 'pure relationship' and 'plastic sexuality'. We examine each of these in turn.

From passionate, through romantic to confluent love

Passionate love, Giddens argues, is a more or less worldwide phenomenon that expresses 'a generic connection between love and sexual attachment' (1992: 37). Although passionate love is liberating in its expression of a break in duty and routine, it is problematic since it may 'lead the individual, or both individuals, to ignore their ordinary obligations' (1992: 38). Giddens likens the disruptive essence of passionate love to charisma with its 'temporary idealisation of the other' (1992: 39); consequently, though exhilarating, for Giddens passionate love is not an adequate foundation for a lasting couple relationship like marriage. In modern Western societies the more enduring emotion of romantic love was seen as a more acceptable basis for such relationships. As we will see, when talking about romantic love Giddens expresses himself in the past tense as he argues that romantic love has been superseded in high modernity by confluent love (discussed below).

Though the more culturally-specific notion of romantic love incorporates elements of passionate love, it entails an emotional involvement deeper than that found in passionate love since romantic love prevails over passion (Giddens 1992: 40). Thus it is more appropriate to enduring relationships since it 'provides for a long-term life trajectory, oriented to an anticipated yet malleable future; and it creates a "shared history"' (1992: 45). For Giddens the idea of this romantic 'narrative' is important since it enables the individual to move beyond the temporary by enabling the individual to locate her- or himself in the romantic story, important if a relationship is to last (1992: 39). Thus romantic love 'became a potential avenue for controlling the future as well as a form of psychological security (in principle) for those whose lives were touched by it' (1992: 41). This is because romantic love presumes 'a meeting of souls' since it involves a 'quest' for confirmation of our self-identity in the site of the other because the other answers a 'lack' in the individual (1992: 45). Thus, for Giddens, it is through this 'meeting of souls' that 'the flawed individual is made whole' (1992: 45). Though still incorporating the idealization of the other person (as in passionate love), romantic love presumes reflexivity, that is the constant self-interrogation of one's own feelings, desires and actions and examination of the feelings, desires and actions of others (1992: 44). It is through reflexivity that individuals remain open to change. However, Giddens suggests that romantic love was 'essentially a feminised love' (1992: 43), the basis of much romantic fiction. In such fiction the search for romance, the 'quest-romance' (Thompson 1989), is foremost and 'sexual encounters are seen as detours on the way to an eventual love relationship' (Giddens 1992: 50). This 'quest-romance' is active in that it rests on an engagement with the future (1992: 51). Romantic love and marriage were seen as connected and the 'quest' involved finding that 'special person'. Thus, '[r]omantic love ... is a gamble against the future, an orientation to the control of future time on the part of women who become specialists in matters of ... intimacy' (1992: 57). Giddens suggests that such an orientation is the province of older women, who are guided by marriage (1992: 53). For older women, marriage was a way of breaking away from the family and of achieving a measure of autonomy. However, Giddens suggests, younger women refer to *relationships* rather than to *marriage*, with a meaningful loving relationship being viewed as the most important goal (1992: 52). Men have also been influenced by the 'ideals of romantic love', but in a different way (1992: 59). Male 'romantics' do not treat women as equals; rather, they become 'specialists in love' as a technique of seduction (1992: 60). Thus '[f]or women, dreams of romantic love have all too often led to grim domestic subjection' (1992: 62). However, Giddens concludes, under the pressure of female sexual emancipation and autonomy in high modernity the ideals of romantic love tend to fragment, with an attendant progression to confluent love (1992: 61).

For Giddens, confluent love has emerged out of the ideals of romantic love, but with fundamental differences. Most importantly, confluent love is ever open to change; it is reflexive (Giddens 1992: 61). Confluent love is associated with a shift in the primary quest from finding that *special partner* to finding that *special relationship* (1992: 62). In consequence, intimate sexual encounters are no longer talked about in terms of a narrative (that is, as a connection to an envisaged future), but rather are viewed as sporadic episodes (1992: 49). Giddens (1992) argues that, in contrast to romantic love (which fixes on and idealizes another person), in confluent love the importance of the individual virtues of the loved one is diminished since the spotlight is turned on the virtues of the relationship itself. So, Giddens (1992) argues, a relationship based on confluent love has a democratic and egalitarian foundation since considerations are centred on the shared and agreed views of the people involved. The relationship is more reflexive and less constricting. These key features of a couple relationship provide the groundwork for what Giddens calls the *pure relationship*, which, according to Bauman (2003), is the prevailing form of relationship today.

The move to pure relationships

For Giddens, a pure relationship is one that is 'entered into for its own sake, for what can be derived by each person from a sustained association with another; and which is continued only in so far as it is thought by both parties to deliver enough satisfactions for each individual to stay within it' (1992: 58). Though they are not confined to intimate couple relationships, since pure relationships can also exist in the context of friendships (Giddens 1991: 98), we concentrate here on intimate couple relationships.

For Giddens (1991), the pure relationship epitomizes relationships in the post-traditional order of high modernity. In high modernity the shielding cocoon of the small community gives way to remote organizations, with the consequence that individuals feel isolated and devoid of a sense of security (1991: 33). It is within the context of this post-traditional order that the self and self-identity become reflexive projects (1991: 32). The reflexive project of the self 'consists in the sustaining of coherent, yet continuously revised, biographical narratives . . . Reflexively organised life-planning . . . becomes a central feature of the structuring of self-identity' (1991: 5). Bauman notes that, for Giddens, 'we are all engaged nowadays in "life-politics"; we are "reflexive beings" who look closely at every move we take, who are seldom satisfied with its results and always eager to correct them' (2000b: 23). Since individuals are reflexive, for Giddens it follows that the relationships that individuals enter into must also be reflexive. Giddens notes that '[i]n contrast to close personal ties in traditional contexts, the pure relation-ship is not anchored in external conditions of social or economic life – it is, as it were, free floating' (1991: 89). Here he provides the example of marriage. He contrasts marriage in traditional contexts (a contract influenced by economic considerations consisting of the division of labour between wife and husband) to marriage in high modernity, which is 'kept going for as long as it delivers emotional satisfaction to be derived from close contact with another' (1991: 89). Giddens notes that, in contrast to 'durable' relationships in traditional societies, present-day pure relationships 'can be terminated, more or less at will, by either partner at any particular point' (Giddens 1992: 137). This is because, in high modernity, individuals have increased freedom and have much more choice, thus the emotional investment associated with 'coasting along' in an unsatisfactory relationship becomes senseless (Giddens 1991: 90). Media texts convey information about close relation-ships (Giddens 1991: 92) and the heavy media focus on marital dissolution influences individual perceptions and expectations of marriage and intimate couple relationships (Elliot 2001: 40). Since '[t]he pure relationship is sought only for what the relationship can bring to the partners involved' (Giddens 1991: 90) continued feelings of individual or mutual dissatisfaction lead more and more to relationship dissolution. This is not to say that commit-ment is not central to pure relationships. Commitment 'replaces the external anchors' (Giddens 1991: 92). For Giddens commitment is wider than love; it is part of an 'effort bargain' since '[c]ommitment is recognised by parti-cipants to buy time: to provide emotional support which is guaranteed to persist through at least some of the perturbations which the relationship might undergo . . . ' (Giddens 1991: 93).

Pure relationships, freedom and autonomy

Giddens contends that many marriages in the 'separating and divorcing society of today' (1992: 61) have benefited from the shift to the pure rela-tionship model, not least because this transformation has led to autonomy and to the 'democratisation of personal life' (1992: 184). In personal life 'autonomy means the successful realisation of the reflexive project of the self – the condition of relating to others in an egalitarian way' (1992: 189). Feminist analyses have held that traditional marriage works to the advantage of men and the disadvantage of women (e.g. Delphy and Leonard 1992). Giddens suggests that women in particular benefit from the move to the pure relationship since the pure relationship is 'a relationship of sexual and emotional equality, which is explosive in its connotations for pre-existing forms of gender power' (1992: 2). The pursuit of sexual intimacy is key and, for Giddens, sexual intimacy depends on the increasing autonomy of women and upon 'plastic sexuality' (1992: 94). By means of contraception and other advancements, plastic sexuality emerges – a sexuality that can be moulded because it has been freed from the constraints of the needs of reproduction. Plastic sexuality is fundamentally bound with self-identity because plastic sexuality can be 'moulded as a trait of personality' (Giddens 1991: 221, 1992: 2). Thus it is suggested that individuals in contemporary Western societies have more fluid sexual orientations and that these can be expressed, in theory at least, through a greater choice of sexual partners. From this perspective, sexual preferences are basically no different from choices that we make in relation to other pleasures, for example regarding the foods that we choose to eat (Armstrong 2003: 134). This 'sexual revolution' not only means that women have more sexual autonomy, but also that we have moved from living in a society of imposed heterosexuality (Rich 1980) to one in which homosexuality can flourish (Giddens 1991: 28). Thus Giddens pictures a democratic personal order in which sexual relationships and other aspects of the personal sphere conform to a model of confluent love in which 'equality in emotional give and take and reciprocal sexual pleasure is a key element in whether the relationship is sustained or dissolved' (Giddens 1992: 62). Giddens regards these changes as democratic rather than repressive (Lewis 2001: 54). The pure relationship is entered into for each partner's benefit and is sustained only by ongoing mutual satisfaction with the relationship (Giddens 1992). Plastic sexuality, confluent love and pure relationships, 'the aspects of commodification or consumerization of human partnerships, are portrayed by Giddens as the vehicles of emancipation and a warrant of a new happiness that comes in its wake – the new, unprecedented scale of individual autonomy and freedom to choose' (Bauman 2000b: 89). Thus the decline in marriage, the increase in divorce, the move towards more cohabiting relationships and individuals moving through relationship careers rather than having life-long relationships are evidence of a progressive rather than a destructive change in the nature of intimate relationships in Western societies. For Giddens, individuals have been freed from traditional norms and values and have become 'two equal individuals making democratic decisions that may be as likely to involve parting as staying together' (Lewis 2001: 54).

However, the growth in such relationships has been hailed as less positive by some commentators. Giddens' thinking is based on the assumption that full individualization for both men and women has been achieved (Lewis 2001: 54). However, families have not become individualized with both partners engaged in full-time paid work and hence economically independent of each other (Lewis 2001: 60). While some research shows that in heterosexual relationships there is a more equal balance of power between partners, with women gaining greater control over material resources (Riseman

1998), and other researchers contend that changes have occurred in gender roles regarding unpaid work in the home and paid work outside the home, these researchers also note that this process will be protracted (Hochschild 1983; Gershuny and Berthoud 1997; Sullivan 2000). Assumptions about gender and care work and gender and paid work remain (Windebank 2001) and caring work within the home is often assumed to be women's work and demanded from and provided by mothers and women more generally (Watson et al. 2004: 333). Wives and mothers continue to be ideologically and empirically associated with unpaid and paid care work (Thomas 1997) and research continues to report that the domestic division of labour remains unequal (Benjamin and Sullivan 1999; Sullivan 2000). While husbands do more domestic work when their wives work full time, they do not do much more (Jamieson 1998). Moreover, gender roles become more entrenched after the birth of children (Ribbens 1994). Lewis (2001) contends that we have not yet arrived at a democratic actuality. Moreover, as we will see, it has been argued that there are winners and losers in the shift to pure relationships, and as the rise of such relationships is said to go hand in hand with the growth of individualism, some critics see this shift as destructive. For a critical approach to Giddens' ideas we turn our attention to Bauman (2000b) who is less positive about pure relationships, which he defines as 'frail, fissiparous, unlikely to last longer than the convenience they bring, and so always "until further notice" ' (2003: 90).

Bauman: liquid love

Zygmunt Bauman sees changes in intimate relationships as part of post-modernization, which he asserts represents a relaxing of the hold of cultural 'codes and rules' over individuals' lives. In the postmodern era the abundance of media images and prototypes renders culture's 'patterns and configurations . . . no longer "given", let alone "self-evident" ' (Bauman 2000b: 7). Thus, he suggests, only flexible intimate relationships that are agreeable to creative reorganization have appeal. However, Bauman (1995, 1998, 2000a, 2000b, 2003) is ambivalent about the positive quality of such 'pure relationships', since he sees the insecurity that they unavoidably engender as having negative consequences for a range of people associated with them. Bauman contends that the positive aspects of such relationships can only be confirmed for the 'stronger and more resourceful members of partnerships, [partnerships] which necessarily include also the weaker, not so lavishly endowed with the resources needed to follow freely their desires (not to mention the children – these involuntary, though lasting consequences of partnerships, who hardly ever view the dissolution of marriage as a manifestation of their own freedom)' (2000b: 89–90). Self-identity is crucial to pure relationships and Bauman emphasizes that though 'changing identity may be a private affair . . . it always includes cutting of certain bonds and cancelling certain obligations' (2000b: 90). He reflects that 'those on the receiving side are seldom consulted, let alone given the chance to exercise free choice' (Bauman 2000b: 90). However, Bauman concedes that children sometimes benefit from the financial settlements resulting from the ending of the pure relationships of the more wealthy, which might provide some diminution of the insecurity associated with such relationships (2000b: 90). He also grants that whatever insecurity remains might not be an excessive price to pay for the right to 'cut one's losses and avoid the need for an eternal repentance for once-committed sins and errors' (Bauman 2000b: 90). However, Bauman argues that the flexibility and mobility associated with this 'shopping around' type of relationship 'are not so much vehicles of *emancipation* as the instruments of the *redistribution of freedoms*' (2000b: 90, original emphasis). Thus, he continues, 'there is little doubt that when "trickled down" to the poor and powerless, the new-style partnership with its fragility of marital contract . . . spawn[s] much misery, agony and human suffering and an ever-growing volume of broken, loveless and prospectless lives' (2000b: 90). So Bauman emphasizes the risky nature of pure relationships. Such relationships are risky because 'if you know that your partner may opt out at any moment, with or without your agreement . . . investing your feelings in the current relationship is always a risky step' (Bauman 2003: 90). There are unquestionable risks in investing strong feelings in a partner since that person might leave at any time; thus such an allegiance creates dependency[3] on another (Bauman 2003: 90). Moreover this dependency, owing to the pure relationship, need not be reciprocated, hence '*you* are bound, but *your* partner is free to go, and no kind of bond that may keep you in place is enough to make sure that they won't' (Bauman 2003: 90, original emphasis). Thus, for Bauman (2003), pure relationships do not foster trust.

Like Giddens, Bauman's analysis of transformations in couple relationships derives from his analysis of changes in wider society. For Bauman, societal change is characterized by a shift from *solid modernity* to the present 'novel' phase in the history of modernity, that of *liquid modernity* (2000b: 2). Solid modernity was characterized by heavy capitalism in which individuals and institutions were engaged in the task of achieving their chosen goals (Bauman 2000a: 56–9). Thus, drawing on the work of Max Weber, Bauman contends that solid modernity was 'instrumentally rational', identified by distinct goals and the search for the most efficient ways of achieving these goals. However, in contrast to Weber's notion that 'heavy' capitalism marks the triumph of instrumental rationality, Bauman (2000b) suggests that heavy capitalism has been succeeded by a more value-based, liquid form of modernity, in which individuals spend most of their lives in torment about which goals to pursue rather than the means of achieving known goals. The focus has moved from production to consumption (Bauman 1995) and liquid modernity is an age of 'universal comparison' that ends for the individual only when they die (Bauman 2000b: 7). Individualization is central to consumption. Unlike production, which rests on cooperation and sacrifice, consumption does not need cooperative or mutually dependent individuals (Bauman 1998). Individuals can consume on their own, they rebel against regulation and the individual 'rules supreme' (Bauman 1997).

Men and women who have no permanent bonds are the elemental figures in liquid modernity. Such individuals can free themselves from their bonds when conditions and requirements change, as they unquestionably do in liquid modernity (Bauman 2003). Since liquid modernity is characterized by a 'permanence of transience' (Bauman 2003: 142), we live in a world of 'mutually assured vulnerability' (Bauman 2003: 156). Like the world in which we live, our sense of our selves, our identities, are never complete since consumption is based on an increasing amount of choice, and our sense of identity is bound up with the choices we make (Bauman 2000a). Relationships, like other choices we make, are centres of self-identities and there are no assurances about which choices will prove successful and which will not (Bauman 2000a). Thus men and women in liquid modernity are in a state of perpetual anxiety, with lives that are infused with the risk of bad choices, even though choice is the bedrock of individual freedom. So liquid modernity seems to provide a profusion of opportunities accompanied by relentless decision-making, thus leaving individuals beset with anxiety (Bauman 2000a: 62–3).

The incessant wants and needs associated with consumption are not limited to consumer durables but also apply to intimate relationships. For Bauman, 'like other consumer goods, a partnership is for consumption on-the-spot . . . and for one-off use 'without prejudice' (2003: 12). Like consumer durables, relationships are not seen as permanent and unconditional, and relationship decisions should not be understood as final (Bauman 1998: 25). Thus links between the past, present and future are severed (Bauman 1997: 89), partnerships are highly disposable and the individuals within them feel disposable (Bauman 2003: 12). Consequently, although '[l]oneliness spawns insecurity . . . in a relationship, you may feel as insecure as without it, or worse' (Bauman 2003: 15). The choice is between being independent, alone (and perhaps lonely) and free from the anxiety that relationships bring or being in a seemingly lasting relationship with its concomitant worry and doubt. Moreover, individuals are wary of the burdens that might ensue from such partnerships (Bauman 2003: viii) since 'the responsibility for failure falls primarily on the individual's shoulders (Bauman 2000b: 8). Thus, '[i]n our world of rampant "individualisation" relationships are mixed blessings . . . which . . . vacillate between sweet dream and a nightmare; there is no telling when one turns into the other' (2003: viii).

Thus *contra* Giddens, who sees new forms of intimate relationships as emancipating, providing freedom of choice and paving the way for a new kind of happiness, for Bauman increased individualization and the manifestation of consumption in all areas of our lives, including our most intimate and personal relationships, have increased anxiety and unhappiness. Though some, typically the rich and the strong, may win in the pure relationship stakes, poorer and weaker individuals are often losers. In particular, children, who often have little say in the break-up of a couple relationship, often lose out. Thus continued structural inequalities hinder the realization of truly democratic and liberating pure relationships (Jamieson 1999). The move away from more permanent relationships, associated with declining legal marriage rates, increasing divorce and serial cohabitation, are, if we agree with Bauman, manifestations of a consumer-led attitude to intimate relationships. It cannot be denied that such an attitude can engender a wonderful feeling of independence and freedom; however, it can also lead to a sense of being weighed down by worry, doubt and insecurity. Thus increasing individualization in couple relationships, as elsewhere, can be marvellous for those who have the necessary resources, but can be dreadful for those who do not have the means by which to attain their desires.

For a more sustained examination of the concept of individualization we now turn to the work of Beck and Beck-Gernsheim.

Individualization – the work of Beck and Beck-Gernsheim

Like Bauman and Giddens, Ulrich Beck and Elizabeth Beck-Gernsheim contend that couple relationships today 'are lived as if they are interchangeable' (1995: 11). They share with Giddens an interest in pure relationships (Gross 2005), but their focus is on the process of individualization. The advance of modernization has resulted in our lives becoming suffused with increasing numbers of decisions that need to be taken quickly (Beck and Beck-Gernsheim 1995: 34). But, they suggest, freedoms today are what Keupp (1988) calls 'risky opportunities' (cited in Beck and Beck-Gernsheim 1995: 99); as individuals we are 'condemned to [the] freedom' (Weyman 1989) of immersing ourselves in such risks (cited in Beck and Beck-Gernsheim 1995: 107). For example, we have the freedom to choose a partner, which 'may look like freedom but actually demands a great deal of effort' (Beck and Beck-Gernsheim 1995: 83). In all decision-making situations, individuals frequently have a vast number of often complex and conflicting options to choose from and have to find a way though these complexities (Beck and Beck-Gernsheim 1995: 82). *Contra* Giddens, Beck and Beck-Gernsheim (1995) contend that individualized and privatized modernity is articulated in opposition to freedom to choose since 'the conditions that encourage individualization provide new unfamiliar dependencies [which means that] *you are obliged to standardize your own existence*' (Beck and Beck-Gernsheim 1995: 7, original emphasis). Thus, they argue, we are driven by a 'craving to be ourselves' and by the 'pressure to conform to internalized demands' (1995: 23). Since individuals are increasingly expected to take responsibility for themselves and to construct a '*life of their own*' (Beck and Beck-Gernsheim 1995: 6) there is a pressure to conform and behave in standardized ways. Thus 'the means which encourage individualism also induce sameness' (Beck and Beck-Gernsheim 1995: 40). So, although we are expected to find our own resolutions to problems and to make our own choices, it transpires that the decisions we make are increasingly predetermined by social circumstances, which are tied to political developments and societal principles over which we have no control (Beck and Beck-Gernsheim 1995: 40–1). Thus, the connection between the individual and society has constrained the level of individual freedom that has been accomplished (Lewis 2001: 54).

Beck and Beck-Gernsheim characterize high modernity as a 'post-romantic world', a selfish place 'where the old ties no longer bind, all that matters is *you:* you can be what you *want* to be; you *choose* your life, your environment, even your appearance and your emotions' (Beck and Beck-Gernsheim 1995: 55). Thus, our capacity to share our lives with another is dogged by our ceaseless concern with our own interests (Beck and Beck-Gernsheim 1995: 53). This leads to a clash of interests between our craving for love and our desire for personal freedom (Beck and Beck-Gernsheim 1995: 11). Though individuals are still looking for an intimate relationship, the penalty of finding one may be far from rewarding. For Beck and Beck-Gernsheim 'the "trap of romantic love" means that love starts out as infatuation and lingers as an expectation which in this term cannot be met, so that all that is left is disappointment' (1995: 86). Because the 'mutual hope of being loved' is the thing that binds couples together, but individualization rests on concerns about 'me' and 'my' yearning to be loved (1995: 95), 'the disappointments inherent in our idea of love, just as much as the hopes we invest in it, are the outcome of our modern concern with being ourselves' (Beck and Beck-Gernsheim 1995: 51). Happiness for me rather than a common aim in life is the main appeal for people in a pure relationship (Beck and Beck-Gernsheim 1995: 99). However, love in the pure relationship is a fundamental form of personal responsibility and thus is essential to self-government (Beck and Beck-Gernsheim 1995: 194). Nevertheless, if a partnership fails, we look for a replacement; consequently, '[l]ove under modern conditions is not an event which takes place once but is a state to be fought for anew everyday' (Beck and Beck-Gernsheim 1995: 99). So, Beck and Beck-Gernsheim declare, '[p]eople marry for the sake of love and get divorced for the sake of love' (1995: 11); accordingly, love 'is losing its mythology and is turning into a rational system' (1995: 141). Thus, they suggest, it is no longer possible to determine the meaning of love, or indeed of family, marriage, parenthood and sexuality, since definitions differ from individual to individual and from relationship to relationship (Lewis 2001).

The effects of individualization are not the same for all and are different for men and for women (Beck and Beck-Gernsheim 1995; Lewis 2001). For women the process of individualization is seen as complex, since there is a tension between 'living one's own life' and 'being there for others' (Beck and Beck-Gernsheim 1995: 22). However, for men, the process is one of emotional dependency since men are required to fit in with the 'job ethos' and thus they feel compelled to fit in with what is expected of them (Beck and Beck-Gernsheim 1995: 23). Thus the degree of freedom attained has been greater for women than for men. Since the 1960s there has been the development of a new 'individual *female* biography' (Beck and Beck-Gernsheim 1995: 61, original emphasis), which has unchained women from family duties. Referring to Beck and Beck-Gernsheim, Lewis notes that women's entry into the labour market has made possible 'individually designed lives' (Beck and Beck-Gernsheim 1992, quoted in Lewis 2001) that are more difficult to integrate with the lives of others (2001: 54). However, Beck and Beck-Gernsheim suggest, 'As traditions become diluted, the attractions of a close relationship grow' so '[i]ndividualization may drive men and women apart, but paradoxically it also pushes them into one another's arms' (1995: 32). Nevertheless, in today's arena of consumption, 'marriage becomes a place which specializes in the development and maintenance of the individual self' (Lewis 2001: 54) and men and women remain 'intimate strangers' (Rubin 1983, cited in Beck and Beck-Gernsheim 1995). Permanence and stability in couple relationships become casualties (Lewis 2001) of this fascination with the maintenance of the individual self within the pure relationship.

In summary, for Beck and Beck-Gernsheim our lives are suffused with risky options, including relationship decisions. Though this might seem to spell freedom, in fact seeing our way through these complexities takes a great deal of effort and the decisions that we make are predetermined by social circumstances. Since our main aims are personal happiness and contentment, as individuals in intimate relationships we are obsessed with the maintenance of the self. The focus is thus on 'me' rather than 'we', and this has led to instability in couple relationships. This is expressed in a move away from more permanent intimate relationships. Beck and Beck-Gernsheim appear to regret the eroding of traditional relationship ties. They suggest that the individualization associated with modern times has led to 'individually designed lives' based on selfishness yet constrained freedom. The upshot is that marriage rates have fallen, the average age at marriage has increased, the divorce rate has risen, remarriage rates have decreased and there has been a rise in serial cohabitation.

Marriage, commitment and detraditionalization

As we have seen, a major concern in this strand of research is the lack of commitment intrinsic to selfish individualism. In popular discourse commitment means staying married (Smart 2005). But such an association overlooks the complexity of commitment. Lewis (2001) contends that commitment is comprised of three elements, each of which is capable of change, all of which interact with each other, and all of which can vary within different relationships.[4] To demonstrate this she uses Adams and Jones' (1997) refinement of Johnson's (1991) model of commitment, specifically:

- 'an attraction component, based on devotion, satisfaction and love (= commitment to spouse);
- a moral-normative component, based on a sense of personal responsibility for maintaining the marriage and a belief in marriage as an important institution (= commitment to marriage);
- a constraining component, based on the fear of the social, financial and emotional costs of ending the relationship (= feelings of entrapment).'

(Lewis 2001: 124–5)

Lewis notes that the separation between the first element, commitment to the other person, and the second, commitment to marriage, is similar to Mansfield's (1999) schema of two forms of commitment; the first to the relationship (which is now oriented to the other person) and the second to the partnership (Lewis 2001: 125). Mansfield (1999) contends that the more future-oriented commitment to the 'partnership' is crucial to long-term stability (cited in Lewis 2001).

All elements are understood to have changed. There has been an erosion of the prescriptive second moral normative component about how a couple relationship should be, which means that the responsibility for working out how to behave in a relationship has passed to the couple (Lewis 2001). The transformation in the third element is seen in the less high (though still high) social, financial and emotional costs attached to divorce compared to 50 years ago (Smart 2005). Smart notes that, with these two elements undergoing change, many sociologists (e.g. Giddens; Beck and Beck-Gernsheim) have focused on the first element: commitment to the other person (Smart 2005). Perhaps stripped of the second and third elements, this first element is not seen as very stable. However, Smart contends that '[t]he values that people hold about family life are recognised to be extremely complex, and also flexible and contextual' (Smart 2005: 553). Thus Giddens' and Beck and Beck-Gernsheim's analyses are problematic since they oversimplify relationships by focusing on conjugal relationships, and take commitment to be deficient rather than changing (Smart 2005).

It has been argued that marriage expectations have altered as a result of changing patterns of family formation, changes in the economy (most centrally, the entry of married women into the labour force) and the increased ease of securing divorce with a consequent general trend toward viewing marriage as a conditional commitment (Furstenberg and Spanier 1984: 27). However, the assumptions behind this argument rest on the yardstick of commitment as marriage. Notwithstanding the complexities associated with the term 'commitment', as outlined above, such an assumption seems to leave unquestioned the nature of marriage itself. Elam (1994: 5) argues that notions of what constitutes marriage are in flux, with the consequence that the term *marriage* can refer to different forms of couple relationship. Moreover, Hochschild maintains that 'modern love has ... become more pluralistic', involving, for example, gay and lesbian people (1998: 8). Although we might still live in a society of imposed heterosexuality (Rich 1980), with rules defining permitted sexual and marital partnerships (Foucault 1979), gay relationships have been more accepted (see Giddens 1992, and as evidenced by recent legislation regarding legally recognized civil gay and lesbian partnerships). Nevertheless, as Waites (2003) notes, the struggle for equality continues, as 'legal equality does not imply recognition of the equal value of homosexuality and heterosexuality' (2003: 637). Formal marriage is not legal for same-sex couples and thus such committed relationships have not been reflected in the marriage statistics. Thus, although the statistics indicate that traditional marriage is declining, committed couple relationships of various kinds are thriving (Lewis 2001).

As we have seen, it has been proposed that the pure relationship has prevailed because intimate relationships have been detraditionalized. Gross argues that the main problem with Giddens' approach is that it falls short of unravelling two analytically distinct forms of tradition (2005: 293). Gross concurs that there has been a decline in what he calls 'regulative traditions' relating to intimacy and the family (2005: 288). Focusing on the United States (though such a trend can also be observed in the UK), he remarks that the strength of the regulative tradition, 'lifelong, internally stratified marriage (LISM)' has declined in recent decades (2005: 288). He defines LISM as 'the set of cultural practices according to which family life and intimacy are organized around a permanent and state or religiously sanctified commitment between members of a heterosexual dyad – a commitment premised on and reproductive of an unequal division of labor, power, resources, or responsibilities between genders' (2005: 288). Though concurring that LISM is in decline, he argues that this is not concomitant with a complete switch to 'reflexivity, understood as unbounded agency and creativity' (2005: 288), because social action is also fashioned by what he calls 'meaning-constitutive traditions', that is meanings passed from generation to generation (2005: 288). Meaning-constitutive traditions 'influence the thinkability of particular acts and projects' (Gross 2005: 296) and, unlike regulative traditions, which operate through the threat of exclusion, meaning-constitutive traditions operate 'by constituting the actor as a being who understands and is oriented to the world in a particular way' (2005: 296). Though, Gross notes, the distinction between the two is blurred in 'real life', '[r]egulative traditions shape action by constraining it from the outside ... whereas meaning-constitutive traditions shape action by enabling it from the inside' (2005: 296). Thus, Gross concludes, although today fewer sanctions are imposed on those who deviate from the practices of LISM, 'the image of the form of couplehood inscribed in the regulative tradition of LISM continues to function as a hegemonic ideal' in many couple relationships and is indebted to the meaning-constitutive tradition of romantic love (2005: 288).

Contemporary theorizing about intimate couple relationships provides a 'rather unromantic view of romance . . . one which resonates with Giddens' pure relationship and the reflexive themes it embraces' (Boden and Williams 2002: 509). Boden and Williams maintain that '[s]uch theorizations seem to imply that romantic relationships are primarily entered into for the purposes of realizing or expanding the self, effectively making the experience of falling in love much more a "self-ish" act than a "self-less" one' (2002: 506). Such an approach implies that the feelings associated with romantic love have been displaced by the logic of the market (Gross 2005: 301). However, Beck and Beck-Gernsheim contend that the narratives of romantic love provide individuals with a source of meaning in this fragmented world (Gross 2005: 301). Though people feel freer to love more fully, but paradoxically feel afraid because love fades and is often replaced by new love (Hochschild 1998: 9), romantic love continues to be sacralized (Collins 1981; Beck and Beck-Gernsheim 1995; Gross 2005). Research has found that younger people see love as a condition of marriage (Sarsby 1983) and those who feel themselves to be in love have a wealth of novels, songs, films, poems and other media to draw on (Jackson 1993). The notion of what constitutes love is contentious and changing (Lutz 1986) and love, so often represented as uniquely personal, follows culturally prescribed patterns (Barthes 1990), although we do not passively accept them (Jackson 1993). However, accepting that definitions of love are diverse, *love* can nevertheless impel us into a monogamous union and can equally be a threat to monogamy, a reason for changing partners or for engagement in extramarital liaisons (Lawson 1988; Jackson 1993). Thus, though Gross notes that the detraditionalization of intimacy implies that the feelings associated with romantic love have been displaced by the logic of the market, he concludes that 'it is nonsensical . . . to imagine that any action can be fully detraditionalized or "reflexive" in the sense of involving a complete break with all prior traditions or habits' (2005: 293). Thus 'departures from the regulative tradition of LISM do not equate with a complete lack of guidance by tradition' (Gross 2005: 306), and love and romantic involvement are currently considered to be more important motivators for intimate couple relationships than any others (Hochschild 1998; Lewis 2001).

Partnering and repartnering in high modernity

Today, people wishing to partner or repartner experience a multifaceted and diverse setting in which to search for a partner and a complex array of social circumstances in which to maintain a couple relationship. More living alone, fewer marriages, higher divorce rates, a growth in cohabitation and relationships where partners 'live apart', and the rise of legally sanctioned civil partnerships mean that the intimate relationship landscape is fluid and varied. Given the relaxation of the legal sanction against parting from a spouse (with the introduction of no fault divorce), intimate couple relationships are perhaps increasingly based on commitment to another rather than on restrictions on leaving. Divorce is now an essential aspect of the marriage system since most married people expect to be able to divorce if their marriage becomes unacceptable to them. Maintaining choice is thus an important aspect of relationship formation, and cohabitation is one way of securing oneself against negative bonds associated with marriage. Consequently, we have seen a move to less repressive and more egalitarian 'pure relationships' (Giddens 1991, 1992). However, the notion that a heterosexual couple relationship involves two equal individuals is contested since, although there has been a move towards a more egalitarian balance of power in such relationships, this is far from complete. As Jamieson (1999) shows, structural inequalities hinder the realization of truly democratic and liberating pure relationships. Although the degree of freedom attained has been greater for women than for men (Beck and Beck-Gernsheim 1995), women continue to bear the brunt of unpaid care work in the home and, for the most part, remain in less financially rewarding jobs than men (Lewis 2001). The positive aspects of such relationships can usually be achieved only by the stronger, more resourceful and more powerful, not by the poor and powerless (Bauman 2000b). Pure relationships, for many, are insecure and thus risky, which can lead to a feeling of being weighed down by worry, doubt and insecurity. Increasing individualization means that our capacity to share our lives with another may be dogged by our ceaseless concern with our own interests (Beck and Beck-Gernsheim 1995: 53). However, although the 'regulative tradition' of lifelong marriage has declined, 'meaning-constitutive traditions' based on lifelong marriage and romantic love provide many of us with an image of an ideal couple relationship (Gross 2005) and love and romantic involvement continue to be considered to be the most important motivators for having an intimate couple relationship (Lewis 2001). Thus, we might conclude, the 'pure relationship' is a work in progress.

Nevertheless, the formation and maintenance of intimate couple relationships are based on individual caution and emotional fulfilment. Since people are generally freer to leave an unsatisfactory couple relationship, the standards for what constitutes an acceptable and satisfying partnership have risen. In consequence, there is no guarantee that one person will stay with another; thus someone (or a number of people if there are children) is usually hurt if a partner leaves. Although this is viewed by some as evidence of a selfish and individualized approach to couple relationships, the freedom associated with it perhaps provides an alternative meaning to the term commitment, with continuing obligations being based on commitment to another person rather than commitment to marriage per se. Although, until the late twentieth century, individual marriages may have lasted, such endurance did not necessarily equate with continued commitment to the other person. Two-timing relationships are not a new phenomenon and it is a moot point whether a partner staying under sufferance is better than a partner leaving. However, the freedom to leave these now more reflexive and less constricting relationships should not be overstated. In addition to commitment to another, there are other constraining components (Lewis 2001) that constitute reasons for staying – for example, financial worries may keep women in a relationship, as may fathers' concerns about losing contact with their children. Moreover, going through relationship dissolution can be a miserable process, especially if it occurs within a legal context, which can have enduring consequences for the well-being of all involved. One way of recovering from the various negative impacts of relationship dissolution is to enter a new relationship. Although some people who have been through relationship dissolution may be cautious about entering a new partnership, many nevertheless choose to do so. However, new partners are often found through leisure activities or social networks (Kalmijn and Flap 2001) and relationship dissolution can have a negative effect on social integration (Kalmijn and van Groenou 2005). Although the setting for finding a partner often differs between those who have experienced the dissolution of an intimate couple relationship and those who have not, needs, attractiveness and opportunity are said to be the three determinants of partnership formation for all (de Graaf and Kalmijn 2003). Women are less likely than men to repartner, but it should not be assumed that they want to repartner and that they only do not do so because, as some suggest, they are unable to find a partner. However, forming a new relationship is the choice of many, and Lewis (2001) suggests committed couple relationships of various kinds are thriving. In the next chapter we examine the repartnering behaviour of formerly partnered people, and their lives and characteristics more generally.

4

The Formerly Married and Former Cohabitees: Their Lives, Characteristics and Repartnering Behaviour

Introduction

This chapter documents the characteristics, situations and repartnering behaviour of the formerly married and former cohabitees in Britain, summarizing research results from the literature to provide a contextual backdrop to our own research, and generating new material via analyses of various quantitative data sources.

The first section starts by considering broad patterns of demographic change of relevance to the formerly partnered and repartnering. Various key studies of the formerly partnered or related groups within the population are then examined, with relevant themes within these being highlighted. We then turn to some important dimensions of formerly partnered people's lives, specifically their material circumstances and employment situation, parenthood, and their health and well-being. Material relating to the social, cultural and policy context of the formerly partnered is then discussed.

Literature relating to the impact of past relationships is then examined, followed by literature relating to repartnering behaviour. Central to the latter is material documenting, or relevant to an understanding of, differentials in the likelihood of repartnering. Finally, there is a brief discussion of evidence showing who the formerly married and former cohabitees repartner.

Notwithstanding the literature discussed in the first section, there are considerable gaps in the 'empirical picture' of the formerly partnered in contemporary Britain, and there are a number of quantitative data sources that can be utilized to document further their characteristics, behaviour and views. Hence the second section uses some of these sources to extend our knowledge of who the formerly married and former cohabitees are, and especially what they think and do with respect to repartnering.

Relevant demographic patterns and trends in Britain, and the 'Second Demographic Transition'

Haskey (1999) has examined the impact on the prevalence of divorced people within the population of the quadrupling of the divorce rate in Britain between the late 1960s and mid-1990s. Between 1976 and 1996, the proportion of adults whose current marital status was divorced rose steadily from about 1 in 40 to nearly 1 in 12. This reflected in part a simultaneous decline in the remarriage rate to less than half of its initial value (1999: 19). About a quarter of people whose legal marital status in 1996 was divorced were, in fact, cohabiting (1999: 21). A more detailed examination of the relationship between marital status and cohabitation has shown that cohabitation rates were higher for younger divorced people (i.e. people in their twenties and thirties), and suggests that the cohabitation rate for divorced people rose between the late 1970s and mid-1980s, but did not continue to do so thereafter (Shaw and Haskey 1999: 12–13). Haskey reports higher cohabitation and remarriage rates among divorced men than among divorced women, leading to a greater number of women than men who were currently divorced and not living with a partner (1999: 19).

Before 1970 fewer than 1 in 20 women marrying for the first time had cohabited pre-maritally with their husband, but by the mid-1990s more than 3 out of 4 had done so (Haskey 2001: 11). A lack of equivalent data on cohabitation that did not lead to marriage makes tracking the trend in this form of cohabitation more difficult. However, Haskey reports that by 1998 more than a quarter of single people in the age range 25–49 had experienced at least one cohabitation of this sort, rising to more than two-fifths of single people in their late thirties (2001: 13). It thus seems likely that, in less than 30 years, former cohabitees have grown from a negligible sub-group of the British population to a substantial one. Berrington (2001) used data from a longitudinal study of the 1958 birth cohort (National Child Development Study: NCDS) to show that pregnancy and the presence of children increased the likelihood of a cohabitation turning into a legal marriage, and possibly also reduced the likelihood of cohabitation breakdown. Such effects may contribute to a differential in the prevalence of children between (unmarried) former cohabitees and the formerly married.[1]

Bernhardt (2000) notes that partnership dissolution and subsequent repartnering are one aspect of a broader 'Second Demographic Transition': a fundamental, interconnected and perhaps irreversible set of family-related demographic changes in advanced industrial societies. These changes are arguably of comparable importance to those constituting the first 'Demographic Transition', wherein, in Britain, mortality and fertility rates declined between the eighteenth and early twentieth centuries (Coleman and Salt 1992: 63; Jackson 1998: 51–2). Lesthaeghe has outlined and interpreted the components of the 'Second Demographic Transition'. The initial demographic changes, which for the most part started or took place during the

1960s and 1970s, were a decline in overall fertility, a growth in the proportion of extramarital births, rising mean ages at first marriage and increasing divorce rates (Lesthaeghe 1995: 36). Changes that took place during the 1970s and 1980s were increased rates of cohabitation and 'procreation within consensual unions', the rise of lone-parent households, a reversal of the decline in fertility for women aged 30 or more, and an ongoing decline in fertility for women aged under 25 (1995: 46).

Lesthaeghe's analysis is relevant to the consideration of the formerly partnered and repartnering in contemporary Britain in a number of ways. Like other theorists (see Chapter 3), he views individualism and a growth in individual autonomy, together with greater expectations regarding relationship quality, as central to recent marital and family changes. However, he argues that such cultural factors are complementary to factors with a clear economic dimension, such as changes relating to women's economic autonomy and to consumerism or consumption aspirations. His cross-national analysis provides empirical support for the argument that the observed demographic changes are a reflection of both cultural, ideational changes and structural, economic changes.

Ideas relating to the 'Second Demographic Transition' thus emphasize the need to take account of structure and agency, and of cultural and economic factors, when examining the lives and behaviour of the formerly partnered. However, it is equally important to recognize the potential significance of the demographic changes themselves, given their magnitude and fundamental nature. Changing patterns of age at marriage, marital fertility and divorce have clear implications for the number and compositional characteristics of formerly married people in Britain. In addition, the growth in rates of cohabitation, extra-marital fertility and divorce, and the prevalence of lone-parent households may, by changing what is normative statistically, have had an impact on what is culturally normative. A more specific consequence of the various changes within the 'Second Demographic Transition' is that, in the United States at least, 'parenthood has become a much less central and stable element in men's lives' (Goldscheider 2000: 530).

The lives (and characteristics) of the formerly married and former cohabitees

Key studies in Britain

A key empirical point of reference for this book is Hart (1976). The fieldwork for her qualitative study of members of a club for the divorced and separated in a Midlands city was carried out in the late 1960s. However, despite the passage of more than a quarter of a century, during which relatively dramatic processes of marriage and family-related change took place, there are many thematic similarities between her results and our own.

Hart was cautious about the scope for generalizing from her sample (1976: xi) and made a pertinent observation in this context: 'Nor would it be an exaggeration to suggest that R.A.D.S. [Rivertown Association for the Divorced and Separated] was especially attractive to the socially isolated, the economically deprived, the stigmatized, and the personally inadequate. The harshness of their experiences may have induced a bias in this study towards the darker side of divorce in Britain . . . ' (1976: 30). However, while the themes of economic and social deprivation and feelings of marginality among the formerly married that she highlighted may not have been, or may not now be, universally applicable, they are still clearly of conceptual relevance.

Conceptually, Hart saw her study as an examination of 'the effects of a critical status passage on the social identity' (1976: xi) and viewed marital breakdown as involving 'the loss of a prominent status in the social identity' (1976: 12), explicitly assuming that 'marital status is a central part of the social identity' (1976: 13). While she reported that all her respondents experienced a period of being 'identity-less' during and immediately after separation (1976: 197), Hart nevertheless identified variability in the centrality of marriage to people's lives and identities, in relation to factors such as age, gender, parenthood and class, and suggested that other sources of social identity, such as paid employment and social networks, needed to be taken into account (1976: 45–9, 226).

Hart also suggested that heterogeneity in the extent to which a joint conjugal identity had been formed had important implications for the degree of trauma experienced after marital breakdown (1976: 56), noting that 'R.A.D.S. members who had experienced a degree of alienation from the conjugal relationship were somewhat better prepared for marital breakdown' (1976: 111). Furthermore, 'A sense of loss and deprivation was felt most strongly by those whose personal investments in a dead marriage had absorbed a large part of their life-time assets and who had few hopes of establishing a new partnership or of finding some other satisfying outlet for their energies' (1976: 215). In addition, Hart's study highlighted the importance of the role taken by a divorced or separated person within the process of separation: active, passive or somewhere 'in between' (1976: 112).

A later study based on a survey of divorced men in the south of England (Ambrose et al. 1983) placed a strong emphasis on the impact of divorce on men. The men frequently made positive or negative comments about 'changes in self', which the authors linked to 'a movement away from dependence and/or connection with others towards self-sufficiency and isolation' (1983: 128). Strong relationships between negative feelings about personal change and various other factors were also identified: 'The men who consider the changes to be negative are largely those who . . . still harbour strongly hostile feelings towards [their ex-wife], who tend to have a much greater incidence of mental health problems and whose financial and, especially, career positions have been most severely affected' (1983: 132).

More recently, notable qualitative, longitudinal research on post-divorce parenthood and family life has been carried out by Smart and her colleagues (Smart and Neale 1999; Smart, Neale and Wade 2001; Neale and Smart 2002). While its emphasis has tended to be on parenting or on children's experiences, the post-divorce identities of parents constitute one area of overlap with our own research. Writing with reference to the work of Giddens (1991, 1992) and Griffiths (1995) on self-identity, Smart and Neale identified among many of their female respondents a need to reconstitute an autonomous self after divorce by disconnecting themself from, and ceasing to be bound up with, their former partner (1999: 141). Their research highlights the potential for conflict between divorced mothers' need for reconstituted identities and the desire of divorced fathers to maintain a particular form of parental role. Smart and Neale conceptualize this as a desire to retain power and control, rather than as a desire to maintain the basis for an identity as a parent (1999: 141–7).

While studies focusing on former cohabitees are infrequent, concerns about the impact of cohabitation breakdown on parenting and children have led to studies by Smart and Stevens (2000) and Lewis et al. (2002). Lewis et al.'s qualitative study also highlighted the relevance of the concept of power in understanding the parenting roles of fathers after separation (2002: 38–45).

Studies of lone parents or lone parenthood sometimes generate results relating specifically to the formerly partnered. Rowlingson and McKay (1998) reported results from qualitative interviews with current or former lone parents, including formerly partnered women. They note that '[h]aving gone through the often difficult phase during which they had established an identity as an independent lone parent, many women were reluctant to lose that identity' (1998: 182). Many of the formerly partnered lone mothers were happier than in their previous relationships, having the same responsibilities for children and home but a greater degree of control over their lives (1998: 155–6).

Like Hart's book, contributions to the literature have often originated in doctoral studies of post-separation life or lone parenthood (Churchill 2004; Kielty 2005; Klett-Davies 2005). Shaw's (1994) qualitative study of separated or divorced mothers makes explicit links between life as a formerly married person and repartnering orientations, and such studies frequently highlight the complexity, ambiguity and diversity of life after separation.

Studies of stepfamilies also sometimes contain potentially useful (retrospective) discussions of life as a formerly partnered person and the repartnering process. For example, a qualitative study of stepfamilies in Sheffield (Burgoyne and Clark 1984) provides evidence of systematic differences between the 'initiators' and 'recipients' of marital breakdown, such as the tendency among the former for the repartnering process to have started before separation (1984: 59).

Much of the existing literature focuses on the legal implications and economic consequences of divorce. Extensive work of this sort has been carried out by Eekelaar and Maclean, including research based on a nationally representative survey of parents who did not currently live with the other, in most cases biological, parent of one or more of their children (Maclean and Eekelaar 1997). Maclean and Eekelaar's sample included over 200 formerly partnered parents; Perry et al. (2000) carried out a smaller, more localized study of the financial circumstances of divorced parents.

Issues of parenthood, parenting and policy provide a strong motivating force for such studies. Of more immediate relevance to our own research, however, is a study with socio-legal origins, but also a psychosocial orientation. This (primarily) qualitative study of adults' experiences of divorce (Day Sclater 1999) used in-depth interviews and focused on 'case studies' within a larger sample of people who (initially) were separated. Key results for our purposes include interviewees' reported experiences of a loss of sense of self and of no longer having a sense of who they were (1999: 145), and the mixed feelings of interviewees about their situation: 'It cannot be said . . . that divorce was unequivocally either a negative or a positive experience for any of our participants. Rather, divorce seems to be characterised by a profound emotional ambivalence . . . ' (1999: 148). Relevant insights from clinical work have also been reported. Burck and Daniel, speaking as family therapists, suggest that 'separation usually involves reclaiming aspects of self which were lost in the relationship' (1995: 198), but also point out that a 'voyage of self-discovery' can act as a trigger for leaving a marriage (1995: 199).

Quantitative studies of the formerly partnered (and also repartnering) have been constrained by the limitations of the available large-scale resources. In their examination of divorce and the divorced, Kiernan and Mueller (1999: 403) comment that they 'were able to identify only a few important and direct factors associated with partnership dissolution', but also that 'the prominence of demographic and economic correlates in divorce research probably reflects the absence of surveys of representative samples of the population appropriate for studying family processes'.

Key studies from the United States

In this chapter we focus primarily on empirical results relating to Britain. The North American literature relating to the formerly married is, however, very extensive, although it focuses to a large extent on the negative consequences of marital dissolution, for formerly married adults and, especially, their children.[2] The North American literature relating to remarriage focuses primarily on remarriages, and in particular stepfamilies, as opposed to the remarriage process.[3] Notwithstanding these orientations, there are a number of landmark studies that can act as a source of potentially useful ideas and hence merit a brief discussion.

In a significant early study, Hunt interviewed approximately 200 separated or divorced people, collected 169 responses to a questionnaire, and also carried out some ethnographic work (1966: 295–6). His respondents were primarily 'middle class', but notwithstanding this limitation, his results anticipated many of those in later studies. Themes of ambiguity and heterogeneity in the lives of the formerly married are evident in his work, but he nevertheless emphasized the existence of 'a veritable World of the Formerly Married, with its own rules of conduct' (1966: 4). He also commented that '[t]he formerly married person is not who he [*sic*] was; he is another person – but who? The process of convalescence requires a redefinition of his identity, the acquisition of a new sense of who and what he now is' (1966: 63), and noted the contribution of 'friends of the same sex who have already been through it' to the 'redefinition of the self' (1966: 70).

More recently, complementary qualitative studies based on interviews with divorced mothers and divorced fathers were carried out by Arendell (1986, 1995). Working from a feminist perspective, Arendell showed how fathers' heterogeneous post-divorce identities were affected by parenthood and informed by notions of masculinity, and how they often experienced challenges to their identities linked to perceived injustices and victimization relating to the divorce process. Her earlier study of 'middle-class' divorced mothers highlighted diverse negative consequences of divorce, and indicated how difficult divorced mothers found it to construct a social identity that integrated being a 'single' woman with being a primary parent. Arendell noted the ambivalence and uncertainty of those of her interviewees (a majority) who wanted relationships of some description with men (1986: 128–31).

Other key studies have focused on the period following separation and examined its impact. One such study undertaken in the 1970s (Spanier and Thompson 1987) involved unstructured interviews followed by a (non-random) survey of separated or divorced people. The most pertinent aspect of this study for our purposes is a discussion of 'dating', which highlights the heterogeneity of dating behaviour among separated people, notes its contribution to post-separation adjustment and self-esteem, and makes a useful, albeit largely implicit, distinction between dating activities and orientation to remarriage (1987: 187–207). A related study focused on remarriage (Furstenberg and Spanier 1984).

In her study of the aftermath of divorce 'at mid-life', Cauhapé (1983) developed a typology of transitional periods or 'passages' after divorce, with the transition ending once a social identity and network of social relationships of the sort to which the individual aspires has been established (1983: 7). Her study focused on in-depth case studies, contextualized by a more extensive range of respondents with whom she talked during six years of fieldwork. The categories of her typology relate to the duration of the transitional period, which she linked to whether a person aspires to a partnership and, if so, what sort of partner, relationship and lifestyle they want.

Results from a study focusing on 'the interpretive process through which individuals make sense of their former marriages and their current lives' were reported by Riessman (1990: 8), who carried out qualitative interviews with recently separated or divorced people. Day Sclater highlights Riessman's view that divorce 'strikes at the roots of identity' (1999: 175), leading to a need to detach oneself from one's past relationship-related identity and forge a new identity (Riessman 1990: 4). In particular, Riessman examined the role of narratives in the reconstruction of self and creation of this new social identity.

In addition to the above studies, various others of a broadly academic nature focusing on the aftermath of divorce in the United States have generated books with a 'self-help' orientation that are self-consciously inspirational in tone (e.g. Hayes et al. 1993; Ahrons 1994).

Some of the key studies are longitudinal, allowing changes relating to the self and identity over time to be established. Chiriboga et al. (1991) discuss results from a longitudinal study (1977–80) of a random sample of separated and divorcing individuals, who were interviewed using a mixture of 'structured and unstructured questions' (1991: 5). Chiriboga et al. conceptualized divorce as a stressful transition with potentially negative or positive consequences, documenting a heterogeneous set of coping strategies employed by separated people (1991: 80), and identifying the maintenance of social support systems as important (1991: 93). They also noted that 'divorce is a transition that robs people of social involvements that form the basis . . . of one's sense of identity' (1991: 291). Moreover, in a detailed consideration of 'the self-concept of divorcing persons', they concluded that, notwithstanding a considerable degree of stability in self-images, 'during the early stages of a transition the individual's self-image may be particularly susceptible to change, especially change of a negative nature' (1991: 173).

Wallerstein and Blakeslee (1989) report results from a longitudinal study of families, recruited via a divorce counselling programme close to the point of marital separation,[4] and followed up for over 15 years. Wallerstein and Blakeslee identify a range of 'psychological tasks of divorce', including 'reclaiming oneself'. This involves establishing a new, separate sense of identity, perhaps by a divorced person reaching 'back into his or her early experience and find[ing] other images and roots for independence, for being able to live alone' (1989: 296). Wallerstein and Blakeslee implicitly emphasize the agency of divorced people. They suggest that 'People who divorce often lose confidence in their own judgement; at some point they must venture forth in order to regain that confidence' (1989: 296), and note that 'adults take up or fail to take up their second chances' or make 'better or worse use' of them (1989: 315).

Results reported by Hetherington and Kelly draw on a number of studies, including a complex study of divorced families, stepfamilies and non-divorced families, extending over more than two decades (2002: 281–4).

Various protective and risk factors relating to 'success or failure' after divorce are identified; the former include social maturity, autonomy and an internal locus of control, together with various forms of external contacts and activities, and the latter include various personal traits and contextual influences, and attachment to the former spouse (2002: 72–89). A typology of divorce pathways is identified, with six categories relating to levels of pro-activity and adaptation to change, together with different orientations to lifestyles and repartnering (2002: 65–6, 98–107). A frequent sense of loss of identity after divorce and associated change in an individual's concept of self were found to lead to 'flurries of self-improvement . . . and social activity', except where divorced mothers were constrained by economic and childcare issues (2002: 61).

Paid employment and material circumstances

Gender and parenthood both affect the employment situation of formerly married people, as is evident from Family Resources Survey (FRS) data (Kiernan and Mueller 1999: 383). These show little difference between the rates of paid employment of married and divorced women without co-resident children, but show divorced men without co-resident children to be less frequently employed than comparable married men, partly as a consequence of a higher unemployment rate. Divorced women and men with co-resident children were markedly less likely than married people to be in paid employment.

Kiernan and Mueller's results highlight the diversity of the employment status of divorced people; while most were found to be employed, a substantial minority were unemployed, and a larger minority were 'economically inactive', including about half the divorced women aged 25–39 with children. Substantial proportions of employed divorced people of each sex were found to be in professional and managerial occupations, again confirming the heterogeneity of divorced people in labour market terms, notwithstanding that they were found to be somewhat more likely than married people to have left education at the minimum age.

Separation sometimes leads to mothers leaving or re-entering paid employment (Maclean and Eekelaar 1997). In a chapter on parenthood and employment after divorce, Neale and Smart comment that 'The identities of the mothers in our sample appeared to be bound up primarily with their relationship with their children . . . where mothers do enter paid work, the motive may be as much to do with the personal fulfilment of paid work as it is with economic necessity', but that 'the identities of most of the fathers in our study remained bound up primarily with their employment', in terms of providing for their children and in relation to personal status and fulfilment (2002: 196). However, the majority of the divorced men surveyed by Ambrose et al. (1983) reported their marital break-up as having had a 'serious' or 'disastrous' impact on their work or career, for a variety of practical, personal and health-related reasons. Smart and Stevens demonstrate that the level of flexibility of the employment, or employment status, of non-resident fathers can impact on how easy it is for them to maintain their desired level of involvement with their children (2000: 38).

Maclean and Eekelaar (1997) have demonstrated the impact of separation on the incomes of both formerly married and formerly cohabiting parents, with formerly married or cohabiting mothers' incomes tending to decline initially after separation and then recover somewhat, but not to their pre-separation levels. Formerly married fathers' incomes also dipped after separation but then recovered, unless they were looking after children, in which case the recovery was only marginally better than that for formerly married mothers (1997: 139). However, income changes are heterogeneous, especially for men, whose incomes rise in some cases (Perry et al. 2000: 13–14). Jarvis and Jenkins (1999) used British Household Panel Survey (BHPS) data from the early 1990s to show that the short-term effects of separation on income are quite heterogeneous for both sexes, and indicated that the immediate impact is more negative for women.[5]

Hart found that both sexes experienced varying degrees of material deprivation, and that '[o]n the whole it was the middle-aged, lower middle class male who suffered the most drastic reverse in material circumstances' (1976: 145). About half of the divorced men surveyed by Ambrose et al. (1983) reported serious effects of the break-up and divorce on their financial position, with negative effects being more frequent among divorced fathers (1983: 119). However, Perry et al. suggest that markedly more divorced mothers than divorced fathers experience difficulties with the costs of basics such as food, clothing and transport, with nearly half of the former but less than a quarter of the latter reporting such difficulties (2000: 19).

Kiernan and Mueller (1999: 384) used FRS data to compare receipt of Income Support[6] between married and divorced people aged 25–59. Divorced people were markedly more likely to receive the benefit, but whilst a relatively small proportion of divorced people without children received it, around half of divorced women with children did, including over two-thirds of those aged 25–39. Maclean and Eekelaar (1997: 117) show that welfare benefits were the main source of income of about half of formerly married mothers, as compared to about one in eight of the same individuals before separation, and that the proportion was even higher for formerly cohabiting mothers.

The authors cited above also show that welfare benefits went some way towards negating the financial consequences of divorce for mothers in Britain in the 1990s. However, the role of benefits in this context is neither consistent across time nor cross-nationally. Dewilde (2002) and Uunk (2004) both identify larger post-separation income losses for women in Britain than in various other European countries, linking this to cross-national differences in welfare state arrangements. In addition, research highlights that a divorced mother's paid employment frequently becomes her main source of income at some point after separation (Perry et al. 2000: 14).[7] A new partner's income may reverse the negative financial consequences of separation, but Hughes (2000) points out that, in Australia, some of the most financially adversely affected categories of formerly married people – people with minimal economic resources and/or total responsibility for children – have the lowest rates of repartnering.

Rowlingson and McKay found that formerly partnered lone mothers who relied solely on income support felt very short of money (1998: 158). However, lone mothers often felt better off than before they separated, because of greater financial control, including the ability to spend money on what was really needed (1998: 160). A study of mothers leaving violent relationships also highlighted that, notwithstanding the particularly poor material circumstances of many such women, control over finances often made them feel relatively 'richer' (Wilcox 2000: 186). Divorced parents vary as to whether they report their living expenses as increasing or decreasing after separation; one study indicates that about half of divorced mothers actually experience a decrease in expenses: 'twelve parents reporting a drop in their living expenses said that expenses had gone down because they no longer had to meet their spouse's expenses' (Perry et al. 2000: 15).

Kiernan and Mueller found that about half of divorced people aged 25–59 were receiving Housing Benefit. For divorced women with children, the proportion was more than 5 out of 6 (1999: 384). Kiernan and Mueller also highlighted the relatively low proportion of divorced people who were home-owners; in particular, only about a third of younger divorced people with children were found to be home-owners. Research suggests that most divorced parents experience a housing move, or moves, at the point of separation or within a couple of years, with the proportion of divorced fathers moving being as high as three-quarters (Perry et al. 2000: 17). Flowerdew et al. (1999) note that divorced people, especially those with resident children, move short distances more often than other migrants (1999: 439).[8] Holmans (2000) found that nearly half of the members of owner-occupier divorcing couples who moved did not continue as owner-occupiers, and that female lone parents with dependent children fared worst in terms of moves to poorer accommodation or problems with mortgage repayments.[9]

Parenthood

Various authors (e.g. Churchill 2004) have argued that motherhood can act, albeit to a varying extent, as a source of identity for lone mothers. However, the results of a study of lone, primarily unmarried mothers in London and Berlin, who were state-dependent or in receipt of state benefit (Klett-Davies 2005), suggest that the degree to which full-time motherhood acts as a satisfactory source of self-identity relates to factors such as perceptions of control/choice, aspects of personal biographies, social class (though not necessarily material circumstances) and the extent to which a lone mother sees her status as comprehensible, manageable and meaningful. Nevertheless, a US study by Wang and Amato indicated that the presence of children post-divorce enhances the life of their resident parent (2000: 664).

In their study of post-divorce parenting and family life, Smart and Neale pointed out that the gendering of parental care activities leads to gendered parental identities, noting that the experience of being a full-time parent, together with dominant cultural constructions of motherhood, result in many divorced women having strong identities as mothers (1999: 51–2). However, Kielty (2005) suggests that where motherhood is a core source of identity for non-resident mothers, adjustment to their status can be very difficult. For some, 'living apart from their children [is] experienced as a physical loss of the very essence of their selfhood' (2005: 9).

Smart and Neale note that the 'good provider' father and the 'new man' father represent alternative identities that divorced men can adopt, with the former leading to their 'deriving a sense of identity from outside the home and family' (1999: 51–2). They also observe that, after separation, a substantial minority of divorced men moved further towards parenthood being a core aspect of their identity, this being facilitated via a shift in their labour market situation or by more time spent with their children as a consequence of at least partial co-residence (1999: 53–6).

Lewis et al. highlighted an assumption among former cohabitees that 'mothers have a "natural" claim to ownership of children', which could lead to a sense of powerlessness among fathers to maintain contact with and parenting responsibilities for their children (2002: 44–5). 'The mothers were depicted as being in control of paternal contact' (2002: 37), and a high level of involvement with their children before separation, in many cases 'equal' involvement (2002: 22), did not prevent fathers becoming distanced from their children after separation. Notwithstanding this, most fathers saw their children every week, and about a third most days or every day (2002: 32). Maclean and Eekelaar found that about two-thirds of formerly partnered parents who were not living with their children were in contact with them, but that many were not providing financial support. About two-fifths of formerly married fathers who were in contact with their children were not providing such support, rising to two-thirds of formerly cohabiting parents (1997: 99, 127).

'Mixed-method' research on non-resident fathers by Bradshaw et al. (1999) found markedly higher reported rates of contact and, especially, financial support. They provide some reflections on the disparity between their study and others in this context (1999: 126–7). Their multivariate analysis of regular contact indicated that geographical distance, a lack of paid employment and a new partner's children (whether stepchildren or their own) significantly decrease the likelihood of such contact (1999: 85–7), with the relationship with their ex-partner also being important. The negative effect of new children implies that levels of contact are, on average, higher among non-resident fathers who are not currently living with a partner, but repartnering also appears to be related to lower levels of contact in its own right, whether as a cause or an effect.

Bradshaw et al.'s results also echo those of Smart and Neale regarding change and diversity in fathers' post-separation parental roles. The role of father appears to be a source of identity for many formerly partnered men, but, as with non-resident mothers, it can simultaneously be a source of tension in relation to their status and self-identity. Simpson suggests that new ways of being a father, linked to the reorganization of contemporary masculinities, may represent an alternative to the difficulties and stress attached to attempting to retain a more conventional notion of fatherhood as a source of identity in a post-separation context (1998: 104).

Health and well-being

Hart illustrated extensively the meaninglessness of existence and lack of reality experienced by many after separation (1976: 189–93). She linked this short-term phenomenon of 'personal anomie' to a sense of normlessness and of crumbling social identity, followed by a reconstruction of self, and interpreted it as reflecting the core role that an individual's marital status once played in their sense of identity (1976: 195). Hart noted numerous instances of 'nervous illnesses, receipt of psychiatric help, and suicidal behaviour' among her respondents during the period of anomie (1976: 201). A study of divorced men found that most experienced new 'mental health' problems – severe ones in a substantial minority of cases (Ambrose et al. 1983: 90–2). Jessop (in Day Sclater 1999) reviews research relating adults' experiences of divorce to their psychological adjustment and well-being, including evidence relating to the disproportionately high rates of psychiatric admissions and depression among divorced people. Wade and Pevalin (2004) analysed BHPS data and found a higher prevalence of poor mental health after the end of marriage. However, disproportionately poor average levels of mental health also preceded separation or divorce, suggesting that social causation and social selection explanations are both credible.[10]

Burgoyne and Clark found that negative health consequences were frequent after separation among 'recipients' of divorce, but that health problems among 'initiators' were often experienced before separation (1984: 76–8). Time since separation was central to Amato's (primarily North American) literature review regarding the consequences of divorce. He suggested that separation has a heterogeneous impact, with a short-term 'crisis model' being appropriate for some people, but a longer-term 'chronic strain' model being appropriate for others (2000: 1275). Amato also suggested that the magnitude of the impact of divorce on psychological well-being and health is not gendered, unlike its economic impact (2000: 1277).

Similarly, analyses of malaise scores by Hope et al. (1999), using NCDS data corresponding to the 1958 birth cohort, showed a marked relative increase in scores within the first couple of years following separation for people who separated as compared to staying married, and an ongoing but smaller relative increase thereafter, the latter being statistically significant only for women. Hope et al.'s results lack generality because of the relatively young age of their separating respondents, but Willitts et al. (2004) reported similar results based on BHPS GHQ score data.[11] Interestingly, the former study found some evidence, albeit statistically non-significant, that the negative effect for women only applied to those with parental responsibilities (1999: 386), and the latter found repartnering to be associated with better mental health, perhaps more strongly for men (2004: 55).

Burck and Daniel note that feelings of loss and powerlessness are common among divorced people. More specific aspects of such feelings include a sense that a 'planned future' has been lost, and, for some men, a sense of threatened masculinity relating to a loss of control inherent in being unable to influence their wives' decisions to leave (1995: 191; see also Arendell 1995). Conversely, while Day Sclater's interviewees found divorce to be a very traumatic experience that adversely affected their psychological well-being, finding the strength to cope was mentioned positively (1999: 136–7). However, Rowlingson and McKay noted a frequently mentioned disadvantage of lone motherhood: 'the burden of sole responsibility for decisions' (1998: 194).

Kiernan and Mueller's analysis of FRS data suggests that people in partnerships are less likely than divorced people to have long-standing illnesses, to have illnesses that restrict the work they can do and to be in receipt of disability benefits. They also found that '[m]ale divorcees under age 40 are more likely than female divorcees to have long-standing illnesses or illnesses that restrict employment, while male divorcees in general . . . are more likely to be in receipt of disability benefits' (1999: 384).[12] Such illness and disability will often have pre-dated separation and divorce, but among the divorced men in Ambrose et al.'s (1983) survey a substantial minority reported new physical health-related problems, many apparently stress-related (1983: 88–9). Simpson suggests that the physical health problems experienced by some divorced men, which are potentially exacerbated by excessive drinking, smoking and paid work, may reflect their avoidance of a 'feminized' channel of expression via 'psychological distress' (1998: 92).

Social lives and networks

While the nature of Hart's sample of divorced and separated people may have led to an overemphasis on the negative consequences of separation and divorce, it is still notable that her respondents typically 'mentioned some form of social isolation as their most pressing problem' (1976: 159). She commented that her respondents 'felt it necessary to distinguish their condition as a peculiar form of loneliness, one characterised by the loss of the most intimate source of companionship in modern society, the marriage partner' (1976: 173). Furthermore, '[t]hose who relied mainly on joint friendships during married life were the most exposed to social neglect after separation and divorce' (1976: 165). Ambrose et al. (1983: 123) found that the survival of joint friendships was highly dependent on how friendly or hostile divorced men were to their ex-wives.

Simpson (1999) notes that life after separation can be characterized by both continuities and transformations in relationship networks. However, since these networks often involve the ex-partner, they may generate confusion and stress (1999: 127). In addition, Burck and Daniel conclude from their clinical work that a cultural norm of couple-located intimacy can undermine the value that separated people place on the roles of friends and members of extended families (1995: 189). Conversely, Shaw reports that friends, families and support groups are an important and valued aspect of formerly married mothers' lives (1991: 145).

Secondary analyses of General Household Survey (GHS) data have shown the social contacts and networks of divorced men aged 65 or more to be more limited than those of other men and all women of a similar age (Arber et al. 2003; Davidson et al. 2003). Arber et al. note that, while both divorced men and divorced women are materially disadvantaged, divorced women, unlike divorced men, 'are almost as integrated into social networks of relatives, friends and neighbours as married women and widows' (2003: 165). However, the price of avoiding social isolation may be a loss of autonomy and self-esteem, as experienced by divorced people who return to live with their parents after separation (Burgoyne and Clark 1984: 81).

O'Brien (1987) found that lone fathers were more engaged with kin where they had become lone fathers via custody disputes. She also found that '[a]s with kin relationships, lone fathers are more likely than married men to lead a life of either social isolation or frenetic socialising' (1987: 230). Lone fathers appeared less likely than married fathers to socialize with couples, but markedly more likely to have cross-sex (usually platonic) friendships, often reflecting a common interest in children (1987: 236). O'Brien suggests that lone fatherhood necessitates the construction of a new identity, finding that many lone fathers had visited one-parent family groups such as Gingerbread. Some found such groups a useful source of social support and a social life, but others felt marginalized by their status as male lone parents, echoing the broader diversity of lone fathers' social lives, and perhaps of their ability to adjust to their situation via a new identity (1987: 239–41).

In their study of stepfamilies, Burgoyne and Clark found that 'recipients' who had not initiated their marriage break-up typically experienced isolation and loneliness after separation and had difficulty breaking out into new social circles, especially where they had heavy domestic obligations or custody of children (1984: 65–8). Some had responded actively by joining clubs for divorced and separated people or by placing personal advertisements.

Cultural and normative context

Hart notes not only that 'divorcees themselves held adverse stereotypes about the status of which they had unfortunately found themselves the incumbent' (1976: 155), but also that 'discrimination and stigma lie without as well as within the mind of the divorcee. They are an integral part of the mental make-up of many "normal" members of British society and as such they are an important determinent [*sic*] of why life can be so difficult for ordinary divorced and separated people' (1976: 156). Her respondents also commented on the prominence of couples and 'happy families' in mass media advertising, and the impact of this on their morale and sense of isolation (1976: 171).

Equally importantly, Hart links the existence of problems after marital breakdown firmly to the 'lack of normative prescription informing the status passage' (1976: 125). She echoes ideas from earlier North American work (Goode 1956), which stresses the absence of 'institutional prescriptions' for the formerly married, and, interestingly, views remarriage as the only viable solution to their problems. Hart also suggests that the status of being divorced lacked 'normative validity' and was something to which the divorced did not become reconciled, viewing it a stage in an ongoing process rather than an accepted status (1976: 221). Nevertheless, her conclusions incorporated her respondents' various attempted 'solutions' to the problems of divorce, which 'went together with continued incumbency of the divorcee status' (1976: 228).

Day Sclater (1999) reports that the divorce discourses that her interviewees could draw on contained 'a plethora of negative, even pathologised, images' (1999: 146), and that 'the prevalent image of divorce in our society continues to be a negative one' (1999: 150). More specifically, various authors have reiterated the stigma attached to lone parenthood (Chambers 2001), and the pressure to recreate a 'proper' family generated by traditional familial ideology (Collins 1991: 160). However, Shaw concluded, albeit cautiously, that lone parenting had become more acceptable and that there was consequently a diminished pressure to remarry (1991: 154).

Similarly, a standard assumption within recent sociology textbooks appears to be that there is little stigma attached to divorce *per se* (Giddens 1989: 399; Browne 2002: 65–7), and that this has contributed to a high divorce rate, as well as reflecting it (Stone 1990: 415). Simpson, citing Giddens (1991), has suggested that 'divorce is more likely to be cast in an idiom of journeying, growth and self-discovery' (1999: 128). On the other hand, in her discussion of various types of 'women without husbands', Chandler (1991: 68) highlights the 'difficulties of forging a new identity and of making sense of a world which disparages women who are alone'. Being on one's own may thus be equally, or more, problematic than being divorced, although any gendered stigma attached to being alone may be diminishing.

Therapeutic and policy interventions

Hart notes the absence of institutional mechanisms in the late 1960s helping structure the separation and divorce 'status passage' (1976: 127). However, since then the 'medicalisation of marriage' (Morgan 1985), a proliferation of 'technicians of human relations' (Rodger 1996) and relevant changes in organizations such as RELATE (Lewis et al. 1992) have occurred. Legislation such as the Children Act 1989, the Child Support Act 1991 and the Family Law Act 1996 illustrate the scale of legal intervention and its frequent association with parenthood.[13] Walker (2001) notes that the piloting of 'information meetings' led to a minority of divorcing people attending counselling, which helped some cope with the end of their marriage, but also pointed out that others did not go on to counselling because they felt it would not help. While it appears that by the 1990s there was a greater, arguably institutionalized, tendency to use formal 'therapeutic' resources to facilitate the separation and divorce 'status passage', recourse to such resources seems to have remained a minority phenomenon. Ambrose et al. (1983) report that divorced men found informal and semi-formal sources of support, mainly within their social networks, to be more helpful on average than formal sources of support, such as doctors, lawyers and marriage guidance, but that the small minority who had approached voluntary or private sources specifically oriented to helping people through their divorces evaluated these sources positively (1983: 67).

The formerly partnered and couple relationships

The relevance of past relationships and current relationships

Shaw points out that previous experiences of marriage among separated or divorced mothers frequently affect orientations to repartnering by generating 'wariness, reluctance or inability to trust, and fear of getting hurt again' (1991: 149), often as a consequence of adultery, betrayal or being left. Past relationships may also inform what people want in future relationships. For example, a qualitative study of divorced people in the US (Schneller and Arditti 2004) identified a desire for greater equality and improvements in communication. Furthermore, past relationships and events tend to influence attitudes and behaviour in general, both during and after the repartnering process (Burgoyne and Clark 1984: 99).

Day Sclater (1999) reports that 'revisiting' or looking back over past relationships seems to 'play a crucial role in the reconstructions of self which divorce renders necessary' (1999: 161), with reinterpretation of the past being a necessary step towards a new, separate self. According to Simpson (1998), 'separated men and women [frequently] feel that their former partners continue to have residual and deeply unwelcome power and control long after they have ceased to be husband and wife' (1998: 134). Day Sclater cites and echoes US research (Vaughan 1987) suggesting that, in addition to the development of an 'ideology of self', the process of 'uncoupling' commonly involves the denigration of the past relationship and partner. Hunt notes that, among formerly married people in the United States, this kind of denigration sometimes featured within the courtship process (1966: 122)

Another US study found that women adjusted more easily to divorce if they had not invested heavily in their marital identity (DeGarmo and Kitson 1996). Kahn (1990) developed, via clinical work as a psychotherapist in the United States, the idea of a psychological disorder, 'the ex-wife syndrome', which 'stops women forming a separate identity away from the ex-spouse and ultimately from completing the psychological tasks of divorce' (Day Sclater 1999: 87). Arendell (1995) suggests that while divorced fathers in the United States who adopted a 'traditionalist' masculinity were preoccupied in a negative way with their ex-wives, it was the minority of more 'innovative' fathers whose time and energy to repartner were most undermined by their parenting role. In general, ongoing ties and obligations often lead to divorced people feeling bound to their former partners (Simpson 1999: 127).

Unsurprisingly, US research by Wang and Amato (2000: 664) showed that where an individual wanted a divorce more than their partner did, their attachment to their ex-spouse was weaker and their general level of adjustment to divorce was greater. A positive attitude to divorce as an act was also found to relate to weaker attachment to one's ex-spouse. Wang and Amato also highlighted the benefits of new relationships for post-divorce adjustment, and Burgoyne and Clark (1984: 84–5) found new relationships to be of therapeutic value in terms of the construction of meaningful explanations of the past. The contribution of 'dating' to the sense of identity of formerly married people was noted in Hunt's early US study (1966: 125).

The value of new relationships is also demonstrated by a small-scale survey of heterosexual, 'Living Apart Together' (LAT) relationships in Sweden. Such relationships were found to offer women, including the formerly married, the balance desired between intimacy on the one hand, and autonomy and control over their daily activities on the other, without an unacceptable, gendered division of household labour (Borell and Ghazanfareeon Karlsson 2003).

Future relationships

In Hart's study, 'Seventy-three per cent of my respondents said that they would like to remarry, but the majority felt that their prospects of doing so were rather limited' (1976: 180). This may have reflected what Hart felt was arguably the greatest barrier to repartnering: 'the loss of self-confidence generated by a sense of failure, rejection and personal inadequacy in so many cases' (1976: 186). Ambrose et al. (1983) found that divorced men varied between keenness, indifference and hostility in their attitudes to remarriage, and suggested that 'the *desire* to remarry might, for many, be unconsciously conditioned by an assessment of their *capacity* to remarry in the light of domestic and financial circumstances' (1983: 139). Rowlingson and McKay (1998) found that most lone mothers neither ruled out nor were keen to establish a new relationship, but 'preferred lone parenthood to an unhappy relationship' (1998: 194). Some of Shaw's sample of separated or divorced mothers expressed a clear preference for cohabiting rather than remarrying (1991: 155), and the vast majority of the married couples in a study of step-families cohabited before remarriage, mainly as a 'trial marriage' or because they simply decided to move in together, rather than as a consequence of barriers to remarriage (Burgoyne and Clark 1984: 88).

Hart observed that the 'internalized models of a suitable partner' of some of her respondents of both sexes had not changed since before they were married, and that such 'redundant norms', relating to factors such as age, parental status and attractiveness, undermined the effectiveness of their repartnering behaviour (1976: 185). Ambrose et al. (1983: 139–43) also noted some interesting apparent relationships between aspects of divorced men's lives and the desire to remarry. Men who reported permanent harm to their career or marked financial ill effects were more often against remarriage, and the subgroup who were most angry about the divorce and its consequences were markedly more hostile to the idea than the least angry subgroup.

Reasons for finding a new partner or for staying as a formerly partnered person

Finlayson et al. (2000: 40) used data collected from the British Lone Parent Cohort (BLPC) in 1996 and 1998 to look at lone parents' reasons for not currently living within a couple, although around a fifth had never been married or cohabited. About half stated that they preferred to live independently, and a similar proportion, with some degree of overlap, agreed that 'I have not met anyone I liked enough to live with'. These two possibilities account for the main reason given in over two-thirds of cases. Among the vast majority of the remainder, the main reasons were split fairly evenly across three types of answer: 'it would not be good for the children', scepticism about the value or durability of such relationships, and economic or practical reasons. Conversely, Collins (1991: 158) suggests that some lone parents may feel under pressure to repartner by poverty and the practical burdens of daily life.

A concern about loss of independence was also cited by many interviewees in another study as a reason to stay as a lone mother (Rowlingson and McKay 1998). A desire for closeness, adult company and sexual intimacy were seen as incentives to find a new partner (1998: 171), but respondents frequently did not see a partner as a personal necessity (1998: 167), and often saw the ideal man as someone 'happy to allow their partner a degree of independence' (1998: 194). Some saw their ideal situation as having a partner who maintained a separate home (1998: 173). Burck and Daniel suggest that, while repartnering may bolster an individual's sense of self, it may also challenge aspects of a sense of self that have developed after separation (1995: 199). Hence, a new, independent identity may act as a disincentive to repartner (Arendell 1986: 142–5; Collins 1991; Shaw 1991: 147–9).

In a study of widowed people aged 65 or more, Davidson (2001) found that widows often associated their current situation with 'freedom', albeit viewed as 'selfish', which 'was associated with not having to look after someone all the time . . . [although] none of the men associated widowhood with a sense of freedom' (2001: 297). In another study of men aged 65+, divorced men were less content with their social situation than other men, and were often found to want another close relationship 'particularly those who had experienced an attenuated relationship with adult children' (Davidson et al. 2003: 180).

Many of Rowlingson and McKay's respondents saw staying as a lone mother as better for their children. Some were scared to trust men with their children, some felt a new partner would cause their children to experience additional confusion, and some felt that they 'should concentrate their time and attention on their children . . . especially if their children were very young' (1998: 169). However, some lone mothers saw potential benefits in having a male figure in their children's (especially sons') lives (1998: 172). Moreover, in Burgoyne and Clark's study of stepfamilies, some women commented favourably on their initial perceptions of the parenting skills of new partners relative to their ex-spouses (1984: 83).

Some lone mothers in Rowlingson and McKay's study recognized the financial advantages of finding a partner (1998: 170), but there was often a perceived absence of any financial necessity to repartner (1998: 167), and many saw both a positive interest in their children and a willingness and ability to make a financial contribution to the running of the household as necessary features of any new partner (1998: 170, 173). In their qualitative study of step-parenting, Ribbens McCarthy et al. (2000: 800) point out that the 'moral imperative to seek to put children's needs first' is very often seen as informing decision-making, because it is a prerequisite for sustaining a 'morally adequate identity'.

New relationships and new children?

In an earlier analysis of GHS data we found that, among formerly married women aged under 35 who had not had children, 4 out of 5 said that they thought that they would probably have a child or children, as compared to fewer than 1 in 5 who already had one or more children (Lampard and Peggs 1999: 453). Jefferies et al. (2000) used GHS data to examine childbearing after marital dissolution and found repartnering to be very strongly associated with women conceiving a child, especially after remarriage to a previously unmarried partner. Interestingly, the conception rate for women without children was found to be *lower* than that for women with young children. Jefferies et al. attribute this to heterogeneity, suggesting that women without children include women 'with a high propensity to have a birth and [also] those that are unable or unwilling to' (2000: 203). They note that it can be difficult to establish whether childbearing is the cause or the consequence of repartnering.

Bearing in mind the above results, one can draw the following conclusions. For many formerly married women, including some without children, childbearing is not an expectation or intention, and thus does not provide an incentive to repartner. However, for others, such an intention exists, although it may or may not provide an incentive to repartner, depending on the woman's attitude to lone parenthood. Furthermore, it seems likely that, for some women, childbearing is an option that is contingent on (or stimulated by) repartnering, and may also be contingent on other factors such as the age(s) of their existing children.

Key studies of repartnering behaviour

This section highlights key studies whose results relating to repartnering are reported below. In an earlier paper (Lampard and Peggs 1999), we used GHS data to carry out a multivariate analysis of repartnering after the end of people's first marriages, over a period of a few decades leading up to the early 1990s. More recently, Ermisch (2002) used BHPS data to examine repartnering among people who dissolved a marriage or cohabiting union in the 1990s.

A number of relevant examinations of (re)partnering among lone parents have involved not just formerly married people and former cohabitees, but also never-married lone parents who have never cohabited. Hence, many of their results are not specific to repartnering, though some of the analyses break lone parents down into pertinent sub-groups. Rowlingson and McKay (1998) analysed data from the Social Change and Economic Life Initiative (SCELI) and focused on a period from the 1960s to the mid-1980s. Payne and Range (1998) analysed NCDS data corresponding to people born in 1958 collected up to and during 1991, and consequently their analysis relates primarily to young lone parents in the 1980s. Various analyses of repartnering behaviour during the 1990s have been carried out using BLPC data (Ford et al. 1998; Finlayson et al. 2000; Marsh and Vegeris 2004).

The above studies support an observation made by De Graaf and Kalmijn (2003: 1462–5) when reviewing 14 key European and American studies of repartnering. They state that 'the number of independent variables taken together is small. Studies are limited to demographic and rudimentary economic determinants of remarriage' (2003: 1467). De Graaf and Kalmijn's own analyses for the Netherlands are more conceptually sophisticated than the existing analyses corresponding to Britain.[14] They treat marriage and cohabitation after divorce as 'competing risks', give due regard to the roles of 'social integration' and opportunities for repartnering, and attempt to 'unpack' the effects of different aspects of employment and economic circumstances on the likelihood of repartnering.

Analyses of repartnering behaviour: age, gender and time

In an earlier paper we found increasing age at end of first marriage to be associated with a decreased likelihood of repartnering, with this effect being somewhat stronger for women than for men. For virtually all ages at end of first marriage and durations separated, we found women to have a lower repartnering rate than men (Lampard and Peggs 1999: 448). Haskey (1999) makes similar observations regarding the impact of age and gender, and Ermisch also found that older people repartner more slowly (2002: 3).

Ermisch notes that about 1 in 12 formerly married people moved directly into a cohabiting union with a different partner (2002: 5). More generally, like our earlier paper, he showed that the repartnering rate declines as the time elapsed since the dissolution increases. Ermisch suggests that this is not simply a consequence of heterogeneity among the formerly partnered (Lampard and Peggs 1999: 448; Ermisch 2002: 3). Finlayson et al. (2000: 57) also found the pace of couple formation to be 'significantly slower among lone parents who had been alone for a long while'. Rowlingson and McKay developed a model of repartnering that suggests that the repartnering rate of formerly married female lone parents is relatively low immediately after separation, subsequently increases for about five years, and then declines continuously thereafter (1998: 149).

The creation and locations of repartnering opportunities

Hart comments that for women in the late 1960s, especially older women, 'although the "institutionalized pressure towards remarriage" may be felt keenly, it is not associated with adequate opportunities to make such a step feasible' (1976: 180). In the Netherlands, De Graaf and Kalmijn found strong support for the theory that opportunities are crucial (2003: 1494), commenting that 'divorced women who are better integrated socially have better chances of meeting a new partner, which is why they are more likely to repartner' (2003: 1488). Participation in leisure activities was found to increase significantly the likelihood of repartnering for women (2003: 1484), but, if anything, to reduce the likelihood for men (2003: 1487), which suggests that the type of activity, and perhaps the way it is viewed, may be of relevance.

De Graaf and Kalmijn's results highlight the point that opportunities to find a partner may be a by-product of other activities, or may alternatively be generated actively. While they found that paid work played a key role in generating repartnering opportunities, a non-negligible proportion of new partners had been located via personal advertisements or some similarly active approach. Moreover, more than 1 in 8 of their sample had made use of advertisements or intermediaries, or had attended meetings specifically for 'singles'. They suggest that this, together with the relative unimportance of 'public places' in the 'remarriage market', indicates that divorced people tend to be poorly socially integrated, and consequently lack repartnering opportunities (2003: 1477).

The way in which a distinction between active and passive approaches to repartnering relates to the 'locations' of repartnering opportunities is evident in Hunt's early US research. He illustrated that, 40 years ago, some formerly married people were already prepared to be proactive in their search for a new partner, even if this meant being 'unconventional', taking risks and setting aside 'middle-class proprieties' (1966: 108).

Marital status, marital histories and repartnering

As noted in Chapter 3, the type of previous relationship and the way in which it ended (whether through cohabitation breakdown, marital separation or divorce, or through the death of a partner), may influence the repartnering rate (Wu and Schimmele 2005). Our earlier paper showed that 'amongst the widowed, only men who are widowed at a very young age . . . have a repartnering rate comparable to that of their divorced/separated counterparts' (Lampard and Peggs 1999: 451). The gender difference in the repartnering rates of widowed people was found to be particularly marked, a finding echoed by Haskey (1999: 21), and their repartnering rate was found to diminish more quickly with increasing age than that for other formerly married people. Ermisch also found that widows repartnered more slowly than divorced and separated people (2002: 6), and that more than two-thirds of people leaving a cohabiting union repartnered within five years, compared to less than half of people leaving a marriage. However, most of the latter difference could be explained by the different age distributions of the two groups. In contrast, a multivariate analysis of BLPC data showed that lone parents whose last co-residential relationship before 1991 had been a cohabitation were significantly less likely than other lone parents to have a partner in 2001 (Marsh and Vegeris 2004: 204).[15]

Other aspects of people's marital histories may affect their repartnering behaviour. Both a higher age at first marriage and a period of pre-marital cohabitation with one's marriage partner have been shown to be associated with a lower repartnering rate (Lampard and Peggs 1999: 451). Marsh and Vegeris found that a report of violence in a lone parent's last relationship had virtually no association with their likelihood of repartnering (2004: 46).

Children and repartnering

Our earlier paper used GHS data relating to fertility histories to show 'that as the number of children born to them before the end of their first marriage increases, the likelihood of formerly married women repartnering decreases' (Lampard and Peggs 1999: 452). However, past births do not constitute a conceptually ideal measure for assessing the impact of children, whereas the longitudinal structure of the BHPS allowed Ermisch to examine, for both sexes, the effect of child custody on repartnering. He found that the formerly partnered repartnered significantly more slowly if they had custody of a child (Ermisch 2002: 6).

In our earlier analysis, the difference between the repartnering rates for men in general and for women who had not given birth by the end of their first marriage was not statistically significant (Lampard and Peggs 1999: 452). Similarly, Ermisch observed that taking account of child custody rendered the difference between men's and women's repartnering rates insignificant (Ermisch 2002: 5). Furthermore, taking account of the number of children born to women also accounted for the interaction between the effects of gender and age on repartnering rates that we found in our earlier analysis (1999: 451). Thus it appears that both the gender difference in repartnering rates and its variation according to age are artefacts of the existence of children.

The ages of formerly married people's children have also been hypothesized to be of importance. In a multivariate logistic regression analysis of BLPC data, Ford et al. (1998: 33) found that lone parents were markedly less likely to leave lone parenthood during the next four years if their youngest child was under five years of age rather than in the range 5–15 years. Similarly, in an analysis of NCDS data focusing on young, formerly partnered lone mothers, Payne and Range (1998: 5) found that having children aged under five at separation reduced the likelihood of moving in with a new partner, but also that a reconciliation with their previous partner was more likely if there was a child aged under 12 months.[16] However, a multivariate analysis of more recent BLPC data showed that having a child under five significantly increases the likelihood of living with a partner ten years later (Marsh and Vegeris 2004: 204). The apparent contradiction between the above results disappears if one assumes that any impact of having young children does not persist as the children grow older. Thus the preceding results suggest that young children reduce the likelihood of repartnering in the short term, but do not necessarily do so in the longer term.

A woman may, of course, have given birth to a child since her last separation. Payne and Range (1998: 5) identified a reduced likelihood of repartnering relative to other separated or divorced lone mothers among women who had given birth more than nine months after separation. Clearly, this group is likely to have included women who had had a relationship of some substance with the biological father but who had not moved in with him. Such women might be expected to have a lower repartnering rate, irrespective of any impact of the child's existence.

Non-resident children may also have an impact on repartnering behaviour. Qualitative research by Bradshaw et al. (1999) highlighted the potential for tension for a non-resident father between maintaining contact with children, especially at a distance, and finding or moving in with a new partner (1999: 106, 111). However, the evidence relating to the impact of non-custodial children in Britain is very limited. In research on children and union formation in Sweden which considered both co-resident and non-resident children, and also both partners' parenting histories, Bernhardt and Goldscheider only found a negative impact on the repartnering rate for women with co-resident children and only in relation to repartnering men without co-resident children (2002: 296). However, in the Netherlands, De Graaf and Kalmijn found that co-resident children had a negative impact on the likelihood of repartnering for both women and (especially) men, and that, for men, non-resident children also had a negative impact, albeit a weaker one. Children reduced the likelihood of finding a partner via paid work, especially for women, and via leisure activities, especially for men (2003: 1484-9).

Other characteristics of children that have an impact on their parents' time, commitment or opportunities may also affect their repartnering behaviour. For example, Finlayson et al. (2000: 57) reported that lone parents 'whose children had long-term limiting illnesses or disability were also slower to repartner'.

Class, paid employment and other factors affecting repartnering behaviour

Our earlier paper showed a more advantaged position in the class structure to be associated with a greater likelihood of repartnering, except for women in professional occupations (Lampard and Peggs 1999: 451). Similarly, Rowlingson and McKay (1998: 150) used SCELI data to show that female lone parent home-owners were much more likely to repartner than those in other housing situations. Again, this suggests that material advantage may somehow facilitate repartnering.[17] Payne and Range (1998: 5) found that lone mothers living in social housing or with their parents were less likely to repartner, but pointed out that this housing effect may reflect other underlying socio-economic factors. They also found a higher repartnering rate for lone mothers in London and the south of England than elsewhere, which may similarly reflect underlying socio-economic factors, or perhaps opportunities for repartnering (1998: 5).

Turning to paid employment, a multivariate analysis of BLPC data showed that lone parents doing 16 or more hours of paid work per week were more likely to end up living with a partner (Marsh and Vegeris 2004: 204). However, an earlier multivariate survival analysis of BLPC data suggested that repartnering was slower among lone parents in paid work than among other lone parents (Finlayson et al. 2000: 55). Conversely, in a multivariate analysis of NCDS data, Payne and Range (1998: 6) found that lone mothers in paid work appeared slightly more likely to repartner than those who were not. These apparently paradoxical results seem to imply that hours of paid work, or more specifically the distinction between full-time and part-time work, may be of relevance to repartnering behaviour.[18] However, Payne and Range did not find any difference between the effects of full-time and part-time paid work.

Finlayson et al. (2000) suggest that paid work may slow down repartnering by conferring choice and independence; conversely, Payne and Range (1998) make the plausible suggestion that paid work outside the home often brings people into contact with potential partners. The economic, interpersonal, temporal and psychological dimensions of paid work may thus have diverse and potentially contradictory implications for repartnering behaviour. De Graaf and Kalmijn took this view in their research focusing on the Netherlands; they found that paid work significantly increased divorce people's likelihood of repartnering, but specifically via this work for women, and primarily via this work for men (2003: 1485–7).

Some other factors affecting repartnering behaviour relate to personal characteristics rather than socio-economic situations. Pevalin and Ermisch (2004) used BHPS GHQ score data to show that poor mental health reduced the risk of repartnering for former cohabitees, but a similar, weaker effect for the formerly married was not statistically significant. In their analysis of longitudinal NCDS data, Payne and Range (1998: 5) utilized a measure of young lone mothers' general 'intellectual ability' when aged about eleven years.[19] They found that women whose 'ability' fell into the bottom fifth of the distribution of scores were relatively unlikely to find a new partner, but that, apart from this, increasing 'ability' seemed to be associated with a lower likelihood of establishing a new partnership. Their results also indicated that the likelihood of reconciliation with a previous partner decreases as 'ability' increases. More generally, the impact of educational achievement was examined by some of the studies reviewed by De Graaf and Kalmijn, whose own research showed that a higher level of educational achievement increased the likelihood of repartnering for divorced men, but not for divorced women (2003: 1486).

Other factors considered by earlier studies include urbanization, family background, migration and religion. De Graaf and Kalmijn's results regarding the impact of religion are quite complex, but they also examined the impact of a broader range of cultural values, generating results which suggest that an individual's values may reduce their likelihood of repartnering by predisposing them against marriage or cohabitation, or both (2003: 1484–7).

Who do the formerly partnered repartner?

Ermisch found that, in a small minority of cases, 'repartnering' involved moving back in with an ex-partner (2002: 5). Similarly, in their examination of partnership formation among lone parents, Finlayson et al. (2000: 37) found that a sixth of new partnerships were reconciliations, although this was less common if the last co-resident relationship had been a cohabitation. Payne and Range (1998: 5) also found reconciliations to be more frequent among formerly married lone parents than among those who were former cohabitees. In addition, they found that the likelihood of reconciliation did not vary with age, but 'fell dramatically as the spell of lone motherhood lengthened' (1998: 5).

It has often been hypothesized that spouses in remarriages are less similar to each other than spouses in first marriages (Dean and Gurak 1978). Ní Bhrolcháin (2005) used official marriage data for England and Wales to examine age differences between spouses, providing evidence of greater diversity within remarriages than first marriages. However, she pointed out that 'very large disparities in age are not in any sense typical in remarriages' (2005: 11), and that the magnitude and direction of the average difference reflect which partner or partners are remarrying. We have shown that the tendency for endogamy, or 'in-marriage', among divorced people does not simply reflect the similarity of marriage partners' ages. An analysis of official data for 1975 and 1993 (Lampard 1997) showed that the tendency remained once marriage partners' ages had been taken into account.

Ní Bhrolcháin (1988) points out that the current and previous spouses of remarried people frequently differ from each other, at least in terms of age and social class. Turning to similarity in relation to class and other stratification-related characteristics, the research evidence is limited, but an analysis of GHS data hints at a greater tendency for dissimilarity of social class background in marriages where the wife had been married before (Lampard 1992: 245).[20] Employment status may be equally pertinent, since 'lone parents [in paid work] who find partners, almost always find partners who themselves have full-time paid jobs. Non-working lone parents are far more likely to join with non-working partners' (Ford et al. 1998: 23).

Important themes evident from the literature

In addition to providing a backdrop of information regarding the formerly married and former cohabitees, the literature reviewed in this chapter serves to highlight important themes that we, as researchers in this area, need to bear in mind. One of the most significant of these is the heterogeneity of the formerly partnered. For example, their life histories and relationship histories vary in ways that impact on their experiences and behaviour. Of comparable importance are the different ways in which individuals engage with and respond to the past. More generally, formerly partnered people do not experience a common set of economic, social and cultural constraints, and they are also far from uniform in how active they have been, and currently are, in making and acting on decisions about their lives and relationships.

Attempts to generalize about the formerly partnered are thus likely to be problematic. The literature also indicates that trying to evaluate the lives of particular formerly partnered individuals in straightforwardly positive or negative terms is likely to lead to oversimplifications, since their experiences are often characterized by ambiguity, and their situations may not be consistently negative or positive across their economic, social, cultural and personal dimensions. However, the literature does document a tendency towards marginality in relation to a number of dimensions of the lives of the formerly partnered. While marginality is not experienced universally or to the same degree, economic, social and cultural marginality are nevertheless recurrent themes.

Ideas relating to transitions and change also feature prominently in the literature. Among these are notions of the reconstruction of identity and self-development. Achieving a satisfactory sense of self after separation is presented as contingent on an individual being able to disengage from their past relationship(s) and assume an independent identity, or being able to maintain or develop roles that provide a source of identity. There are hints here of the emphasis on individualism that can be found in the contemporary theoretical literature (see Chapter 3), but the literature reviewed in this chapter also highlights the specific normlessness of the formerly partnered status. The absence of clear-cut and well-established societal guidelines for 'appropriate' behaviour, together with the declining salience of traditional ideas and expectations regarding the life course, and their lack of fit with formerly partnered people's lives, create a cultural vacuum within which formerly partnered people have to operate.

Given the salience of gender to many key aspects of the lives of formerly partnered people, such as parenthood, it seems inevitable that their experiences and behaviour will vary in ways that reflect this. However, heterogeneity within each sex and the fact that it is largely the same aspects of men's and women's lives which are crucial, albeit sometimes in differing ways, mean that broad similarities may be as striking as any gender differences.

Quantitative analyses of secondary data: introduction and technical issues

The rest of this chapter consists of secondary analyses of survey data from a number of sources. The purpose of these analyses is to document some of the key characteristics of formerly partnered people, and key features of their repartnering behaviour, in a way that complements the analyses of our qualitative data (presented in later chapters). Among other steps forward relative to past research, the secondary analyses provide a picture of the characteristics and behaviour of former cohabitees, comparing them to formerly married people. The analyses also extend our earlier analysis of repartnering behaviour (Lampard and Peggs 1999) and give an insight into attitudes and behaviour of relevance to the repartnering process, specifically repartnering orientations and non-resident sexual and couple relationships.

The analyses that follow use a conventional value for assessing statistical significance (5 per cent). However, the reader can assume that any differences or effects that are discussed are significant at the 1 per cent level ($p < 0.01$), unless otherwise stated.[21] Explicit information regarding p-values is given where differences or effects are significant, but not at the 1 per cent level, and also for some differences or effects which just fall short of significance.

Bivariate relationships (relationships between two variables) have been tested for statistical significance using chi-square tests, unless it is otherwise stated. However, Yates's continuity correction has been used for analyses of 2×2 cross-tabulations.[22] The multivariate analyses (analyses involving more than two variables) make use of binary logistic regression, unless otherwise stated.[23] Wald tests have been used to assess the statistical significance of the effects of explanatory variables within the logistic regressions.

A sample of formerly partnered people from the General Household Survey

To complement our qualitative sample, data from the 2001–2 General Household Survey (GHS) were used to construct a sample of people who were formerly married or former cohabitees in April 1996. The GHS is a multipurpose continuous, usually annual, survey collecting information from people living in private households in Great Britain.[24]

The retrospective relationship history data collected by the GHS are central to its value for our purposes. They allow repartnering behaviour to be examined with reference to detailed aspects of individuals' marital histories.[25] While retrospective data have some disadvantages relative to data collected longitudinally, the sample size of the GHS and its breadth of coverage of the formerly partnered population outweigh the advantages of longitudinal studies such as the BHPS (Berthoud and Gershuny 2000), NCDS (Ferri et al. 2003) and BLPC (Marsh and Vegeris 2004).

More specifically, the 2001–2 GHS, which collected data from April 2001 to March 2002, allows us to look at the repartnering behaviour of the formerly married over the five-year period directly following our qualitative fieldwork. Furthermore, the cohabitation histories collected by the GHS since 2000–1 allow us not only to identify and examine former cohabitees, but also to identify more accurately the role played by cohabitation in the repartnering process.

However, there are some problems with using GHS data for our purposes. For example, the cohabitation histories only contain information about the timing of the current and first three completed cohabitations. In addition, only respondents aged 59 years or under were asked the questions in the Family Information section. Perhaps most seriously, data about the timing of a substantial minority of marital separations are missing. This made it difficult in some instances to establish whether or not an individual was formerly partnered in April 1996 and, if so, for how long they had been separated.[26]

More generally, our use of a survey of private households clearly excludes the small minority of the formerly partnered living in other contexts. Furthermore, migration into and out of private households between 1996 and 2001 (as well as to and from Britain) weakens the representativeness of our GHS sample with respect to the population of formerly partnered people in private households in Britain in 1996. Finally, it should be noted that the GHS sample does not match our qualitative sample geographically. Matching the samples in this way would have necessitated a radical reduction in sample size and would have involved a loss of generality.

However, notwithstanding the above issues, and the more general concerns that one should have about results from secondary analyses of survey data – for example in relation to the impact of non-response and missing data, and to the accuracy and truthfulness of respondents' answers – we are confident that our results based on the GHS sample paint a broadly accurate picture of the formerly partnered and their repartnering behaviour.

Before we move on to an examination of the characteristics and repartnering behaviour of our GHS sample, it should be noted that the distinction between former cohabitees and formerly (legally) married people used in the analyses that follow is a conceptually crude one. For example, in terms of their *last* co-resident relationship, some formerly (legally) married members of our GHS sample may be former cohabitees. However, the primary distinction that we make here, albeit not the only important distinction, is between sample members who have *ever* been married and those who have *never* been married.

Details of the GHS sample

Our GHS sample of formerly partnered people contains just under eleven hundred individuals ($n = 1081$). However, the exclusion of respondents who had not completed the GHS Family Information section, or for whom crucial marital history data were missing, means that this sample size is smaller than it otherwise would have been.

Single people who did not complete the Family Information section, including those who were cohabiting, may or may not have completed a period of cohabitation in the past. Similarly, married people who did not complete the section may or may not have been married more than once.

The numbers of people who were formerly married or former cohabitees in April 1996, but who did not complete the section and were thus excluded, were estimated via comparisons with respondents who did complete the section.[27] The estimated overall shortfalls for formerly married people and for former cohabitees were found to be 3.25 per cent and 12 per cent respectively.[28]

Once these shortfalls have been taken into account, the implications of the sample size of 1081 for the size of the formerly partnered population in Britain in April 1996 can be established by using the weights provided with GHS data (ONS 2002: 3) to 'gross up' the sample (correcting for known patterns of non-response), so that it corresponds to the British population as a whole. The overall estimate generated in this way is more than 3.25 million people: nearly 2.3 million formerly married people (70 per cent) and over 980,000 former cohabitees (30 per cent).[29] While well under half of the former group of people are men (37 per cent)[30], most of the latter group are men (55 per cent). Overall, 42 per cent are men.

The above values correspond only to adults aged 54½ or less living in private households. Formerly partnered people constituted 10.7 per cent of the overall population with these characteristics in April 1996, with formerly married people making up 7.5 per cent and former cohabitees 3.2 per cent. However, the proportion of people who had *ever* been formerly married or a former cohabitee is clearly greater than this. To illustrate this, the number of people aged 16–59 who were formerly married or former cohabitees at their GHS 2001–2 interview date can be compared with the number of people who had *ever* been formerly married or a former cohabitee, estimates of the values in question being 1755 (14 per cent) and 3763 (31 per cent).[31] The higher percentage of formerly partnered people in 2001–2 (14 per cent) as compared to 1996 (10.7 per cent) is in part an artefact of slightly different age ranges, but also appears to reflect a relatively large number of cohabitations ending in separation between 1996 and 2001. Periods of cohabitation ending in separation seem to have been rapidly increasing in frequency at that time, leading to a correspondingly rapid expansion of the number of former cohabitees.[32]

Returning to our GHS sample, it consists of a majority of formerly (legally) married people (73 per cent) and a substantial minority of former cohabitees (27 per cent). Just over a third of the former (269 = 34 per cent) and about half of the latter (148 = 50 per cent) are men. While formerly married people and former cohabitees may have something in common conceptually, they differ markedly as groups in terms of age structure: Table 4.1 shows that most of the formerly married were aged 40 or more, as opposed to about one in six of the former cohabitees.

Of the members of the sample for whom separation durations were available (*n* = 1001), a clear majority (57 per cent) had been separated for less than five years, but a substantial minority (9 per cent) had been separated

Table 4.1   Age composition of the GHS sample according to previous marital status

Age	Formerly married	Former cohabitees	Total
Under 30	10% (77)	48% (141)	20% (218)
30–39	34% (263)	36% (106)	34% (369)
40–49	39% (310)	14% (40)	32% (350)
50–54	17% (136)	3% (8)	13% (144)

for 15 years or more.[33] The separation durations of the former cohabitees were on average shorter than those for the formerly married people, with 70 per cent of the former having been separated for less than five years, as opposed to 51 per cent of the latter. Conversely, only 5 per cent of the former cohabitees had been separated for 15 or more years, as opposed to 11 per cent of formerly married people. However, these differences become statistically insignificant when the younger age range of former cohabitees is taken into account (via a log-linear model).

Of the sample members, 7 per cent belonged to minority ethnic groups.[34] While 9 per cent of the women in the sample belonged to these groups, only 6 per cent of the men did, although this difference is not quite statistically significant ($p < 0.08$).

Dependent children, employment status and social class

Since the GHS does not collect detailed work histories, and did not collect detailed cohabitation histories before 2001, neither the 2001–2 GHS nor the 1996–7 GHS can be used to examine the employment status of both formerly married people and former cohabitees in 1996. A similar problem applies to household composition in 1996, including the presence of dependent children. Consequently, to allow a comparison of former cohabitees and formerly (legally) married people, we here look at the current employment status of respondents to the 2001–2 GHS, and also the presence or absence of dependent children in their family units.

A sample was constructed of 1,641 individuals aged 16–59 years who were formerly partnered at the time of their GHS 2001–2 interview.[35] Compared to other people aged 16–59 in the GHS 2001–2 sample, these individuals were less likely to be in paid work: 65 per cent compared to 76 per cent. They were also markedly more likely to be classified as permanently unable to work: 11 per cent compared to 4 per cent. There were also smaller excesses of formerly partnered people who were unemployed, keeping house or otherwise economically inactive,[36] with these groups constituting 5 per cent, 11 per cent and 3 per cent of the individuals respectively. This pattern of short-falls/excesses was found to apply to both sexes when considered separately, although (predictably) a much higher proportion of women (16 per cent) than of men (1 per cent) were keeping house.[37]

Only a small proportion (10 per cent) of formerly partnered men were found to have a dependent child or children living with them in their family unit. The proportion corresponding to former cohabitees was lower than that for formerly married men, with the values being 7 per cent and 12 per cent respectively. While this difference is not quite statistically significant ($p < 0.09$), the difference becomes significant ($p < 0.04$) when age is taken into account in a multivariate analysis using a log-linear model. For formerly partnered men, there is a relationship between age and the presence of a dependent child or children, with the proportion of men with a co-resident dependent child rising with age to 16 per cent for men in their forties, before declining to 4 per cent for men in their fifties.

For women, the proportion with dependent children was found to be 48 per cent. The difference between formerly married women and formerly cohabiting women was not statistically significant, but became significant when age was taken into account in a multivariate analysis using a log-linear model. For formerly cohabiting women aged under 50, the proportion did not vary with age, and was 54 per cent. For formerly married women aged under 50 the proportion was 68 per cent, but varied according to age, being highest for women in their thirties (84 per cent). The proportion for women in their fifties was only 6 per cent, and did not vary between former cohabitees and formerly married women.[38]

We now consider the impact of dependent children, alongside the effects of age and whether an individual was formerly married or a former cohabitee, on whether they were in paid work. A separate multivariate analysis was carried out for each sex, with in paid work or not as the dependent variable.

Among women, former cohabitees without dependent children in their family units were more likely to be in paid work (82 per cent) than comparable formerly married women (63 per cent). Conversely, former cohabitees with co-resident dependent children were less likely to be in paid work (43 per cent) than comparable formerly married women (60 per cent). The contrasting employment characteristics of former cohabitees with and without co-resident dependent children relative to the formerly married remained statistically significant when age was taken into account within a multivariate analysis.

The above may appear to imply the absence of any substantial effect of dependent children on paid work among formerly married women. However, this is misleading, since the effect is highly dependent on age. For women who live with dependent children, increasing age is related to an increasing likelihood of paid work, whereas for women who do not, increasing age is related to a decreasing likelihood, although the latter relationship is not quite statistically significant ($p < 0.06$ according to the linear-by-linear association variant of the chi-square test). For formerly married women under 40, more of those without dependent children do paid work (76 per cent) than those with dependent children (56 per cent). Conversely, for formerly married women aged 40 or more, the values (61 per cent and 67 per cent) do not differ significantly.

Predictably, the presence of dependent children in a formerly partnered woman's family unit was associated with a greater tendency towards part-time paid work, of up to 30 hours per week, irrespective of whether the woman was a former cohabitee or formerly married. Among women who were not living with dependent children, the proportion of all those in paid work who were in part-time work increased significantly with age, from 10 per cent of those under 40 to 30 per cent of those in their fifties. This may reflect in part women who have had dependent children in the past, have worked part-time at that stage and have not returned to full-time paid work. Among women living with dependent children the proportion working part-time was 57 per cent and did not vary with age.

The proportion of women who were classified as permanently unable to participate in paid work was higher among the formerly married (13 per cent) than among former cohabitees (5 per cent). However, a multivariate analysis showed this difference to be almost entirely attributable to the different age distributions of the two groups, since the proportion classified as unable to do paid work also rose with increasing age, from 3 per cent among women under 30 to 23 per cent among women in their fifties.

For men, the likelihood of paid work did not differ between the formerly married and former cohabitees, and a multivariate analysis also showed that there was no interaction between this distinction and the effects of age or the presence of dependent children. The proportion in paid work declined with age ($p < 0.02$), with 78 per cent of men aged under 40 working as opposed to 66 per cent of men in their fifties. While the effect of dependent children for men aged under 40 was not quite statistically significant ($p < 0.10$), 80 per cent of men who were not living with dependent children were working, as opposed to 64 per cent of those who were. However, for men in their forties and fifties with and without dependent children in their family units, the proportions in paid work were very similar.

As was the case for women, the proportion of men who were classified as permanently unable to do paid work was higher among the formerly married (15 per cent) than among former cohabitees (8 per cent). Once again, this difference could be attributed to the different age distributions of the two groups, since the proportion classified as unable to work varied with age, from 3 per cent among men under 30 to 20 per cent among men in their fifties.

Turning to social class, based on an individual's current or last occupation, the relevant classification schema available within the GHS 2001–2 data is the National Statistics Socio-Economic Classification (NSSEC) (Rose and Pevalin 2003).[39] Compared to other people aged 16–59, formerly partnered people were less likely to be full-time students: 3 per cent, as compared to 7 per cent. Presumably this partly reflects differences between the two groups' age distributions. Formerly partnered people were also more likely to be long-term unemployed, with 3 per cent classified as such compared to 1 per cent of other people. A similar proportion of each, just over 3 per cent, had never participated in paid work.

Differences were found in the distributions of formerly partnered people and of other people across the main NSSEC analytical categories. For men, fewer formerly partnered people (31 per cent) than other people (41 per cent) were in managerial and professional occupations. Conversely, proportionately more formerly partnered men (51 per cent) than other men (41 per cent) were in routine or manual occupations. The proportions of men in intermediate occupations were similar (18 per cent). However, when formerly partnered men were divided into former cohabitees and formerly married men, it became evident that the two groups differed. Formerly cohabiting men were spread across the three categories of occupations in a virtually identical way to the other people (41 per cent, 17 per cent and 43 per cent). Conversely, formerly married men differed even more markedly from other people than formerly partnered men in general did, with the proportions in the three occupational categories being 25 per cent, 19 per cent and 56 per cent.

Turning to women, 29 per cent of formerly partnered women were in professional or managerial occupations, as compared to 33 per cent of other women. The values for women in intermediate occupations were 22 per cent and 27 per cent, leaving an excess of formerly partnered women (49 per cent) in routine or manual occupations when compared to other women (40 per cent). The proportions of formerly cohabiting women and formerly married women in each of the three occupational categories did not differ significantly.

Thus, while the overall picture is that formerly partnered people are skewed towards the lower end of the class structure, especially in the case of formerly married men, they are nevertheless spread across the class structure sufficiently evenly to be quite diverse. Clearly, the higher proportion of formerly partnered people who are in routine and manual occupations in part reflects the higher rates of marital dissolution for people in such occupations.[40] However, looking ahead to the repartnering analyses later in this chapter, one needs to bear in mind that people in such occupations may be slower to repartner, and hence remain in the formerly partnered population for longer, although this may in turn be offset by a tendency for the marriages of people in such occupations to end at younger ages, at which repartnering rates are higher, and hence for them to leave the formerly partnered population more quickly.

Repartnering behaviour: marital status, sex, age and separation duration

The GHS data allowed us to identify people who started a marriage or cohabitation during the five-year period April 1996–March 2001. The differences in

Table 4.2   Repartnering rates by sex and previous marital status for the five-year period April 1996–March 2001

	Formerly married	**Former cohabitees**	**Total**
Women	28% (145/517)	44% (64/147)	31% (209/664)
Men	38% (103/269)	55% (82/148)	44% (185/417)
Total	32% (248/786)	49% (146/295)	36% (394/1081)

repartnering rates between women and men and between formerly (legally) married people and former cohabitees are shown in Table 4.2.

Table 4.2 shows that more than a third of the sample repartnered within the five-year period, with the rates being higher for men and for former cohabitees. The rates for formerly married women and men also differ significantly, but the difference between formerly cohabiting women and men is not quite statistically significant ($p < 0.06$). Formerly married people and former cohabitees also differ significantly when each sex is considered separately.

However, the repartnering rate decreases with age, falling from 61 per cent among people aged under 30 in April 1996 to 46 per cent for people in their thirties, 22 per cent for people in their forties, and 10 per cent for people aged 50 or more. Since former cohabitees are, on average, markedly younger than formerly married people, they should be expected to have a higher repartnering rate. In fact, a multivariate analysis shows that most of the difference between the repartnering rates of the two groups disappears, and the difference becomes statistically insignificant, when their age structures are taken into account. Hence, in this respect at least, former cohabitees appear behaviourally similar to formerly married people. However, as will become evident, this is only superficially the case.

It is interesting to examine whether there are any differences between the repartnering rates for formerly partnered people and the partnering rates for people who were single in April 1996 and had never cohabited. A sample of the latter category comparable to the sample of formerly partnered people was constructed, and Table 4.3 contains a comparison of the rates for these two groups. Since very few (about 5 per cent) of the formerly partnered sample who were aged under 30 in 1996 were also less than 20, whereas most of the single sample who were aged under 30 were also less than 20, the latter group is restricted in Table 4.3 to people aged 20 or more in 1996.[41]

A multivariate analysis based on a log-linear model shows that the trend in repartnering rates by age does not vary significantly between formerly partnered women and men.[42] For single people of each sex the partnering rate declines with increasing age; once again, applying a log-linear model shows there to be insufficient evidence to conclude that this trend varies

Table 4.3 Partnering rates by sex, partnership status and age for the five-year period April 1996–March 2001

Age	Formerly partnered women	Single women	Former partnered men	Single men
Under 30	58% (77/133)	52% (473/912)	66% (56/85)	46% (461/1013)
30–39	39% (89/230)	33% (44/133)	57% (79/139)	40% (70/177)
40–49	18% (36/206)	5% (2/38)	29% (42/144)	12% (10/86)
50–54	7% (7/95)	4% (1/23)	16% (8/49)	4% (1/24)

according to sex. The rate for single men in their twenties is, unsurprisingly, significantly lower than that for single women in their twenties.

Perhaps the most interesting pattern visible in Table 4.3 is that, for both sexes and for all ages, the repartnering rate appears to be higher than the partnering rate for single people. In fact, multivariate analyses based on log-linear models show that, both for men and also, just, for women ($p < 0.03$), the repartnering rate for formerly partnered people is significantly higher than the partnering rate for single people.[43] More specifically, the difference between the repartnering and partnering rates is larger for men than it is for women.[44]

The higher (re)partnering rates for formerly partnered people in general, and for men in particular, may reflect a selection effect, whereby formerly partnered people were (when single), and remain, disproportionately strongly motivated to form cohabiting or marital relationships, although not necessarily disproportionately strongly motivated to stay in them. In other words, they may have, on average, started off as more 'marriage-oriented' in some sense than other single people. An alternative is that formerly partnered people have *become* more marriage-oriented as a consequence of living with a partner, perhaps through habit or as a consequence of a greater appreciation of any advantages.

One possible explanation of the observed gender differential is that formerly partnered women and men started off as more marriage-oriented than other single people to a similar extent, but that formerly partnered women became *less* marriage-oriented as a consequence of having lived with a partner, whereas the level of marriage orientation of formerly partnered men remained constant. In other words, the experience of living with a partner may have left women less positively oriented than men towards cohabitation or marriage, possibly because of negative aspects of their past relationship(s), or possibly because some of the incentives for living with a partner have been removed – for example, the 'rite of passage' to adulthood, or the desire to have more children. Of course, this assumes that such relationship experiences and incentives are gender-related.

Table 4.4   Repartnering rates by separation duration by sex for the five-year period April 1996–March 2001 (duration since last co-resident relationship)

Duration separated	Women	Men	Total
Under 5 years	44% (148/338)	54% (126/232)	48% (274/570)
5–9 years	28% (39/138)	41% (32/79)	33% (71/217)
10–14 years	10% (8/78)	22% (9/41)	14% (17/119)
15 or more years	10% (6/58)	24% (9/37)	16% (15/95)

In our earlier paper, we examined repartnering behaviour after first marriage from the point of separation onwards (Lampard and Peggs 1999: 446). However, here we are looking at the repartnering behaviour of people with a range of marital histories, who have been separated from their last co-resident partners for different durations. It is thus relevant to consider the impact of separation duration on repartnering over the subsequent five years.

Table 4.4 shows that repartnering rates decline with duration separated for both men and women.[45] However, a multivariate analysis based on a log-linear model shows that there is insufficient evidence to conclude that this trend differs in magnitude between the sexes. Since separation duration is correlated with age, and since age in April 1996 has been shown to impact on the repartnering rate, the possibility has to be considered that the pattern in Table 4.4 is induced by age. In fact, a multivariate analysis indicates that a substantial minority of the effect of separation duration can be accounted for by age, and that a smaller minority of the effect of age can be accounted for by separation duration. Hence both increasing age and increasing separation duration reduce the repartnering rate, to an extent in an overlapping way.[46]

Repartnering behaviour: a multivariate analysis

Having established the effects of a handful of key characteristics of formerly partnered people on their likelihood of repartnering, we move on to a broader multivariate analysis of repartnering behaviour. We take into account a range of additional factors and assess their impact on repartnering behaviour once all the other factors, including sex, age, separation duration and whether an individual was formerly married or a former cohabitee, have been taken into account.[47]

Children

In our earlier paper, we reported that the number of children that a woman had given birth to by the end of her first marriage had a significant impact on repartnering. We found a lower rate for women who had given birth to any children than for those who had given birth to none, and an even lower rate for women who had given birth to three or more children (Lampard and Peggs 1999: 450). Here we carry out a similar analysis, based on how many children women had given birth to by the end of their last marital or cohabiting relationship.[48] Just under half the women who had not given birth repartnered in the five-year period (49 per cent), as compared to just over a quarter of the women who had given birth once or twice (28 per cent) and only about a fifth of the women who had given birth three or more times (19 per cent). The three groups differ significantly from each other ($p < 0.03$ for all comparisons).

However, since age and number of births are related, and age affects repartnering rate, it is important to take account of age. Once age in April 1996, separation duration and whether or not the woman was a former cohabitee have been taken into account within a multivariate analysis, the difference between one or two births and three or more births is no longer statistically significant. However, while the magnitude of the multiplicative effect of not having given birth on the odds in favour of repartnering is reduced, from 2.91 to 2.30, it is still statistically significant, and of a broadly similar magnitude to the effect found in our earlier analysis (1999: 450).[49] The GHS 2001–2 data allow the sexes of a woman's children to be taken into account, but an extension of the multivariate analysis does not show any significant variations in this context.

At this point we consider the impact of children's ages, thus extending this analysis beyond our earlier one, which only considered this issue in qualitative terms (1999: 461). We constructed a measure of the age of a woman's youngest child in April 1996, or, more precisely, the duration since her most recent birth. An examination of this measure's impact, within a multivariate analysis taking account of the factors considered at the end of the preceding section, shows that the effect of having a child of under ten years of age is substantial, increasing the odds against repartnering by a factor of 2.67 relative to a woman who has not given birth. However, the effect of having a youngest child aged ten or more is small (a factor of 1.32), and is not statistically significant. Hence it appears that having a young child or children has a marked negative effect on the likelihood of repartnering, but that having an older child or children may not have any effect.

Marital status revisited

The multivariate analysis that takes whether women have given birth or not into account also indicates that the repartnering rate for formerly cohabiting women is significantly *lower* ($p < 0.05$) than that for formerly married women. In other words, since former cohabitees had, on average, given birth to fewer children, the positive effect of this on their repartnering rate offsets a lower latent repartnering rate to give the broadly comparable repartnering rates for former cohabitees and formerly married women noted earlier. These different underlying repartnering rates highlight the importance of distinguishing between former cohabitees and formerly married people, at least for women. Marsh and Vegeris's (2004) finding that formerly cohabiting lone parents had a lower repartnering rate than other lone parents thus presumably reflects the lower repartnering rate for all former cohabitees identified here, once children have been taken into account.[50]

Our earlier analysis indicated that the repartnering behaviour of widows and widowers is also distinctive in some respects (Lampard and Peggs 1999: 451). Here we focus on people whose last co-resident relationship ended in their partner's death, including nine 'widowed' cohabitees. Incorporating widowed people within the multivariate analysis generates differences that are statistically insignificant, but are broadly consistent with our earlier results of a lower repartnering rate for widowed people and a higher rate for widowers than for widows.[51]

Marital and cohabiting histories

Compared to our earlier analysis of repartnering, the analysis here considers people with a wider range of relationship histories: for example, people who have been married more than once and people who have only cohabited. One potentially relevant aspect of these histories is the number of past co-resident relationships that individuals have had. One straightforward hypothesis is that a greater number of past relationships will lead to a higher repartnering rate. Nearly four out of five people had had only one such relationship (79 per cent), with just under a fifth (18 per cent) having had two, and fewer than 1 in 25 having had three or more (4 per cent). Number of past relationships is very likely to be correlated with age. Nevertheless, when it is incorporated within the multivariate analysis, the results show the odds in favour of repartnering to be 1.59 times as high for people with two or more past relationships as for people with one past relationship.[52]

Our earlier analysis showed that the repartnering rate diminishes as age at first marriage increases (Lampard and Peggs 1999: 450), possibly reflecting a tendency for people who start their marital or cohabiting histories later to be less positively oriented to living with a partner. For the analysis reported here, we constructed a variable representing age at first cohabitation or marriage.[53] When this variable is incorporated within the multivariate analysis, the results show that people who first cohabit or marry when aged under 30 years are more likely to repartner ($p < 0.02$), with their odds of repartnering being 2.87 times as high as for people cohabiting or marrying later.[54]

A more detailed multivariate analysis shows there to be a gender-specific effect for women first cohabiting or marrying when aged 24–29 years, with these women being significantly less likely ($p < 0.04$) to repartner than women who cohabited or married at a younger age, who have odds of repartnering that are 1.95 times as high. In other words, the point at which increasing age at first cohabitation or marriage becomes an indicator of a less positive orientation to living with a partner seems to come markedly earlier for women than it does for men.[55,56]

While our earlier paper indicated that pre-marital cohabitation with one's first marriage partner reduces the likelihood of repartnering to a significant degree (1999: 450), the impact of pre-marital cohabitation when incorporated into the multivariate analysis reported here is negligible.[57]

'Race', class, education and employment

As noted earlier, the GHS sample contains a disproportionately large number of women from minority ethnic groups. One possible explanation for this is that these women have a lower repartnering rate. Extending our multivariate analysis to test this shows that minority ethnic women have odds of repartnering that are less than half as high (0.45) as for other women and men ($p < 0.04$).[58]

Our earlier analysis identified a positive relationship between social class (Registrar General's Social Class) and repartnering rate, with the notable exception of women in professional occupations (Lampard and Peggs 1999: 450). Here we use the more recent NSSEC schema (Rose and Pevalin 2003). In the absence of detailed work history data, we use information on individuals' jobs at their interview dates (or their last jobs), although this clearly introduces the problem that, in theory at least, repartnering could have had an effect on their current job.

An examination of the impact of NSSEC on repartnering indicates a distinction between Class 1 (higher managerial and higher professional occupations) and Classes 6–8 (semi-routine and routine occupations, and those who have never worked or are long-term unemployed), with the other classes occupying an intermediate position: the repartnering rates for the above-mentioned groupings were 61 per cent, 39 per cent and 29 per cent, with the difference between each pair of groupings being statistically significant. Incorporating NSSEC into our multivariate analysis results in these differences diminishing in magnitude, with the difference between the second and third groupings ceasing to be statistically significant ($p < 0.09$). However, the first grouping remains very clearly distinctive.[59]

While research on remarriage has sometimes found educational effects on repartnering rates (typically positive for men and negative for women), our earlier analysis did not identify any net educational effects.[60] However, a crude distinction between having and not having qualifications at CSE/GCSE/'O' level or above has a statistically significant effect, with the repartnering rates being 42 per cent and 25 per cent for people with and without qualifications respectively.

When this distinction is added to the multivariate analysis (alongside NSSEC), its effect diminishes and ceases to be statistically significant. However, an examination of the way in which the effect varies according to sex suggests that it exists for women but not for men. Looking at the impact of qualifications for women specifically, the effect is to increase the odds of repartnering by a factor of 1.69 ($p < 0.03$). At first sight, this seems inconsistent with the existing literature regarding the effect of education on women's repartnering behaviour. However, the educational effect identified here does not relate to women's position within a detailed educational spectrum, and would be consistent with highly qualified women having a lower repartnering rate than women with lesser qualifications.[61]

A closer examination suggests that the observed effect of education is distinguishing specifically between sub-groups of women within the second and (especially) third NSSEC groupings, with its addition to the multivariate analysis reducing the difference between the repartnering rates for women in these two groupings to zero. In other words, for women what appears to matter is having some form of qualifications, rather than (as is the case for men), being engaged in non-routine paid work.

In summary, when considered together, NSSEC and educational qualifications have the following impact within the multivariate analysis:

- For both sexes, being in Class 1, which almost inevitably means having educational qualifications, leads to a relatively high repartnering rate.
- An intermediate repartnering rate is found among men in Classes 2–5, and among women who are outside Class 1 but have qualifications.
- A relatively low repartnering rate is found among men in Classes 6–8 and among women with no qualifications.

Our results show these three levels to have significantly different repartnering rates ($p < 0.02$ for all comparisons), with the odds of repartnering for the highest level being 3.45 times as high as for lowest, and the odds for the intermediate level being 1.71 times as high as for the lowest.[62]

Earlier it was shown that, in 2001–2, formerly partnered people were disproportionately likely to be classified as permanently unable to participate in paid work. While there are problems with using information from 2001–2 in analyses of repartnering during the period 1996–2001, it nevertheless seems worth incorporating this factor within the multivariate analysis. Doing so results in a significant effect: people classified as permanently unable to do paid work have odds of repartnering that are only 0.45 times as high as the odds for other people. Hence, whatever factors affect the ability of these people to work may also affect their ability to repartner.

A separate multivariate analysis (controlling for age at separation) indicates that the odds of being classified as permanently unable to do paid work are higher by a factor of 1.47 for people who had been separated for at least ten years when compared to people who had been separated for less than ten years. While this effect is not quite statistically significant ($p < 0.08$), it is consistent with the suggestion that a lower repartnering rate contributes to a higher proportion of people who are permanently unable to participate in paid work within the formerly partnered population at higher separation durations.

The next relationship: cohabitation or remarriage?

Recent analyses of partnership formation have sometimes used a competing risks approach to examine cohabitation and marriage as alternative outcomes (Berrington and Diamond 2000; De Graaf and Kalmijn 2003). So far we have treated cohabitation and remarriage as equivalent, but we now examine whether any of the factors that influence the likelihood of repartnering among our GHS sample also affect what form of relationship occurs next.

This is, of course, complicated by the fact that an individual's first relationship after April 1996 may have been a cohabitation that has since ended, a pre-marital cohabitation that has since become a marriage, an ongoing cohabitation that might or might not end in marriage, or a marriage without pre-marital cohabitation. To start with, we focus on 'direct' marriage – that is, marriage without prior cohabitation.

Very few (8 per cent) of the repartnering former cohabitees went directly into a marriage, as compared to a substantial minority (21 per cent) of the formerly married people who repartnered.[63] Rising age is also associated, approximately linearly, with a growing proportion of direct marriages: only 5 per cent for people aged under 30 in April 1996, rising to 40 per cent for people in their fifties. Former cohabitees cease to be significantly different from formerly married people when age is taken into account within a multivariate analysis. However, when former cohabitees are combined with those formerly married people who had cohabited at some point before April 1996, a multivariate analysis controlling for age shows that a history of cohabitation comes close to significantly reducing ($p < 0.06$) the odds of direct marriage, multiplying them by a factor of 0.56. Given the plausibility of such an effect, it seems likely that past cohabitation still has a negative impact once age has been taken into account.

With regard to the other factors that have been shown to influence the likelihood of repartnering, the only other significant effect is that members of 'white' ethnic groups are less likely to have married directly (15 per cent) than people from minority ethnic groups (39 per cent).

We now broaden our marriage outcome by including cohabiting relationships that had led to marriage before the 2001–2 interview. Again, former cohabitees and formerly married people differ, with 35 per cent of the former having married, as opposed to 53 per cent of the latter. When the latter group is subdivided according to past cohabitation, a significant difference exists between those who had cohabited, of whom 45 per cent had remarried, and those who had not, of whom 60 per cent had remarried ($p < 0.03$). The difference between the remarriage rates of former cohabitees and formerly married people who had cohabited in the past is not, in fact, statistically significant. Thus any history of cohabitation appears to reduce the likelihood of remarrying, both initially and later. No other relationships appear to exist between this broader outcome and the factors affecting repartnering.

Finally, we focus on cohabiting relationships that had ended by the 2001–2 interview. These were more common among former cohabitees (28 per cent) than among formerly married people (9 per cent), and were also more common ($p < 0.05$) among formerly married people who had cohabited in the past (13 per cent) than among those who had not (5 per cent). Such relationships can be shown, within a multivariate analysis controlling for the distinction between former cohabitees and formerly married people, to have had higher odds of occurring (2.0 times as high) among people with more than one past co-resident relationship than among people with only one ($p < 0.03$). However, this effect diminishes slightly (to 1.8) and just ceases to be statistically significant ($p < 0.07$) when all past cohabitation is taken into account. Again, number of past relationships, while of some relevance, appears to be of less empirical importance than other aspects of formerly married people's relationship histories, in this instance whether or not they have ever cohabited. New, 'transient' cohabiting relationships appear to be positively related to having cohabited in the past and negatively related to having been married in the past.

With whom do formerly married or cohabiting people form partnerships?

Since the GHS collects data from all the individuals in the sampled households, the characteristics of married or cohabiting partners in combination can be examined. The 2001–2 GHS collected information about 5,328 couples.[64]

Marital and cohabitation histories

In an earlier paper (Lampard 1997) the extent to which divorced and widowed people remarry endogamously, that is, marry partners of the same marital status, was addressed. The 2001–2 GHS can be used to distinguish further between former cohabitees and the formerly married, giving us the scope to identify whether, in terms of whom they repartner, former cohabitees are more like 'single' people (people who have never married or cohabited), or whether they more closely resemble the formerly married.[65]

To maximize comparability with our analyses of repartnering behaviour, we focus on current partnerships at the GHS interviews in 2001–2 that had started since the beginning of April 1996. Clearly, these may not correspond to the first repartnering event during this period for each formerly partnered person. People who repartnered during the period, but were no longer in partnerships by the time of the interviews, are also excluded. Nevertheless, focusing on partnerships formed over a relatively limited period gives a reasonable indication of the tendency to repartner someone of the same marital status.

During the period in question, 893 couples' partnerships started. Of these, 749 couples' joint marital histories could be examined.[66] Table 4.5 shows their joint marital status, with the first partner being a woman (except in two same-sex couples), and the second partner being a man (except in three same-sex couples).

Table 4.5 The marital status in combination of partners before partnering

ALL COUPLES (n = 749)

First partner	Second partner		
	Single	Former cohabitee	Formerly married
Single	343 (75%)	65 (14%)	49 (11%)
Former cohabitee	49 (41%)	45 (38%)	25 (21%)
Formerly married	42 (24%)	22 (13%)	109 (63%)

ODDS RATIOS

Marital status combination	Source of odds ratios			
	From above	Model 1	Model 2	From below
Single/former cohabitee	4.9	4.4	4.9	9.5
Single/formerly married	18.2	7.7	13.0	5.6
Form.cohab./form.mar.	8.9	5.7	6.4	4.3

COUPLES BOTH AGED 30–39
AT GHS INTERVIEW (n = 161)

First partner	Second partner		
	Single	Former cohabitee	Formerly married
Single	57 (72%)	9 (11%)	13 (17%)
Former cohabitee	12 (30%)	18 (45%)	10 (25%)
Formerly married	15 (36%)	8 (19%)	19 (45%)

Table 4.5 illustrates that most single people partner single people, whereas most formerly married people partner other formerly married people. Former cohabitees are more likely to partner single people than to partner other former cohabitees, but are more likely to partner other former cohabitees than to partner formerly married people. However, these patterns partly reflect the relative sizes of the three groups, and, furthermore, may have been induced, at least in part, by the groups' differing age distributions.[67]

The extent to which members of any two groups tend to partner people within their own group as opposed to the other group can be summarized in a way that take account of the two groups' sizes using an odds ratio.[68] For example, the odds of a single person partnering another single person as opposed to a former cohabitee are 4.9 times as high as the odds of a former cohabitee partnering a single person as opposed to another former cohabitee. Table 4.5 indicates that the biggest difference, with an odds ratio of 17.8, corresponds to single people compared to formerly married people, with the difference between former cohabitees and the formerly married being greater than that between single people and former cohabitees, with the respective odds ratios being 8.9 and 4.9. Thus former cohabitees occupy an intermediate position between single people and the formerly married, being more likely to partner members of either of these two groups than members of these two groups are to partner each other.

However, as noted above, the difference between single and formerly married people might largely reflect a disparity between the age ranges within the two groups. We use a multivariate analysis based on log-linear models to take account of the partners' ages. Within these models, age is categorized into under 30, 30–39, 40–49 and 50 or over. Model 1 takes account of the relationship between each individual's marital status and their age, and of the relationship between partners' ages. Model 2 also allows for the possibility that one partner's age relates to the other partner's marital status. Table 4.5 shows that the difference between each pair of groups is reduced when partners' ages are taken into account. However, substantial differences remain, and the more sophisticated model implies that the negative impact on the size of the differences of controlling for age is less than the simpler model suggests.[69]

An alternative way of illustrating the persistence of the marital status relationship once age has been taken into account is to focus on couples whose ages both fall into a relatively narrow range. Since the age range where the three groups' age distributions most overlap is 30–39, Table 4.5 demonstrates that, for couples where both partners were in their thirties at their GHS interviews, there are still differences between each pair of groups ($p < 0.03$ for all the comparisons). Interestingly, in this subset, formerly married people are more likely to partner outside their own group than within it.

Of the 749 couples, 43 per cent were married and 57 per cent were cohabiting at the time of the GHS interviews. An examination of whether the relationship between the marital statuses of partners before partnering varies according to this distinction only identifies one significant difference, corresponding to the comparison between single people and former cohabitees. The overall odds ratio of 4.9 splits into values of 11.6 for married couples and 3.0 for cohabiting couples ($p < 0.02$ for the difference, according to a log-linear model).[70] This variation between the relationships for married and for cohabiting couples was not induced by the partners' ages, and reflects a very high level of endogamy among the married people who were previously single. Eighty-three per cent of the currently married people who had previously been single were married to other single people and 8 per cent were married to former cohabitees, as opposed to 71 per cent and 17 per cent of the currently cohabiting people who had previously been single. One implication of these results is that single people who partner former cohabitees are much less likely to marry directly or relatively quickly than are single people who partner other single people.

Another aspect of an individual's relationship history that we have shown to be of relevance to their repartnering behaviour is the total number of past marital or cohabiting relationships they have had.[71] An examination of the relationship between partners' numbers of former partners indicates that the key empirical distinctions are between people with no former partners, people with one former partner and people with two or more former partners. Of individuals with one former partner and a partner with one or more former partners, only 22 per cent had partners with two or more former partners, as compared to 46 per cent for individuals with two or more former partners themselves. Another way of expressing this is to say that the odds of partnering someone with two or more former partners as opposed to one former partner are 3.0 times as high for someone with two or more former partners as for someone with one former partner. This effect remains statistically significant when partners' ages are taken into account within a multivariate analysis using a log-linear model, diminishing only slightly in strength, from 3.0 to 2.7.

Of equal interest is the impact of number of former partners on an individual's likelihood of partnering a single person. Thirty-six per cent of people with one former partner had a single partner, as opposed to only 25 per cent of people with two or more former partners. Another way of expressing this is to say that the odds of having a single partner are 1.8 times as high for somebody with one former partner as for somebody with two or more former partners. This relationship again remains significant (and does not diminish in strength) when partners' ages are taken into account.

To summarize the last two results, people who are in a second or later period as a formerly partnered person, judged in terms of their number of former partners, represent a distinctive group within the formerly partnered population more generally, inasmuch as they are disproportionately likely to partner each other and disproportionately unlikely to partner single people.

Age and age differences

We continue by examining partners' ages in combination among the 749 couples. Where two heterosexual partners had the same marital status before they partnered, the age difference between them is, on average, 2–3 years, with the male partner on average being older. The average difference where both partners had been single is 2.3 years, with the corresponding figures for former cohabitees and formerly married people being 2.9 and 3.4 years. However, the differences between these averages are not statistically significant.[72] Where the pre-partnership marital status of each partner is not the same, the average age differences are significantly different from those for 'symmetrical' couples. For example, formerly married men partnering single women were, on average, 7.6 years older, whereas single men partnering formerly married women were, on average, 3.5 years *younger*. Clearly, this is partly a consequence of the different age distributions of single people and formerly married people.[73]

Returning to couples where both partners had the same pre-partnership marital status, there is evidence that repartnering is associated with a greater diversity of age differences between partners. Assuming that a gap of five years between partners' ages is (in some sense) large, then 48 per cent of couples where partners were both previously married have large age differences, with the male partner being older in 40 per cent and the female partner in 7 per cent of cases. However, where the partners were both previously single, only 25 per cent of couples have large differences, with the male partner being older in 23 per cent and the female partner in 2 per cent of cases. The difference between these two sets of percentages is statistically significant. Among couples where both partners were former cohabitees, 38 per cent have large age differences, a value that does not differ significantly from those for the other two groups.

If all couples where one or both partners had previously cohabited or been married are taken together, 49 per cent have large age differences. Of these, 38 per cent are heterosexual couples with an older male partner, 10 per cent are heterosexual couples with an older female partner, and 1 per cent are same-sex couples. Thus there are almost twice as many large differences in couples that involved repartnering as in couples that did not. More specifically, there are more than four times as many heterosexual couples with markedly older female partners.

Another way of considering the impact of repartnering on the diversity of age differences between partners is to look at the spread of the age differences for each marital status combination. The standard deviations for combinations including single people and/or former cohabitees do not differ significantly.[74] However, the standard deviation for each combination involving one or more formerly married partners is significantly larger than that for couples where both partners were previously single.

Class and education differences

Restricting attention to the 690 couples in which both partners fall within the main three analytical categories of the NSSEC schema (Rose and Pevalin 2003), proportionately more couples in which one or both partners had repartnered differ markedly in terms of the class of their current or past occupation. In 20 per cent of these couples one partner belongs to the managerial and professional occupational category and the other to the routine or manual occupational category, as compared to a figure of 15 per cent for couples where both partners were in their first co-residential relationship. A multivariate analysis using a log-linear model shows this difference to be statistically significant ($p < 0.04$).[75]

There is less evidence of a greater frequency of educational dissimilarity between partners among couples in which one or both partners had repartnered. Judged in terms of a four-level educational hierarchy, partners differ educationally in 59 per cent of these couples, as compared to 52 per cent of couples where both partners were in their first co-residential relationship.[76] While this difference is not quite statistically significant ($p < 0.07$), when couples where one or both partners had previously cohabited but never married are examined, partners differ educationally in 63 per cent of couples, as compared to 54 per cent of other couples, a significant difference ($p < 0.04$).

The evidence provided by the last two paragraphs that repartnering is associated with an increased incidence of class or educational heterogamy, that is, dissimilarity between partners for these characteristics, is rather limited. Hence the factors that predispose or channel individuals towards a partner with similar social stratification characteristics appear to operate nearly as strongly within the repartnering process as within the couple formation process more generally.

Repartnering orientations and recent sexual activity

Since the GHS does not collect data on attitudes or relating to relationships that are not co-residential, this section uses alternative sources of data to look at these aspects of formerly partnered people's lives. In the absence of any appropriate survey data for 1996 regarding the repartnering orientations of formerly partnered people, the analyses that follow use data from the 1990 National Survey of Sexual Attitudes and Lifestyles (NATSAL; Johnson et al. 1994). In addition to collecting data on sexual behaviour and attitudes, one version of the survey questionnaire asked respondents two related closed questions about ideal lifestyles in terms of sexual or couple relationships, namely: 'Which of these lifestyles would you regard as the ideal one for you at this stage of your life?' and 'What about the future, say in five years' time, which one do you think will be your ideal then?' Respondents were shown eight answers relating to various combinations of co-residential status, legal marital status and number of concurrent partners.

Neither question is ideal for our purposes, namely identifying broad orientations to repartnering. The first question, focusing on the respondent's current ideal, cannot distinguish between short- and longer-term orientations, and may often generate answers that reflect an individual's desire for a reconciliation with a former partner, or for a transitory period 'on their own', or to enter a new relationship gradually. While the second question is not without such problems, it seems more likely to generate answers that have a consistent meaning, that is, longer-term relationship preferences. In addition, the second question echoes the five-year prospective period used in our repartnering analyses. However, the second question is inherently speculative and cannot establish the substantial proportion of formerly partnered people who do not want certain types of relationship yet. Hence both questions are used here.

Clearly, orientations may vary according to whether or not an individual has a current non-resident partner, or partners. NATSAL allows the numbers of heterosexual and homosexual sexual partners that an individual has had during a specified period leading up to their interview to be identified. Hence an individual's repartnering orientation can be linked to this.

The NATSAL sub-sample corresponding to the long version of the questionnaire (which contained the questions required for our analyses) includes 814 relevant respondents, aged 16–59, of whom 70 per cent were formerly married and 30 per cent former cohabitees.[77] The former cohabitees can be identified from a question that asked whether single people had ever lived with a partner or partners.

Sexual partners within the last month

We focus first on whether individuals had had at least one sexual partner within the preceding four weeks. Focusing on that period has the advantage of excluding the last co-resident sexual partner in all but a very few cases, and of ensuring that the sexual activity was more or less current, as opposed to towards the beginning of a longer retrospective period, such as a year. Of the individuals for whom information was available, 48 per cent had not had a sexual partner, and 52 per cent had had one or more, including 6 per cent who had had at least two sexual partners.[78]

Sexual partners in the last month were reported by 60 per cent of men, including 10 per cent reporting two or more, as opposed to 47 per cent of women reporting at least one partner and 3 per cent reporting two or more, a statistically significant gender difference overall. There are also marked differences according to marital status. Only 20 per cent of widowed people reported a sexual partner in the last month, as opposed to 52 per cent of separated or divorced people and 62 per cent of former cohabitees. Eleven per cent of former cohabitees reported having had more than one partner, as opposed to only 3 per cent of formerly married people. However, the differences between former cohabitees and separated or divorced people are statistically insignificant once age is taken into account within a multivariate analysis. Age differences are very marked, with 70 per cent of people under 30 reporting a sexual partner or partners, as opposed to 25 per cent of people in their fifties, and 50 per cent of those in between; 11 per cent of people aged under 30 reported more than one partner, as opposed to 3 per cent of those aged 30 or more. With regard to the time since a formerly partnered individual last lived with their partner, a weak negative relationship between separation duration and having a sexual partner becomes negligible when the effect of age is taken into account within a multivariate analysis.

People who reported attending a religious service at least once a month were significantly less likely (35 per cent) to have had a sexual partner in the last month, but once again this relationship diminishes, and just ceases to be significant, when age is taken into account ($p < 0.06$). Perhaps unsurprisingly, having had a sexual partner relates to age at first heterosexual intercourse, with the relevant percentages for those for whom this age was under 16, 16–19 and 20 or more being 71 per cent, 54 per cent and 31 per cent respectively.[79] The first group were also more likely (12 per cent) to have had more than one partner than the other two groups (4 per cent). The first of these two relationships also persists, albeit to a markedly reduced extent, within a multivariate analysis controlling for age.[80] There is a subtle but important gender difference in the impact of age at first heterosexual intercourse within the multivariate analysis, with the effect relating primarily to a distinction between under 16 and 16 or over for men, but to a distinction between under 20 and 20 or over for women.

For men, the number of children aged under 16 in an individual's household was negatively related to having had a sexual partner, with 39 per cent of men with children in their household having had a partner, as compared to 62 per cent of men with no children in their household ($p < 0.02$). This relationship persists when other variables are taken into account within a multivariate analysis. However, a positive bivariate relationship corresponding to women becomes insignificant within a multivariate analysis.[81]

An examination of the effects of social class and highest educational qualification on whether or not an individual had had a sexual partner identifies only one bivariate relationship that persists within a multivariate analysis. Specifically, men in the unskilled manual class were significantly less likely to have had a partner (17 per cent) than other men (64 per cent). Interestingly, the only relationship arising from an examination of the impact of employment status is that full-time students were significantly less likely ($p < 0.04$) to have had a sexual partner (24 per cent) than other people were (53 per cent), an effect that strengthens within a multivariate analysis. A more detailed examination shows this effect to relate to women students.

Perhaps unsurprisingly, sexual attitudes are linked to whether people had had a sexual partner. The small minority of people, virtually all women, who saw sex before marriage as always being wrong were very unlikely (8 per cent) to have had a partner, and less likely than other people were (53 per cent). People viewing 'one night stands' as mostly or always wrong were also less likely than other people (47 per cent compared to 63 per cent) to have had a partner, and much less likely to have had more than one partner (4 per cent compared to 10 per cent). The significance, and most of the magnitude, of the effects of both of these attitudes on the likelihood of having had a partner persists when they are included simultaneously within a multivariate analysis which takes into account the other significant effects ($p < 0.01$ and $p < 0.05$).

The NATSAL questionnaire also contained questions relating to how respondents saw themselves and their lives. Individuals agreeing with the statement 'I often wish I could be a different sort of person' (presented as an alternative to the statement 'On the whole I am happy with the way that I am') were more likely ($p < 0.04$) to have had a sexual partner (58 per cent) than other respondents were (49 per cent).[82] The effect is still of borderline significance when included in a multivariate analysis taking into account the other significant effects noted above.

Current and longer-term partnership orientations

A well-defined combination of current and future partnership orientations was specified by 753 individuals (92 per cent). Of these, 5 per cent favoured celibacy in the longer term, that is in five years' time. A multivariate analysis examining factors affecting the likelihood of favouring celibacy shows it to have been much more unusual among those who had had a sexual partner in the last month ($p < 0.02$), markedly more common among older people, especially those aged 50 or more, and several times more common among those who had two or more natural children. It was also far more common among the small sets of individuals who viewed sex before marriage as always wrong, or were in the unskilled manual social class. Finally, the analysis shows it to be more common for longer separation durations ($p < 0.03$).

A further 6 per cent of individuals favoured sex with multiple, non-resident partners in the longer term. A multivariate analysis shows factors increasing the likelihood of favouring this lifestyle to have been having had more than one sexual partner in the last month, viewing one night stands as not at all wrong, and having cohabited or married for the first time either relatively early (at an age of less than 20), or relatively late (at an age of 25 or more). Favouring this lifestyle was very unusual without at least one of these characteristics, and while men were three times as likely as women to favour this lifestyle, this is accounted for by the first and second of the preceding factors.

Favouring having a non-resident but 'monogamous' partner in five years' time was quite common, with 16 per cent of individuals seeing this as their ideal lifestyle. A multivariate analysis shows factors increasing the likelihood of favouring 'living apart together' to have been increasing age, a low age at first heterosexual intercourse (specifically under 16) and having had two or more natural children ($p < 0.02$). The analysis also shows the small number of full-time students, largely women, to have been more likely to have favoured 'living apart together', and also provides evidence, albeit of borderline significance, that the likelihood of favouring it grew with increasing separation duration ($p < 0.07$).[83]

Nearly three-quarters of people (73 per cent) favoured cohabitation or marriage in the longer term. For just over half (52 per cent) of these it was also their ideal current lifestyle.[84] The only factors that a multivariate analysis shows as significantly increasing the likelihood of favouring cohabitation or marriage now as well as later are increasing age and attending a church service or meeting at least once a month. Thus, while more than one in three people favoured cohabitation or marriage in the long term, but not in the short term, these people do not appear to be markedly different from those who favoured cohabitation or marriage now as well as later, at least in terms of the factors used in our analysis.

Of all the individuals who favoured a live-in partner in the longer term, 37 per cent preferred cohabitation to marriage. The factors identified by a multivariate analysis as significantly increasing the likelihood of this view are attending church services or meetings less than once a month, viewing one night stands as not always being wrong and having had more than one sexual partner in the last month ($p < 0.02$). In addition, none of the individuals who viewed sex before marriage as always being wrong favoured cohabitation rather than marriage ($p < 0.02$ in a bivariate analysis). People whose ideal current lifestyle involved a live-in relationship were more than twice as likely to favour marriage as cohabitation, whereas people who saw this as ideal only in the longer term were fairly evenly split between the two.

Formerly partnered people and partners who live elsewhere

Social surveys that collect data on couple relationships usually do so only for co-resident relationships. However, in line with the increasing attention paid in the literature to couple relationships where the partners live in separate households (e.g. De Jong-Gierveld 2004; Levin 2004), the ONS Omnibus Survey of April 2002 contained a module relating to this (ONS 2003a: 4, Haskey 2005). Respondents aged 16–59 years were told, 'This next section is about relationships . . . ', and those who were not married or cohabiting were asked, 'Do you currently have a regular partner?' shortly thereafter.[85] The survey also collected data on marital status and on past non-marital relationships, co-resident or otherwise. Both formerly married people and, in most cases, former cohabitees can thus be identified.[86]

We constructed a sample of 250 formerly partnered people from the survey, and weighted the data to take account of the survey's sample design, retaining a base sample of 250.[87] Of the weighted sample, 37 per cent were former cohabitees. This higher value compared to the figure for 1996 from our GHS sample (27 per cent) may in part reflect change over time, but nevertheless provides some reassurance that former cohabitees are not substantially underrepresented. In response to the question quoted above, 31 per cent of individuals stated that they had a current regular partner. Thus nearly a third of people who were formerly partnered, in the sense that they had had, but did not currently have, a co-resident partner, were nevertheless part of a 'couple' in a less demanding sense of the word.[88]

The factors affecting having a regular partner might be expected to be similar to those that we have shown to relate to repartnering behaviour. However, the differences in proportions with a partner between men and women and between formerly married people and former cohabitees are negligible. A significant difference in proportions does exist with respect to age, with 40 per cent of people aged under 40 having a partner, as opposed to 24 per cent of older people ($p < 0.02$). Once again, the absence of a significant bivariate relationship between marital status and having a regular partner is deceptive; when age, sex and the distinction between formerly married people and former cohabitees are incorporated within a multivariate analysis the odds of having a partner are shown to be only 0.46 times as high for former cohabitees as for formerly married people ($p < 0.02$).

Neither the number nor the age of children in an individual's household relates to their having a current, regular partner, whether or not the other factors considered above are taken into account. At first sight this seems surprising, but non-resident partners may be rather heterogeneous, with some being future live-in partners and others being 'alternatives' to this. The presence of children might reduce the likelihood of having a partner of the first sort, but increase the likelihood of having one of the second sort.

A form of diversity among the partners that may relate to this distinction is how long-standing they are. The distribution of partnership duration is approximately negative exponential in form: 24 per cent of the relationships were less than a year old, 31 per cent 1–2 years old, 31 per cent 3–9 years old, and the remaining 14 per cent 10 or more years old. Length of partnership was correlated with age ($r = 0.25$; $p < 0.03$), with every extra ten years of age increasing the average length by 18 months. In addition, former cohabitees' partnerships were on average just over 2 years old, compared to just over 6 years for formerly married people.[89]

The distribution of partnership lengths implies that a substantial proportion of the less long-standing relationships end each year, with more than a quarter ending per year in the early years of the relationships. Such relationships either become a co-resident relationship or end when the couple splits up. Earlier, we showed that 36 per cent of formerly partnered people repartnered over a five-year period. This finding translates into a yearly rate of around 8.5 per cent, or about 21 instances of repartnering per 250 formerly partnered people, as compared to the 20 or so instances of current, regular, non-resident partnerships ending implied by the Omnibus Survey data.[90]

If one assumes that all co-residential repartnering follows a period as a couple living at separate addresses, then the above figures imply that partnerships where the partners live at separate addresses more or less invariably end in co-residence rather than relationship splits. However, both this assumption and its implication are clearly implausible, although the above figures suggest that the proportion of 'living apart' partnerships ending in splits may not be substantially different from the proportion of (self-acknowledged) partnerships that start with cohabitation or marriage, which is presumably relatively small. Of course, the estimate of 20 or so non-resident partnerships ending is quite vulnerable to inaccuracy as a consequence of sampling error. Nevertheless, it seems reasonable to conclude that a substantial proportion – probably even a majority – of the regular partnerships reported by the Omnibus Survey sample are, in effect, stepping stones to cohabitation or remarriage.[91]

Some themes evident from the secondary analyses

While the results of the preceding secondary analyses are too detailed and wide-ranging to be summarized concisely, some of their collective features nevertheless merit comment.

A key factor and source of diversity in relation to repartnering is age, which not only has a marked effect on orientations and behaviour, but also largely accounts for the apparent differences between formerly married people and former cohabitees. Former cohabitees are nevertheless distinctive. They appear less different from single people than formerly married people, and appear to have a greater tendency than the latter to enter into, and possibly leave, cohabiting relationships, as opposed to marrying or having a non-resident partner. However, the similarities between former cohabitees and the formerly married seem as striking as any differences, and both groups are sufficiently heterogeneous to render generalizations crude and unsatisfactory.

Like earlier quantitative studies, our secondary analyses have identified ways in which repartnering orientations and behaviour are affected by gender, parenthood and widowhood, as well as by characteristics such as class, ethnicity and religiosity. However, these factors go a very limited distance towards explaining the observed variation in orientations and behaviour, suggesting that this also needs to be understood via a qualitatively different set of factors or form of explanation.

Some of the other explanatory factors that our analyses have shown to be of significance may echo underlying forms of heterogeneity as much as they document relevant forms of diversity. For example, numbers of past relationships and the ages at which particular aspects of individuals' relationship histories started both appear to be relevant, but their significance may reflect the importance of other, unmeasured personal characteristics or structural factors. The observed impact of separation duration within some analyses highlights the filtering effect that repartnering has on the population of formerly partnered people, and also suggests the possible presence of unknown but pertinent forms of heterogeneity.

The effects of a number of the factors shown to be of relevance, including some of those already mentioned, can be interpreted as reflecting the importance of individuals' personal views and beliefs about the nature and value of couple relationships, and also their expectations of such relationships and perceptions regarding the roles that such relationships could play in their lives. While the observed effects are open to alternative interpretations, the individual's perspective on relationships, and its links to their identity and sense of self, nevertheless seems to be a potentially important source of variation in repartnering orientations and behaviour.

5
Past, Present and Future – Orientations towards Repartnering

This chapter looks at our interviewees' orientations towards repartnering. It examines whether they want new couple relationships, when they want them (assuming that they do) and whether they are currently looking for a new partner.[1] It also discusses the kinds of relationships and partners for which they express a preference, and those they intend to avoid. In addition, it brings into consideration remarks made by the interviewees that are of relevance to the repartnering process. Some of these relate to their repartnering behaviour, if any, during their time as a formerly married person or former cohabitee. Others relate to aspects of their lives and situations that they perceive as having, or anticipate as being likely to have, an impact on their likelihood of repartnering or on the repartnering process more generally.

The approach taken to the discussions and analyses of interview material is broadly consistent with the Grounded Theory approach advocated by Glaser and Strauss (1967). Hence there is an emphasis on providing an account of our results derived from and consistent with our interviewees' viewpoints as expressed in the interview transcripts. More specifically, an attempt is made to generate a 'repartnering typology', based on the interviewees' orientations and behaviour. Inevitably, such a typology reflects our analytical frame of reference as well as the interviewees' viewpoints, which is also the case for the analyses in this chapter more generally.

Is repartnering on the agenda?

For a minority of our interviewees, repartnering is not viewed as a relevant consideration, at least not at present. Some do not currently want a couple relationship of any sort and can envisage never wanting one again. For a minority this reflects specific past experiences such as domestic violence, but for many it seems to reflect a more general fear of being hurt again:

> I felt as though I was nothing. I just felt like nothing and completely worthless. I don't want to end up in that position again.
>
> (Carol, divorced and in her mid-forties)
>
> ... I just wouldn't want to risk being hurt that much again and the only way that you can make sure you're not is to never, ever get involved with anybody.... I prefer loneliness to the prospect of maybe being let down again.
>
> (Ellen, divorced and in her early fifties)

Some of the interviewees who have this outlook have been separated from their most recent partner for a relatively short period of time, leaving open the possibility that their views may change:

> But, I mean I can't look into the future and that, you know I can't say that if I sort of came into contact with somebody next week or next year or whatever I might feel totally different but, umm, I'm not the same person that I was before and I don't know that I could be easy with somebody else ...
>
> (Samantha, separated and in her early forties)

Some of the interviewees who do not view repartnering as a relevant consideration have experienced more than one problematic marriage or cohabiting relationship. While their viewpoint may consequently be less likely to change, their past experiences do not necessarily mean that they do not view a couple relationship as their ideal situation, albeit one that they view as 'impossible' to achieve:

> So, ideally now, I would want to be sharing my life with somebody, but I don't see that as a possibility. So I suppose I try to separate wants from my needs ...
>
> (Claire, separated and in her mid-thirties)

In addition to those interviewees who do not currently want a relationship, there are others who have not been sufficiently motivated by any attractive features of having a new relationship to seek one actively. Sometimes this reflects a degree of scepticism regarding the prospects of finding someone appropriate or 'worth having':

> I suppose theoretically I'm open to the idea of having another relationship, but I don't know how it [would] work practically and I don't feel like

doing a lot about it either. I think I'd have to work hard to find another relationship, and I have some doubts about finding someone who would fit in with the kind of relationship that would work for me, so I don't think about it any detail.

(Paula, separated and in her mid-thirties)

Even if repartnering is on an interviewee's agenda, it is not necessarily a high priority. Some of the interviewees who have been looking for a partner, quite often in an active way, do not currently view finding a partner as of sufficient importance to put any particular effort into doing so in an ongoing way:

I've decided to just not bother really . . . I'm independent, I'm financially sufficient on my own and I've geared my life so that I don't need a man, it would be nice to have one, but I certainly don't need one, you know.

(Louise, divorced and in her late thirties)

The initial relevance of repartnering after separation

In the preceding section we suggested that orientations to repartnering may fluctuate over time, and it certainly appears from our interviews that the initial relevance of repartnering may be different from its later relevance:

I spent three years living at home by myself thinking that I would never ever have another relationship again . . .

(Nicola, divorced and in her early fifties)

Some of the interviewees have learned from their own or others' experiences:

I want to have my own freedom, space and time, rather than go straight from one person to another, which is what I did last time. I'm only just starting really getting over the last one.

(Charlotte, a former cohabitee in her mid-twenties)

At this point in my life, I'm more determined than ever not to be caught on a rollercoaster, because I've seen people who have broken up their relationships and then started another one almost straight away, and before you know it, to me, it's back to where they were at the beginning.

(Alison, divorced and in her mid-thirties)

While finding a new partner has sometimes acted as a boost to an interviewee's confidence, starting a relationship soon after separation can sometimes be counterproductive:

So I was feeling on a bit of a high, you know. Yes, someone wants me, someone wants me. I can be loveable, I can be attractive, I can be all the rest of it, and then it just fell flat on its face.

> (Maria, separated and in her early thirties)

However, an initial period of isolation, despair or coping sometimes renders repartnering irrelevant, at least initially:

It was a nightmare, a nightmare, but a feeling of being really, really cold. It was a hot summer, but I was cold. I was physically isolated. Absolutely on my own. Everything was – there was just so much to do.

> (Kate, divorced and in her early fifties)

. . . I did stop working and I just locked myself in the house really and just survived from day to day, even hour to hour to some extent . . . I was really, you know, just in a small shell . . .

> (James, divorced and in his mid-thirties)

If I'd have had the guts, I would have killed myself. . . . I never went and got any tablets or did anything to attempt to die, but I just knew I wanted to . . .

> (Emma, a former cohabitee in her early thirties)

As discussed later, thoughts about their last partner and relationship were often at the forefront of our interviewees' minds in the period immediately after separation and, in some cases, for a long time thereafter. However, some interviewees who are preoccupied with their last relationship and who report a new relationship as being the 'last thing' on their mind, nevertheless found themselves involved with a prospective partner shortly after separation or divorce.

Readiness to repartner

A few of our interviewees are explicit that they have reached a 'turning point' at which they feel ready to repartner, or at least feel that it may be a possibility worth considering:

. . . you are in the back of your mind thinking about the future, so it's not all devastation and loss is it, and so that's where I'm at. I think I'm at that kind of turning point.

> (Fiona, a former cohabitee in her late twenties)

I'm not, I'm not going to chase anybody . . . But I'm, I, if some-, somebody invites me out, I will go out, and I will see [if it works].

> (Frank, divorced and in his mid-forties)

The last extract illustrates the blurred nature of the concept of 'readiness to repartner', when compared with the following extract from earlier in Frank's interview:

> ... I'm not ready for anything at all. I don't think it would be right to be ready for anything at all yet ...
>
> (Frank, divorced and in his mid-forties)

Frank is also explicit that 'I'm not over my relationship', an example of one of the ways in which many of our interviewees still feel constrained or affected by their last relationship. The diversity of the ways in which ex-partners are still directly or indirectly of relevance is illustrated in the next section.

Our interviewees sometimes view 'readiness to repartner' as contingent on being at ease with themselves or as depending on having adequate economic circumstances or prospects, the latter appearing especially significant for some male interviewees:

> So, as I say, I can see my debts going on, never ending and will never clear, and I cannot start another relationship while I have them.
>
> (Joe, separated and in his late twenties)

The legacy of the last relationship

Many of our interviewees refer to their last relationship in a way that either makes it explicit that it has a continuing impact of some sort on their repartnering attitudes or behaviour, or suggests that its legacy may still be of relevance in that context. However, previous relationships are certainly not of universal relevance, and the extent to and ways in which they continue to be significant appear to vary considerably.

For a small number of the interviewees resuming a relationship with their last partner still seems a possibility, albeit an unlikely one:

> ... in the future relation camp, I still see him. I still think maybe there's a possibility that after six months' rest, he will turn up and fall in love with me again.
>
> (Fiona, a former cohabitee in her late twenties)

However, sometimes such interviewees view the possibility of resuming their previous relationship with considerable ambivalence, or feel that it makes it difficult for them to move on. Irrespective of their feelings about their ex-partner, some have felt constrained by still being legally married:

> I deliberately didn't want to go out with anybody until I had got my divorce absolute. Because I was still married in my eyes . . .
>
> (Louise, divorced and in her late thirties)

However, not yet being divorced is occasionally felt to have some advantages:

> But as yet that isn't sorted out and I'm not about to sort of hand him everything on a plate . . . And it's the only bargaining tool I've got at the moment.
>
> (Samantha, separated and in her early forties)

For Samantha and some of our other interviewees, however, unresolved financial or housing issues relating to the divorce process are viewed as delaying forward movement, whether in relation to repartnering or more generally:

> . . . I think once the divorce is sorted out and the house is sorted out, I'll probably feel a bit more able to perhaps take the next step then. . . . I feel that I've got to get that behind me before I'm able to think about where I'm going.
>
> (Samantha, separated and in her early forties)
>
> . . . until the house sells I'm just really in limbo.
>
> (Ellen, divorced and in her early fifties)

Ellen still lives in the same house as her ex-husband, and, like some of the other interviewees of both sexes, still performs some domestic tasks for him. More frequently, ongoing involvement with an ex-partner, and any consequent complications, is a consequence of shared responsibility for children:

> . . . a lot of that is because [my ex-wife] wants to do things at particular times and I won't really allow a breach in what we've agreed. I've got [my son] for a couple of weeks over the Easter holidays, but basically the way it happens we try and agree things. If we have a real big argument about something, [she] can be really quite physically violent in that way which is quite difficult for me . . .
>
> (Duncan, separated and in his mid-thirties)

Whatever the reason for continued contact, it creates the opportunity for domineering or abusive behaviour on an ongoing basis by some ex-partners.

A number of the interviewees feel, or have felt in the past, that they or potential partners may be at risk from their ex-partner's behaviour:

> ...also he said: 'Oh, you'll never be free of me'; he said, 'I'll maim you for life before I let you go off and lead your own life', and that frightened me.
>
> (Ellen, divorced and in her early fifties)

> So of course [his obsessive behaviour] would have a bearing on future relationships because he will never leave me alone. ...I can't put another man at risk from him really unless that man is quite assertive and self-confident that he doesn't [feel] threatened by that.
>
> (Louise, divorced and in her late thirties)

Occasionally our interviewees are visibly concerned about the potential impact of their repartnering behaviour on their ex-partners:

> ...if she sees me walking around with somebody else, then you know ... I'm not going to do that just to make her jealous. ... if I did, she could end up killing herself anyway, so that's one reason why I'm not going to do it ...
>
> (Martin, separated and in his mid-twenties)

As what Martin says above illustrates, the scope for chance encounters with an ex-partner can sometimes viewed as problematic, and as consolidating an unwelcome link with the past. Samantha has experienced this, as her ex-husband lives nearby and sometimes attends the same social events:

> I see him walking past and you know, I feel as though he is still, I feel as though he's watching me, as though he wants me to, to sort of react in some way.
>
> (Samantha, separated and in her early forties)

> ...I don't know why it matters, I've asked myself that, you know, what, why do you worry about what he thinks of you? You know, it doesn't make any difference and I suppose really, it's probably selfish, a bit childish I suppose, in that I think, well, I don't want him to see me not looking my best ...
>
> (Samantha, separated and in her early forties)

So far in this section the emphasis has been on the impact of ongoing contact with ex-partners. However, the relevance of emotional ties to ex-partners, however viewed and whether alive or dead, transcends actual contact:

> I know I'm still tied to him and that's another thing about going into another relationship isn't it, because I know in some way I'm still emotionally tied to him even though some days I don't want to be.
>
> (Emily, divorced and in her late forties)

> In my case I just don't feel that I can let go. He will always be there wherever I am. I mean I've moved from where we used to live and I've moved to here, but it still doesn't make any difference.
>
> (Pauline, widowed and in her mid-forties)

Pauline feels that she has promised her dead husband that there will not be anybody else and that her commitment to their marriage should be ongoing. However Janice, another widowed interviewee, while exhibiting a comparable sense of irreplaceable loss, feels that her partner wanted her to repartner:

> I've got to honestly hand on heart be able to say to [him], I really am giving it the 110 per cent we always gave it and I would dearly love to be in another relationship in time.
>
> (Janice, widowed and in her late forties)

On the other hand, Janice feels that she will have to be cautious in her expectations of any new relationship in terms of the level of intimacy and intensity that it will be realistic to expect, at least in the first instance, relative to her last relationship.

Our interviewees often feel that they need to learn from their past co-resident relationships and to deal with any emotional baggage before repartnering, in part to avoid repartnering 'on the rebound', or hurting a new partner:

> There's too much, I think, I've got to sort out and come to terms with to be able to move on clearly, otherwise you're just dragging things, I'd just be dragging things with me . . .
>
> (Claire, separated and in her mid-thirties)

However, some interviewees seem resigned, albeit unhappily, to moving forward without a clear understanding of why their last relationship failed or ended acrimoniously.

Even in the absence of contact with or emotional bonds to ex-partners, the legacy of past relationships appears substantial. Occasionally, an interviewee's overall outlook seems to have changed:

... I don't have a lot of faith, I don't have a lot of faith in the future because, you know, I suppose your experience colours your perception of things, doesn't it?

(Cheryl, separated and in her mid-forties)

More specifically, a fear of being hurt again means that some of our interviewees do not want new relationships. More generally, the interviewees are frequently cautious about repartnering, in case history should repeat itself:

... I think I would end up getting hurt again, because I think I've thrown myself fully into a relationship, being honest, being totally committed, being faithful and [I] tried to be totally honest, and for what? It just gets thrown back at you.

(Rob, a former cohabitee in his mid-thirties)

In consequence, some of the interviewees approach repartnering in a pessimistic way, or are concerned that they will be unable to trust or commit themselves to a new partner:

... when he left here, I mean, when he left here he didn't only take his, sort of clothes and personal possessions with him, he took things from me that I don't feel will ever be replaced, he took my ability to trust ...

(Samantha, separated and in her early forties)

The next time that situation arises with a different person, you're looking for the signs and although it might be a completely different person, if you sense or see the signs as it happens, it makes you reluctant to commit what you would normally do as instinct, commit anything towards the situation.

(Kevin, a former cohabitee in his mid-twenties)

Some of the interviewees are particularly unwilling to risk the upheaval of losing another home. (Issues associated with risk are discussed more fully in Chapter 6.)

The 'failure' of their last relationship sometimes appears to have undermined an interviewee's self-esteem or confidence in a way that is of relevance to repartnering:

The second [relationship] I thought, well, I thought it was going to go fine, but it went downhill like the other one did, so that makes me feel a bit more uncomfortable about me trying to meet somebody else.

(Martin, separated and in his mid-twenties)

Our physical relationship was terrible and that's what's hurt me, that's what's knocked my confidence, and [is] probably why I haven't had a relationship [since], because I've just lost all confidence in myself, in how I would react . . .

> (Michelle, divorced and in her mid-twenties)

More specifically, some of our interviewees feel that their 'second-hand' status reflects badly upon them:

> . . . I mean it's not a very good track record – twice divorced and a young child. There's not many people, if anybody, that would want to get mixed up with somebody like that, so you have to look at it realistically . . .
>
> (Claire, separated and in her mid-thirties)

Some of the interviewees have an explicit fear of being rejected, which discourages them from seeking a partner. Others have reacted differently, and have sought relationships in part to boost their self-esteem:

> I don't know if it's interest or whether it's just the need to be wanted. For whatever reasons, be it sexual or whatever, it's knowing that someone wants you, that you are not on the scrapheap. You have been pushed aside, but that was the mind of somebody else.
>
> (Sylvia, divorced and in her late forties)

The indirect impact of past relationships on repartnering behaviour can be seen to operate via the financial as well as the personal consequences of separation. Interviewees of both sexes are explicit about the impact of post-separation financial constraints:

> . . . it wasn't the sort of be-all-and-end-all of my life, but it was something that was holding me up from going out and doing things to get on with my life.
>
> (Kevin, a former cohabitee in his mid-twenties)

To repartner or not to repartner? Factors affecting orientations

Some of the interviewees are clearly motivated to repartner, in the long term if not sooner, by a sense that a close relationship, whether based on intimacy or shared experiences or both, is an ideal that suits them:

> . . . in an ideal world I would have a living-together relationship because I am a born sharer: I like sharing things and sharing experiences and doing things with other people.
>
> (Rosa, divorced and in her late forties)

While some interviewees who express such views are nevertheless content to be on their own at present, many clearly miss having a partner:

> I do things to fill in my time now, I've started doing jigsaw puzzles and silly things like that to just do something with my time really, and I'd rather be with another person.
>
> (Louise, divorced and in her late thirties)

> The way I feel at the moment I actually quite like living alone, and yet there are times when I don't, when I think I would like a shoulder to cry on or something, you know, to have that person to share how I feel . . .
>
> (Colin, a former cohabitee in his mid-thirties)

However, a substantial number of our interviewees have established a sense of independence, freedom or control that may be difficult to give up, irrespective of whether they miss having a partner:

> Yes, I think that is one of the things that I'm scared about, if I did have a relationship. I know that I will have to adapt the way that I live. I'm so used to just doing what I want to do.
>
> (Alison, divorced and in her mid-thirties).

> So I can see my independence and freedom, I have this freedom which is very valuable to me, very valuable indeed, and I'm not going to give it up easily, and I'm at the stage now where I'm not lonely although I'm on my own . . .
>
> (James, divorced and in his mid-thirties)

> . . . I quite like living on my own. I quite like having my freedom. I have been out with other men, but I just find that they're, their expectations are too much, are too tight.
>
> (Emily, divorced and in her late forties)

While interviewees of both sexes appreciate having control over their own lives, if anything, women appear more likely to have reached a point where they cannot envisage sacrificing this, and would be prepared at most to have a non-resident partnership.

Children, or the absence of children, might be expected to be a significant factor affecting repartnering orientations. Some, but not all, of the younger women interviewed who were without children would ideally like to have children at some point, and view this as a potentially positive aspect of repartnering. However, the preference of some of these women for having children within a partnership is based on personal or practical issues rather than on family-related ideology. Additional children seem to be less of a motivating factor for women who already have children, including those with only one child. The dangers of making naïve, gendered or simplistic assumptions about children as an incentive to repartner is usefully high-lighted by a comment by Kevin, who is already father to a number of children, but would like more:

> ... I like kids around me all the time. It's just, you know – how can I put it? – it's like a male version of maternal instinct. It might sound a bit daft, but I like the kids, I love seeing kids play because of the innocence of it and after some of the experiences I've had, it's nice to just basically have them around ...
>
> (Kevin, a former cohabitee in his mid-twenties)

Existing children, whether resident with the interviewee or living else-where, have more diverse and complex effects on our interviewees' repart-nering orientations and behaviour. The interviewees often view themselves and their children as a 'package' that potential partners will have to engage with as a whole, and regard the time, attention and commitment that they devote to their children as a given. Superficially at least, the gender of an interviewee and whether or not their child or children live with them seem to be of little relevance. Such interviewees are, however, clearly conscious of the tensions in the repartnering process created by being part of a 'package':

> ... but I mean I've got to find a lady who's going to put up with my trips to [a distant location] to see my children, that type of thing ...
>
> (Barry, divorced and in his early fifties)

> ... there have been a few minor relationships along the way, where – including ones where people thought they were good with children and I thought they were just abominable ...
>
> (Penny, divorced and in her mid-forties)

> Some women are not willing to, sort of, take on a bloke who's got kids, because obviously if that woman, if that particular woman's looking for a relationship to have kids, she's going to be wondering how the situation is going to arise ...
>
> (Kevin, a former cohabitee in his mid-twenties)

Occasionally, of course, children are of negligible significance in the context of repartnering behaviour or orientations, for example where an interviewee is not in contact with them. Conversely, a co-resident parent can be as much a part of an interviewee's 'package' as a child would have been. Our interviewees' views regarding the rights of children, or other household members, to contribute to their repartnering decisions vary:

> ... [my children] respect the fact that if it was to be my choice, it's my choice and not theirs.
>
> (Pauline, widowed and in her mid-forties)

The saying is whatever they want and I just think they're funny, but whoever comes into my life doesn't just get me, they get my children as well and they think, they've just as much right, they haven't got like, the ultimate right to say he's not for you or whatever because I've said to them it's my decision . . .

(Emily, divorced and in her late forties)

. . . you know I just I couldn't say to her 'Right, we're both moving in with [my boyfriend]' because you know I've got no right to say that to her . . .

(Cheryl, separated and in her mid-forties)

Feelings about the degree of involvement that children should have with prospective partners also vary. Some interviewees feel that children would want or should have the opportunity to 'vet' prospective partners; others are disinclined for children and prospective partners to come into contact with each other, at least not in the first instance. Our interviewees have often monitored and reflected on how well their children have got on (or not) with prospective partners, and with any children that they have had. While the interviewees typically, and unsurprisingly, prefer their children to get on well with a prospective partner, a willingness to respect their parent's (the interviewee's) choice and tolerate the person seem in some instances to be viewed as adequate:

. . . I just felt that whatever I did it had to be with – if not with their blessing, at least with their knowledge. They had to know who I was with and they had to be happy about it, or at least not distressed about it.

(Kate, divorced and in her early fifties)

Irrespective of what their children's views may be about specific potential partners, some of the interviewees report that their children have encouraged them to find a new partner, and a substantial number feel that their children would be pleased, or even relieved, if they did, because of their concern for their parent's happiness and well-being:

[My son] always says it's time you found yourself a nice, rich bloke. So they're being very encouraging.

(Rosa, divorced and in her late forties)

So, to answer your question, how would he feel as he would be the most affected person, if I was to enter into a proper relationship where somebody moved in? I think he'd be very glad. He would like to see dad happier than what he is because dad isn't as happy as he should be.

(Barry, divorced and in his early fifties)

... I don't know, it would probably be a bit of a shock to them, but they might be relieved. It could well be that they think, 'Oh, thank goodness my mum has got herself sorted out at last'.

(Ellen, divorced and in her early fifties)

Unsurprisingly, the ways in which children are felt to view, or be likely to view, parental repartnering seem to vary according to the children's age, their feelings about their other parent, and the time elapsed since the end of their parents' relationship. Children are sometimes perceived as viewing potential new partners as a threat, whether to their own relationship with their parent, or to their parents' relationship, or to their parent's well-being:

... I think he will accept it, but, it's going to hurt him. It will hurt him. Because, he doesn't think it's really finished yet, and I think, if I found somebody now, he will think, it's finished.

(Frank, divorced and in his mid-forties)

I actually think that I would get – they would be the same whoever it was. I think they would find a reason not to like them. I really do.

(Pauline, widowed and in her mid-forties)

For some of the interviewees, having children places constraints on what is currently appropriate in terms of repartnering. One view is that finding a relationship should be delayed until any children have left home, and our interviewees are often uncomfortable about the idea of bringing a new partner into their home, even if their children are close to adulthood or if it is perceived that doing so would not bother them. Sometimes, having a series of relationships is also viewed negatively:

... that's probably why I don't want to enter a relationship because I actually did make this kind of promise to myself that I wouldn't enter, I wouldn't get into a relationship until they'd left home, because I actually think it's very difficult for them ...

(Emily, divorced and in her late forties)

I would find that very difficult, to start with anyway, to bring somebody into my home and share my bedroom with them.

(Sylvia, divorced and in her late forties)

So I just wouldn't want a stream of men coming to the house. I should be so lucky!

(Heather, widowed and in her early forties)

According to a number of our interviewees, a prospective partner should be 'right' for their children, or should be liked by them, or should have parenting skills (although without interfering with their own way of bringing up their children).

Finding a new partner: the repartnering process

In this section we discuss what our interviewees have to say about the process of finding a new partner. The extent to which the interviewees have made an effort to find a new partner varies considerably, as does the extent to which they have had relationships of any sort since last living with a partner. Being open to the possibility of a relationship has not necessarily translated into any active attempt to find one. For some of the interviewees the prospect of looking for a relationship is unappealing; others rely on opportunities occurring without their making any particular effort:

> I haven't said 'I will choose to be on my own', but on the other hand neither have I gone out and sought any relationship.
>
> (Eleanor, divorced and in her mid-fifties)

> No, definitely not going to look for one. I don't know. It depends how lonely you feel; I don't know whether I would want one. How I feel now is no, that's it; you know if something happened without me having to put any effort into it at all then that's fine . . .
>
> (Cheryl, separated and in her mid-forties)

> . . . I don't know how I'm going to form any relationships. I just have to have faith I will, and just believe that I will form a relationship wherever I go, and just keep telling myself that because I'm a nice person, I'll naturally form relationships. It's going to happen, but I haven't a clue how.
>
> (Fiona, a former cohabitee in her late twenties)

The idea of forming relationships 'naturally' is, for a substantial number of the interviewees, more of a preference than just an expectation. Alternatively, while some have sought a new relationship to boost their confidence, for others issues of self-esteem or fear of rejection have led to a passive approach to repartnering or to their social life more generally:

> . . . I will not follow her example, and go out and try and find it. I want, I want it to come along, sort of thing.
>
> (Frank, divorced and in his mid-forties)

> I'd keep my fingers crossed because I believe what's meant to be is meant to be.
>
> (Louise, divorced and in her late thirties)

... it's very easy to sink into doing the gardening, doing the, er, you know, working at night and all that, and I think we all do it because it's safest. It, as I say, it doesn't involve any effort, it doesn't carry any risk of, of rejection.

(Eleanor, divorced and in her mid-fifties)

An examination of our interviewees' views regarding, and experiences of, personal advertisements, dating agencies and singles' nights and clubs provides some interesting evidence in relation to the distinction between actively seeking a partner and being passive in this respect. Some of the interviewees see singles' clubs as an obvious vehicle for constructing a new social life, and a number of interviewees have formed dating relationships with people that they have met via singles' clubs or through personal advertisements:

I think the idea of joining [a singles' club] is more or less recreating a spontaneous meeting raising the likelihood [of finding a partner] because all of these people are going to be unattached. If you think that you go to, whatever it is, you go to somebody's barbecue and there may be fifty people there, but what are the chances of, or what will be the percentage of unattached people, unless your friend is desperately trying to fix you up, which happens at times.

(Rosa, divorced and in her late forties)

Some of our interviewees have found singles' clubs to be a valuable source of friendships and mutual support, and a number of interviewees are resentful that some people attending such clubs treat them solely as a kind of dating agency. Others view some singles' clubs as too close in character to other forms of social club:

When I joined that singles' club for six months, I used to enjoy going. They had discos and that and I used to enjoy going to that and I used to normally take a friend with me, a girlfriend, and I'd be quite happy there in my own little world dancing away and then men would come up and try and dance and woof, immediately, I felt that they were intruding on my space...

(Pauline, widowed and in her mid-forties)

... the danger I think with these singles' clubs is that they become not a singles' club, but just a club. You get to know those people and it's more of a social thing rather than perhaps what you'd expect it to be, go and meet somebody.

(Sylvia, divorced and in her late forties)

This conflict of views highlights the potential tension between the development of a satisfactory post-separation social life and finding a new partner. For some of the interviewees, the ideal singles' club would seem to be one that focuses on the former but allows scope for the latter:

> After the third time I thought I don't want to join because – no disrespect to any of the people there – it was like a bloody meat market at the end of the day. I thought, no, this ain't what I'm looking for.
>
> (Barry, divorced and in his early fifties)
>
> . . . if it was a sort of friendship club, if you like, with a possibility of developing further . . .
>
> (Duncan, separated and in his mid-thirties)

The interviewees have sometimes discovered that singles' clubs they have attended do not suit them. Sometimes this reflects a mismatch between the interviewee and the clubs' other members, in terms of age, social characteristics or outlook, and sometimes a negative view of these other members:

> The best way I can put it, I'll be quite frank, I walked in there and the impression I got was that they were a lot of rich kids trying to play at being working class. Although they might have been single, it just seemed – I just felt so out of place . . .
>
> (Kevin, a former cohabitee in his mid-twenties)
>
> I just felt that in some particular groups, I just felt they were all misfits basically. I didn't feel they were people on the same wavelength as me at all.
>
> (Heather, widowed and in her early forties)

A substantial number of the interviewees view the costs of being involved in such clubs, in terms of time and of money, as prohibitive, especially if they do not fit in particularly well with the club's members. A few are held back from attending them by a lack of confidence.

Some of the interviewees who have never been to a singles' club visualise them in rather negative terms, and some who have attended singles' clubs perceive many of the members to be 'desperate' or burdened by extensive 'emotional baggage':

> . . . I don't know what they're like or what they involve and you tend to get the general picture that it's full of sad people, don't you? Sad, desperate people and no, I don't want that to be me.
>
> (Claire, separated and in her mid-thirties)
>
> The people who turn up at singles' clubs are people that have nowhere else to go. They're at their wits' end and they need to go somewhere,

so they go somewhere like the singles' clubs. . . . they bring baggage with them that most of it is insurmountable.

(Davina, divorced and in her early fifties)

Placing or replying to a personal advertisement or using a dating agency is similarly viewed by some as the act of a 'desperate' person, and is furthermore sometimes seen as 'unnatural'. However, other interviewees embrace what in the past would have been something that they would never have done or contemplated doing:

It's almost like you're going to try and buy them off the shelf which is not really how I want it to happen.

(Michelle, divorced and in her mid-twenties)

I've found myself doing things out of character as far as going places where I wouldn't normally go, doing things I wouldn't normally have considered before and that I would have classed as like a last resort . . .

(Kevin, a former cohabitee in his mid-twenties)

As with singles' clubs, many of our interviewees view using personal advertisements and dating agencies as an approach to finding a new partner as flawed in practice, whether because of the cost, or because it is an ineffective way of finding the 'right' type of person, or because the unfamiliarity and awkwardness of the process undermine their confidence:

. . . I know instinctively whether I like someone or not as soon as I meet them. . . . and then I'd say to them, 'Well, I'm sorry, I don't think so', and that's the end of that, so I went through about ten of these doing this and I was really quite fed up with it in the end and then one of them, towards the end, was OK . . .

(Maureen, separated, subsequently a cohabitee, and in her early fifties)

If we ever met somebody that we liked, either one of us, neither of us could pick up the phone and ring that person and say 'Would you like to meet again?' and that's the fear of rejection.

(Sylvia, divorced and in her late forties)

Some of the interviewees have replied to advertisements but have not received a responses to their reply. Others have been put off using dating agencies or personal advertisements by a concern that they would find it too embarrassing or even meet someone odd or frightening:

. . . I'd be terrified that I would get some weirdo that I couldn't get rid of.

(Samantha, separated and in her early forties)

As with singles' clubs, some of the interviewees favour agencies or advertisements that are oriented to friendship rather than sexual or couple relationships. This echoes the more general preference of a substantial number of the interviewees for a gradual escalation to a relationship from friendship as a starting point:

> ... by the time the man answers or puts an advert in the paper, he's so desperate and all they want to do is talk about marriage and all the rest of it.
>
> (Sharon, divorced and in her late thirties)

> Well, to start off with, probably someone for friendship first and then leading on to a relationship later on. Finding somebody for friendship and someone to talk to for a start off...
>
> (Martin, separated and in his mid-twenties)

> Now, if I fell in love again, it's more likely to be with someone that I've built a friendship up with because the friendship is the strongest thing with me. That's the important thing.
>
> (Jean, separated and in her early fifties)

Some of the interviewees feel strongly that increasing one's chances of finding a new partner does not necessarily depend on using approaches such as singles' clubs or dating agencies. New or resurrected leisure activities, and even taking courses or changing jobs, are viewed by some as appropriate approaches to broadening one's social networks:

> ... I think in a way it's a disaster to go out doing things to find somebody, which is why I don't really like the singles' thing, but I mean the singles' things they organize lots of activities, go to the theatre, have a walk, whatever. Well, why not do that anyway? It seems to me that in the end the way that I will make other friends is by doing the things that I enjoy...
>
> (Janice, widowed and in her late forties)

> I'm not particularly very sporty, but I've just decided that as my social life has gone downhill to join something like that which has a social aspect to it... you may meet a female who's got male friends and it's just this widening of everything really that you just need to keep ploughing away at.
>
> (Heather, widowed and in her early forties)

However, Janice and Heather, as well as other interviewees, view such activities primarily as part of the process of reconstructing a social life as an end in itself. A less than satisfactory social life sometimes exists in parallel with the absence of a partner:

> ... I've actually come to a standstill as far as social activities are concerned really.... I'm tired. I think it's a vicious circle. If there was somebody in my life I wouldn't be tired, I would have something to, motivate me. Motivation. And it's so easy to get stuck in a rut.
>
> (Sylvia, divorced and in her late forties)

It is clear from the fact that many of our interviewees have used or considered using singles' clubs and personal advertisements, and the fact that other interviewees have considered other ways of meeting a greater number of potential partners, that these interviewees do not perceive their day-to-day lives as generating adequate opportunities to find a new partner. Neither private nor public social contexts bring them into contact with significant numbers of new, unattached people of an 'appropriate' sort, and they are sometimes unsure of how to address this:

> I am now considering joining a dating agency ... I figured I'll do that and see what comes of it, you know, because I don't see that I'm in a position to do it any other way. I don't go out socially.
>
> (Caroline, divorced and in her late forties)

> ... you're always sort of, wherever you go, you're always the odd one out, you're always in couples and it makes you feel, I think it actually makes you feel worse the fact that everybody's in couples.
>
> (Pauline, widowed and in her mid-forties)

> I have friends round here or I am invited to friends' houses, but it's all a very closed circle. I don't have the opportunity financially or the time to sort of go out and meet other people.
>
> (Samantha, separated and in her early forties)

> I'm sure the up-market dating agencies have good names, but again tradition, I don't see why you should go and pay for that kind of service when you can try and meet them, but how do you meet them? I don't know.
>
> (Rob, a former cohabitee in his mid-thirties)

Workplaces are often seen as obvious settings in which to meet a partner. While some of our interviewees endorse this view, and quite a number have met potential partners through their employment, for a substantial number this is evidently not the case:

> ... if I was in a working environment, I would probably find somebody ...
>
> (Frank, divorced and in his mid-forties)

My place of work at the moment, I work with elderly people. I think there's one man that crosses my path at work.

> (Rosa, divorced and in her late forties)

I mean there's lots of people at work that have the qualities that I'm looking for in a man, but they're married.

> (Sylvia, divorced and in her late forties)

Meeting people is always very difficult. . . . I'm self-employed, I work by myself, so I hardly see anybody.

> (Edward, divorced and in his mid-forties)

Well the only drawback with work is the fact, I mean [I do dirty, manual work] which doesn't really do your confidence much good when you're out there . . .

> (Kevin, a former cohabitee in his mid-twenties)

Conventional locations like nightclubs are viewed as of limited value as places to meet people, assuming that the interviewees feel that they can afford to go out:

I go to nightclubs, which is something I never thought I'd do . . . it's not the sort of place where I feel that I'm going to meet someone who I could start a serious relationship [with].

> (Kevin, a former cohabitee in his mid-twenties)

. . . so, like everything else, it's down to money. If you haven't the money, you can't go out and you can't go out if you haven't got the clothes to go out in . . .

> (Sylvia, divorced and in her late forties)

Some of our interviewees have met potential partners through chance, day-to-day encounters with people known to their friends or relatives, or whom they have come into contact with via personal or leisure activities. However, the more socially isolated an interviewee is, the less she or he has been able to rely on such chance events. The same applies to existing friendships developing into couple relationships; our interviewees have sometimes come to view a friend as a potential partner, and on occasions an existing friend has made advances, sometimes unexpectedly. In addition, friends, family or colleagues have sometimes attempted to act as matchmakers, though perceived pressure to repartner is not always welcome or necessarily felt to be helpful:

. . . it actually works out worse, because they'll try and fix you up or they'll suggest things, which to me personally makes me feel even more sort of useless.

> (Kevin, a former cohabitee in his mid-twenties)

In some cases, both repartnering orientations and behaviour seem to relate to the importance or intensity of other demands on the interviewees' time. As noted earlier, our interviewees' orientations are often consciously shaped by a parenting role. However, parenthood can also act as a significant demand on an interviewee's time and energy, irrespective of whether their children live with them or elsewhere. As the central focus of the lives of some of the interviewees, parenthood can act as a substitute for some aspects of having a partner, or at least act as an obstacle to finding or carrying on with a new relationship. On occasions our interviewees were conscious of this and viewed it as problematic:

> A lot of people find life busy anyway, so I do find it very busy. It's better now as [my daughter has] got older. . . . in many ways I feel my life is on hold at the moment whilst my daughter is growing up. I don't care if I meet somebody in the meantime though.
>
> (Peter, widowed and in his mid-forties)

> [*Interviewer*: So what's most important to you in your life at the moment?]
>
> Having enough money to keep going and seeing my kids really. It really is. I'm not bothered about having enough money to socialize or go out . . .
>
> (Barry, divorced and in his early fifties)

> . . . I've got two healthy children and they're no problem. I shouldn't say this really, but they're my life, they're my reason for living, but even that's a bad thing because I just wrap my whole life and reason for living round them and they're going to be fleeing the nest sooner or later, and then I'm empty again.
>
> (Ellen, divorced and in her early fifties)

Our interviewees report a number of other activities that either explicitly or implicitly compete with repartnering for their time and attention. Paid employment is important to the sense of self of some, but is seen by others more as a heavy demand on their time and energy. In addition to children and work, our interviewees reported spending significant amounts of time on their grandchildren, parents and grandparents, renovating or improving their homes, education or training, leisure or political activities, socializing with friends and day-to-day practicalities (especially in the period immediately following separation). In some instances our interviewees are clear that they have either filled, or plan to fill, the gap left by a couple relationship

1-303

M. Gorra!

Money attenuates old friendships— also one's self—

130

with such activities. However, they are not always sure that they can do this:

> You can't be a mum, look after a house, do a job and have a social life and meet other people. It's just impossible. With all the will in the world, it's really, really hard.
>
> > (Alison, divorced and in her mid-thirties)

> ... straight after my divorce I enrolled for that and now I've done it again, I've [enrolled in further training]. I think what it is – I channel myself into learning something because I haven't got a relationship so I need something to focus on in the meantime that's different...
>
> > (Louise, divorced and in her late thirties)

> What's central now, I really have no idea. I just can't answer that really. I think [my partner] changed that in terms of making relationships with people central to life in a way that [it] had never been before and to a degree I can't seem to go back to what I was because I'm changed, but I can't be what we were, so I don't know what I will become.
>
> > (Janice, widowed and in her late forties)

As in any assemblage of 'single' people, some of our interviewees exhibit a degree of self-consciousness about their age or appearance, or something specific such as a disability. Occasionally, an interviewee is self-conscious about being perceived as having had a 'failed' relationship, although there is little evidence of concern about any residual stigma attached to divorce. However, such concerns seem to be far less of an issue, in the context of our interviewees' views of the repartnering process, than a sense of being rusty or 'out of place' is:

> It's so long since I've not lived with somebody that I find it quite hard to imagine dating someone. That's quite comical.
>
> > (Fiona, a former cohabitee in her late twenties)

> ... where do people my age go where they're not sort of sticking out like a sore thumb or where they're not giving out this message, you know, 'I'm here, come and get me' sort of thing?
>
> > (Samantha, separated and in her early forties)

> And a couple of the lads went off to have a dance and I still felt a lack of confidence. I didn't know how to chat up a girl, I'd no idea, you forget [that] what came naturally that you didn't have to think about had gone...
>
> > (Barry, divorced and in his early fifties)

Some of the interviewees are more comfortable than others with the 'experimental' nature of the dating process:

> In fact, I've been thinking about these past few years and I hope people I've been out with don't think that I was treating them experimentally. I would hate to think that. I wasn't aware of it at the time, but in retrospect it was one big experiment.
>
> (Kate, divorced and in her early fifties)

> There's one friend of mine who goes out with anybody that asks her because it's a night out and I admire her for that and sometimes I wish I was more like that but I'm not, I just can't force myself.
>
> (Heather, widowed and in her early forties)

The pros and cons of different types of relationships

Some of our interviewees are, or have been, 'dating', or are otherwise sexually active. While some report a strong disinclination to engage in 'one night stands', others have engaged in casual or short-term sexual relationships:

> . . . I don't want to, sort of give people the impression that, you know, I kind of like got rid of him and, you know, I'm having a different man every other week.
>
> (Samantha, separated and in her early forties)

> I'm looking for something where if it takes three to six months to get to know a female well enough before we start an intimate relationship, then I'll be more than happy to do that than to basically jump into bed with whatever woman's sort of drunk that night and wake up in the morning and she says, 'Right, I'll see you around' and leave[s]. I want something a lot more solid . . .
>
> (Kevin, a former cohabitee in his mid-twenties)

> . . . she said, 'Oh, don't you feel guilty?' and I said, 'What for?' And she said, 'Well you know, you['ve] slept with him and gone'. I said, 'No. Why should I?' And I had this feeling inside that I had control, and I did not feel guilty by doing something, and I don't regret what I did.
>
> (Sylvia, divorced and in her late forties)

Some of the interviewees appear to have succeeded in shutting out sexual feelings, while others feel that coping with them is preferable to casual encounters. For some interviewees, experiencing or acting on such feelings seems to have constituted part of the process of coming to terms with the aftermath of their last relationship:

I suppose [I] just ignore it at the moment because I just don't want to get into a situation where I can get into a mess again . . .

(Claire, separated and in her mid-thirties)

I think the physical loneliness, the lack of love and sex is enormously difficult to cope with, but I don't think that that would be satisfied by just having casual sex.

(Janice, widowed and in her late forties)

Wonderful night and [it] worked, because it was natural. It wasn't something I was trying to do to prove that I could do it and after that I wouldn't say things have been perfect in the sex life, no, they haven't, but I know I've improved.

(Barry, divorced and in his early fifties)

I went through the stage of just sleeping with anybody. It used to take my mind off it and perhaps it made it worse because it wasn't me.

(Emma, a former cohabitee in her early thirties)

Our interviewees have often been involved with someone on a longer-term basis since they last lived with a partner. These relationships have been quite diverse in character, varying from what might be regarded as embryonic cohabiting relationships or marriages to relationships where such an outcome would seem very unlikely, for example in some of the cases where the other person has been living with a spouse or partner. While it might arguably be appropriate to classify some of these relationships as 'living apart together' relationships (LATs) or as 'affairs', this would seem to be an unduly restrictive way of categorizing a rather heterogeneous phenomenon.

Some interviewees are clear that they would not knowingly have a relationship with someone who is living with a partner, often because they have 'had it done to me', but sometimes because they are concerned that they might end up hurting the other person, or vice versa. In some cases an opportunity has arisen for an interviewee to become involved with someone whose partner is already known to them, ending or putting at risk an existing friendship. For some interviewees, the attraction of being able to talk intimately with someone they know and like has been a strong magnet. For others, a relationship with someone who already has a partner has provided sexual intimacy, a sense of excitement, or simply a pleasant time.

I would never do that. I know what it's done to me and I don't want to do that to somebody else.

(Ellen, divorced and in her early fifties)

...I wanted to avoid the embarrassment and that actually finished the friendship with the two of them. I don't know to this day whether the wife is aware of why.

(Rosa, divorced and in her late forties)

I do know some women who have fallen into that and you think, well, it's, it's hard. It's hard coming out of a relationship and then not having somebody, and somebody to talk to.

(Emily, divorced and in her late forties)

...you know, I suppose one of the things about affairs is you haven't got all the day-to-day problems. You've just got the nice times.

(Heather, widowed and in her early forties)

According to some of our interviewees, relationships of this sort may in some instances be rendered less inappropriate by the specific nature of the relationship between the other person and the other person's partner. Such a view often reflects a perception that the relationship in question is no longer rooted in sexual or emotional intimacy, or is coming to an end.

...I think for a long, long time the sexual side of their marriage has been you know not very good and I think basically they're perfectly happy [with their] friendship. They belong together very well. They're very comfortable and secure.

(Heather, widowed and in her early forties)

They've had separate bedrooms for [many] years.... they cannot split up for financial reasons.

(Barry, divorced and in his early fifties)

It was a shock for me and then I said, 'I'm not coming between a man and his wife', and he said, 'You're coming between, you are coming between absolutely nothing', and whether I choose to believe that, I don't know. He's still with her.

(Sheila, separated and in her late forties)

While not always seen as ideal, relationships with people who already have partners have offered some interviewees something of value. However, the constraints associated with such relationships mean that they may be abandoned in favour of a relationship with an unattached partner, which in some cases is something that has clearly been discussed.

...we stopped having a sexual relationship and that wasn't my choice it was his choice because he thought I deserved to have somebody that was free...

(Louise, divorced and in her late thirties)

... I think she would initially be gutted if I met somebody else I think, but in a way she would also be happy as long as we could remain friends.

(Barry, divorced and in his early fifties)

Relationships with people who are already married or cohabiting constitute a subset of a broader category of 'dead-end' relationships, which on occasions have suited the interviewees, but which are also, in some instances, viewed as a possible barrier to other, more satisfactory relationships:

Oh, he's quite aware that at any time I may disappear. I would say that in some respects having this relationship probably stops me from pushing myself into something else, but it wouldn't stop me altogether if the right person came along.

(Heather, widowed and in her early forties)

... yes, he has done things for me because he has brought me out and we know lots of people, but I'm just in this dead end and I'm getting older.

(Alice, divorced and in her early fifties)

Even when considering unattached people as potential partners, a substantial minority of the interviewees, predominantly women, would prefer, and in some cases have had experience of, a relationship with a partner who lives elsewhere. Where this is seen as an ideal, it is typically a reflection of a desire to maintain an independent life, with one's own territory, while at the same time having someone with whom to spend time and be sexually intimate. The prominence of a relationship with a partner who lives elsewhere as an ideal echoes the high value placed on 'space' by many interviewees of both sexes:

My ideal situation is never to live with anyone or marry them, but [to] have them sort of close, so we can spend a lot of the time together ... but also have separate lives. That would be nice; that would be ideal. I can't see me meeting someone that would agree to that, not long term.

(Jean, separated and in her early fifties)

My ideal would be a person who is obviously unattached but who lives an independent life as well and to me that would be the absolute ideal: to meet up at weekends, to stay over at weekends, but have your space as well.

(Heather, widowed and in her early forties)

So now I don't actually have to think about it. I can go to bed when I want to, eat when I like and just have space really. I just like space.

(Teresa, divorced, subsequently a former cohabitee, and in her early forties)

However, a disinclination to live with a partner sometimes seems to reflect a lack of trust and a consequent desire to remain in control, whether emotionally or financially. In other cases, a non-resident partner seems to have represented a compromise, because something has been acting as a block to the partners living together, for example the presence of children, or the other person not being viewed as the 'right person' to live with.

> For quite a while until I was absolutely sure that he felt the same about me or that he loved me a little bit more than I loved him then I'd be sure he wouldn't treat me badly.
>
> (Louise, divorced and in her late thirties)

> ... right at the beginning one of the things that I felt it wasn't right living together was because I still had some kids at home and I felt this wouldn't be right for them at this point.
>
> (Rosa, divorced and in her late forties)

In some instances a non-co-resident relationship seems to have been viewed as relatively transient, something that might progress to, or perhaps be replaced by, a cohabiting relationship. The interviewees have also sometimes had short-term, 'dating' relationships. In general, our interviewees are often positive about the non-co-resident relationships that they have had, but which have since ended, since they seem on occasions to have offered the interviewees something important in a 'transitional' sense:

> It helped. It helped me cope with all sorts of things because again he was very supportive and encouraging and he gave me a lot of advice. It really helped get me back on my feet and I think he helped a lot in my personal growth as well.
>
> (Rosa, divorced and in her late forties)

> I had a relationship a couple of years ago for only a few months with a much younger chap and he was very immature. It was just a bit of fun really and it was nice, it was just nice to go out with somebody...
>
> (Heather, widowed and in her early forties)

Other interviewees have found emotional support or companionship within platonic friendships, with friends of both sexes. Frequently, such support has come from people who have had similar experiences, whether existing friends or fellow members of a support group:

> He just came round for coffee and things, but he was, he was a good talker and he was a good listener and he could express himself very well in terms of feelings, but that was nice.
>
> (Emily, divorced and in her late forties)

... they understand my need to be hugged, that there is a huge physical need to be touched and reassured and they're very careful and very caring to give one deep hugs.

(Janice, widowed and in her late forties)

My woman friend, her marriage broke up within two weeks of mine, two boys the same age, and so we went on 'the journey' together...

(Sandra, divorced and in her early fifties)

... just being able to come in and sit down, and to know these people knew about your history, and not having to explain anything to anyone was just being so good because they really knew you and what you were going through.

(Maureen, separated, subsequently a cohabitee, and in her early fifties)

However, Duncan's platonic friendship with a married female friend seems to be a potential barrier to his repartnering:

What tends to happen is when I don't have a relationship that particular friendship is there for me, but that probably isn't actually such a good thing.... She's quite happy for me to pop round there and phone up every night and all the rest of it. She phones me up half the time of day, but it's not really, it's not really healthy...

(Duncan, separated and in his mid-thirties)

Interviewees who want, or think that they may want, to live with a partner in the future have a range of views regarding the desirability of legal marriage at some stage. For some it retains the status of an ideal, and for many others it still represents the appropriate, final outcome of finding the 'right person'. Some feel it to be an appropriate, 'public' sign of commitment. Occasionally it is viewed as preferable for pragmatic reasons, for example in relation to financial security. Predictably, marriage is viewed with scepticism or hesitancy by some because of past experiences. Others feel it to be unnecessary given an adequate degree of commitment or the absence of children, or to be ideologically objectionable, or simply to be unimportant.

... in my dreams I see me married with [a] little child...

(Louise, divorced and in her late thirties)

I would have no objections to getting married again so long as the ground rules were understood, but I think if I'd met the right person and felt like getting married it would be because of that.

(Kate, divorced and in her early fifties)

I mean you can live with somebody but there's always the freedom, there's no actual legal bind that says basically you've got to stay...

(Kevin, a former cohabitee in his mid-twenties)

... I think there's no way I'd get married again unless I was going to have children, and you know I'm too old to have children, so I think 'Why get married?' you know, it doesn't make sense.

(Cheryl, separated and in her mid-forties)

Perhaps surprisingly, many interviewees who currently favour LAT-style relationships do not rule out the possibility of marrying again. More generally, interviewees who are open to and actively seeking a new relationship typically seem to view marriage as a future possibility, even if they are sometimes ambivalent about its relevance.

Preferred features of a new relationship

The concept of commitment seems more significant to many interviewees than the distinction between cohabitation and marriage. Commitment seems to be particularly salient for some widowed people, perhaps because they view it as having been a core feature of their marriage or cohabiting relationship, but making or publicly celebrating a commitment also has more general appeal:

I think you can have just as much commitment in a living together relationship without a marriage document as you can within a marriage, yes.

(Giles, divorced and in his mid-fifties)

... maybe because I [had] such a relationship as I did with my husband that I feel that if [my non-co-resident partner] did decide that he wanted to stay with me that he would have to give the same commitment as what my husband did to me and I did to him...

(Pauline, widowed and in her mid-forties)

I mean obviously if there were different options making the same sort of commitment and not being called marriage or not marriage itself, then obviously that's something I'd look into as well.

(Kevin, a former cohabitee in his mid-twenties)

Legally, no [I would not marry], but I would, if I was sure of myself that I wanted to be with this person for life for all intents and purposes, then I would come hell or high water have celebrations of that at a much earlier stage.

(Fiona, a former cohabitee in her late twenties)

Our interviewees report various other features of relationships as being desirable, with their last co-resident relationship often acting as a point of reference. A monogamous relationship or fidelity is often viewed as essential, but the key underlying issues seem to be trust and respect. These qualities are also often perceived as important in their own right. There is perhaps more variation in whether our interviewees feel that a relationship with an appropriate level of trust and mutual respect will come along than in whether they see these qualities as important:

> Well yes, I think I'm pretty choosy. I think, as well as the fidelity thing and there being absolute trust, there has to be mutual respect.
>
> (Rosa, divorced and in her late forties)

> I wouldn't sleep with him again because he let me find out about what was going on. He didn't respect me enough to keep it hidden from me.
>
> (Louise, divorced and in her late thirties)

> I was betrayed and the lies that came with that and I hate lies. I can cope with most things, but I can't cope with being lied to.
>
> (Claire, separated and in her mid-thirties)

While good communication is sometimes viewed as an important route to a close, intimate relationship, our interviewees also often perceive it to be a way of staying aware of a partner's feelings or to be a sound basis for resolving conflict. Some of the interviewees intend open communication in general, or negotiation and compromise in particular, to be more of a feature of any new relationship than they were of their last relationship:

> ... I think because in my marriage we didn't talk about anything ever, that it's made me more determined to try and open up more with [my new partner].
>
> (Brenda, divorced and in her early forties)

> ... I could sit down and we could start a discussion or a conversation and we could argue the dos and the don'ts all night long with good reasonable explanations and so forth, because that's something I must admit that I didn't have with my ex-partner.
>
> (Kevin, a former cohabitee in his mid-twenties)

An underlying theme of power is evident in some of the interviewees' comments on the sort of relationship that they would prefer. A power imbalance is sometimes characterized as unattractive, and our interviewees often seem to have as an ideal a relationship in which the partners are two independent people who respect each other's individuality and who do not exercise power in an attempt to change or control their partner:

> I also think I'm very controlling and this is the business about [it], on the one hand I do need somebody who is strong enough to kind of stand up to me, but on the other hand I need to be less controlling.
>
> (Fiona, a former cohabitee in her late twenties)

Somebody who can respect your – I don't know, what am I trying to say? – respect what you want to do in life and doesn't make any – I'm searching for the right words – who doesn't want to stop you from doing [it].

(Heather, widowed and in her early forties)

In addition to our interviewees' references to equality in terms of power and control, some of which make explicit reference to gender, a substantial number of the women are clear that they do not want a gendered division of labour in any new partnership, though occasionally women favour a relatively 'traditional' arrangement, and men sometimes favour a symmetrical one:

The wife does everything and I just think that I don't want that. I would want something, I would want a much more equal relationship with somebody than what I've had . . .

(Emily, divorced and in her late forties)

That's a great difficulty, isn't it, because you're almost in danger of trying to repeat the pattern [of a past, equal relationship], but on the other hand, I can't see me compromising and living with a man who expects me to do the ironing and the washing and the cleaning and the shopping and everything.

(Janice, widowed and in her late forties)

There is a range of other things that our interviewees would be looking for in a new relationship: a loving relationship, mutual care and support, shared interests. Again, what is most interesting is the way in which these requirements tend to echo the strengths or weaknesses of an interviewee's last co-resident relationship, together with the level of optimism or pessimism that an interviewee appears to have about finding a relationship with the desired qualities.

Preferred characteristics of a new partner

These key themes of the strengths and weaknesses of their last co-resident relationship and their perception of their chances of finding something that they want are also present in the comments of many interviewees on what they would look for in a new partner. For some, their last partner is a model for what they are seeking. For others, someone with different attributes is preferable:

Well, I [*sighs*], I – to tell you the truth, I'd be looking for somebody the same as what I looked for, what I found actually; I mean, I thought I'd found the perfect person . . .

(Frank, divorced and in his mid-forties)

Maybe that is [the problem], I'm looking for another him, but I suppose [the] chances of ever finding him are very, very remote.

(Pauline, widowed and in her mid-forties)

... I think I would probably consciously avoid somebody who I felt was similar to him.... Because I wouldn't want to be reminded in a sense.

(Samantha, separated and in her early forties)

... I suppose the ideal is somebody – 'normal' is a dreadful word to use – 'ordinary', but I suppose I always found ordinary so boring.... I always wanted an exciting life I suppose, but now, to me, 'ordinary' is somebody going out to work and not drinking all the rent money or not wanting to beat you up or kill you; sounds [like] heaven, but I suppose I don't believe that's there.

(Claire, separated and in her mid-thirties)

Some of the interviewees have an explicit preference for new partners whom they feel are, like themselves, able to be open and reflexive about their past relationships. On the other hand, some of the interviewees view potential partners who are inclined to discuss unresolved issues relating to past relationships less favourably:

... I think you've got to be very open with each other and you've got to talk about all sorts of things and where you feel you are in the process ...

(Emily, divorced and in her late forties)

You've got them trying to resolve their problems, me trying to find out where I am and I don't think the answer lies in our coming together as mutual wet shoulders.

(Janice, widowed and in her late forties)

A frequently expressed preference among our women interviewees is for characteristics in a new partner that might be viewed as more 'feminine' than 'masculine'. This often seems to be a consequence, at least in part, of past experiences. Some women exhibit a degree of pessimism about the number of available men, especially younger men, who are free from the specific 'masculine' characteristics that they wish to avoid:

I just feel that most of the men I've met, they're a bit like leeches. They come out of one relationship and think, 'Oh, well let's find the next available woman', and they like to stick themselves [to her], and I really, I really don't want that. I would actually like a man who was capable of being on his own and doing everything for himself, so that he's like a whole person really.

(Emily, divorced and in her late forties)

Somebody who was also secure in themselves not to, to be able to be faithful in a relationship and not to always need somebody else's, another woman's [interest].

(Kate, divorced and in her early fifties)

... I think this is the trouble: there are so many who have been brought up in, with the power play, and the inherent sexism.

(Eleanor, divorced and in her mid-fifties)

... basically someone who's honest and can say how they feel. I don't think there's many men around like that.

(Sylvia, divorced and in her late forties)

To go out with an old man or a woman. I think that's the answer.

(Fiona, a former cohabitee in her late twenties)

More generally, it is evident that some of the interviewees are fully aware that their preferences constrain the supply of potential partners, and that 'being picky' means that they rarely meet anyone suitable.

A substantial number of women would prefer a tall, or taller, partner, sometimes in combination with less gender-stereotypical characteristics. More generally, external appearances seem to vary in importance to the interviewees, but are typically not as prominent in their accounts as personal qualities. According to our interviewees, other desirable qualities, often cited with reference to the 'limitations' of ex-partners, include maturity, self-awareness, a strong, secure and independent personality, and financial independence or prudence.

Money and social status are often viewed as unimportant, but having a well-educated, intelligent or thoughtful partner, or having a degree of social, cultural or attitudinal compatibility, is more frequently seen as important. However, some of the interviewees have had relationships with partners who differed from them markedly in age. While they were conscious of, and reflected on, these age differences, they do not seem to have been problematic, at least in the context of non-resident relationships:

I should have said someone who's not scared to use their brain because he was a very intelligent man who was constantly intimidated by anybody else who was intelligent and that just drove me crazy. I want somebody who is intelligent and isn't scared to use it ...

(Fiona, a former cohabitee in her late twenties)

Someone really from my sort of background, maybe middle-class, but not someone that's like got, who's life is dedicated to intellectual [matters], but equally not someone whose solution to life is to knock the crap out of somebody.

(Duncan, separated and in his mid-thirties)

I'm a very sexual person you know, I really am and if I have someone younger, that's better.

(Maureen, separated, subsequently a cohabitee,
and in her early fifties)

Interviewees' varying perspectives on the desirability of forming a new relationship with someone with children echo some of the themes that arose earlier when the relevance of their own children or parental status was discussed. For some, the idea of a partner with children is a positive one, either because they view a family situation or parental role positively, or simply because they 'love kids'. For some fathers, it is something that they would expect and is viewed as providing common ground or a potentially useful degree of symmetry. Some of the interviewees, however, are less comfortable with the idea of playing a step-parenting role, or fear being recruited primarily as a substitute parent. A potential partner's children's demands on the partner's time and energy are a concern for some. The possibility that it might make it difficult to have their 'own' child is also a concern for some interviewees without children. The number of children and their ages are viewed as being of some relevance:

That's sort of actually going into an extended family [and] is something that would be, something different that [my partner] and I didn't have and it would be quite a bonus. Definitely.

(Janice, widowed and in her late forties)

I've been conscious that really I get on best with women I know in a similar situation to myself with children, especially of my daughter's age for obvious reasons . . .

(Peter, widowed and in his mid-forties)

. . . he was trying to get custody of [his son] and I started to get the vibes that he wanted me to be a substitute mother for the boy . . .

(Louise, divorced and in her late thirties)

I don't think I'd want to, if I wanted to spend time with somebody, I would not want them to have a young child . . . it would be his free time and that perhaps would be the time when he would have his own children.

(Samantha, separated and in her early forties)

While many of the interviewees have rather fragmentary ideas regarding the types of partner and relationship that would suit them, there are two broad 'ideals' with enough coherence to be worth presenting here. The first, which is particularly evident in the case of some of the widowed interviewees, is a committed, sharing relationship with a partner with a good sense of humour, based on respect for each other as individuals and a good sexual relationship. While positive aspects of a past relationship may have contributed something to this, the emphasis seems to be on the new partner and the relationship's own merits rather than on finding something different or similar to the past. The second ideal can perhaps best be summarized as a relationship with an independent, intelligent 'new man', which appeals to a substantial number of the women interviewed, sometimes but not always as a consequence of negative past experiences. It is interesting that the first ideal seems to be more compatible than the second with the new partner already having children, perhaps because the former is more traditional in tone, and the latter more individualistic.

A number of our interviewees feel that the notion of an 'ideal' partner is an artificial construct, and that what a new partner would actually be like is inherently unpredictable and likely to require a degree of compromise, especially since the interviewee would be chosen as much as choosing:

> Oh yes, you've got to compromise because there's no such thing as the ideal person; that is just a romantic dream. We've all got our flaws haven't we?
>
> (Louise, divorced and in her late thirties)

> So, my perception is still that not of, um, what I would choose, but who would be likely to choose me.
>
> (Eleanor, divorced and in her mid-fifties)

A typology of repartnering orientations

On the basis of the reported repartnering orientations and behaviour of our interviewees, as outlined above, we have developed a typology of repartnering orientations. The categories of the typology contain individuals with relatively similar repartnering orientations and behaviour, and were developed by constructing an initial typology using a sub-sample of the interviewees, and by extending or revising this initial typology, as and when necessary, with reference to the remaining interviewees.

The construction of the initial typology was facilitated by exploratory multivariate analyses of a dataset containing variables relating to the various repartnering themes and issues that arose during the interviews with the sub-sample. The techniques used to analyse this dataset were factor analysis, cluster analysis and multidimensional scaling. However, precedence was given to a holistic assessment of each interviewee's repartnering orientation.

Inevitably, the complexity of repartnering as an issue, together with the diverse and sometimes idiosyncratic orientations of the interviewees, meant that it was difficult to generate a set of clearly defined and mutually exclusive categories. Nevertheless, the categories of the typology do highlight key distinctions between individuals in terms of their outlook and actions.

Furthermore, in many instances where an interviewee seems to fit reasonably well into more than one category, this is indicative of a process of change or transition in their life and/or orientation.

The conceptual importance of transitions and change over time is also illustrated by a sub-group of the interviewees who were difficult to classify. This sub-group consists of some, but by no means all, of the interviewees who have only recently separated from a partner. However, all but a few of these interviewees can be matched to categories, albeit a little speculatively, as can the small number of interviewees who are close to entering a co-residential relationship, who have been classified on the basis of their orientation during the latter part of their time as a formerly partnered person. A small number of interviewees who are beyond the (notional) upper age bound of our study are distinctive inasmuch as they seem to view themselves as having passed the stage at which repartnering is an issue.

An indication is given below of the proportions of our interviewees that fall into each category. However, it should be remembered that the sample cannot be viewed as representative of formerly married people and former cohabitees, since a range of factors may have made individuals disproportionately likely or unlikely to volunteer to participate in the research. Furthermore, formerly partnered people who are strongly oriented to repartnering may in consequence repartner more quickly than average. Hence a cross-section of currently formerly partnered people might be expected to be less strongly oriented to repartnering than a cross-section of formerly partnered people taken immediately after separation.

The categories of the typology

Broadly speaking, the seven categories of the typology divide into two subgroups: four categories in which the interviewees are positively oriented towards having a new couple relationship, and three categories in which the interviewees are not. However, as will become evident, this distinction is an over-simplification.

The first category, containing about one in seven of the interviewees, is made up of those individuals who appear resistant to the idea of having any sort of couple relationship at present. These interviewees, who are disproportionately women and disproportionately live with dependent children, have typically had bad experiences in their past relationships, and are not confident that a new relationship would be any different. In many ways they seem quite self-contained, although they do not necessarily view couple relationships as inherently problematic, at least in theory. Some of them have only been separated for a short period, and acknowledge that their views may change, for example in the case of younger women who anticipate having children in the future. Others have been separated for a relatively small number of years, although the likelihood of their views changing appears to vary from interviewee to interviewee.

The second category, containing about one in eight of the interviewees, and also consisting disproportionately of women, has within it those individuals who until recently have been held back from the idea of repartnering by the legacy of a past relationship, but who are now at a point where they can envisage the possibility of entering a new relationship, even though they are not currently inclined to seek one actively. Their relationship histories and views about their ex-partners vary considerably, from being the widow of a much missed partner to being divorced from a spouse who is now viewed quite negatively. Nevertheless, these interviewees share the common feature of being at the stage of a process of disengagement from ties to the past when it seems appropriate to view the prospect of a new relationship more favourably.

The third category consists of a small number of individuals, less than one in fifteen of the interviewees, whose repartnering orientations and behaviour have been affected by the legacy of their last relationship, which seems to be acting as a barrier to their finding a new, co-resident partner, but who have nevertheless become involved with someone who is neither a 'one night stand' nor of equivalent significance to their last partner. Such a relationship seems to represent a compromise, although not necessarily a wholly satisfactory one, that allows the interviewee to avoid celibacy or being wholly on their own, without their finding or making a commitment to a new partner. In some instances the new relationship is with someone who simultaneously has another relationship or relationships.

The above three categories share the characteristic of consisting of interviewees who, at least until recently, have not been positively oriented to repartnering, and whose relationship histories have something to do with this. Members of the fourth category, which contains about one in six of the interviewees, view having a new partner as a potentially attractive idea, but for one reason or another do not feel inclined to do anything active to find one. The demands of parenthood, paid work or other activities, sometimes coupled with an independent trait or with a lack of self-esteem or confidence, help bolster this passive stance. Once again, the legacy of past relationships appears to be of some relevance, but in this case its contribution to the interviewees' passivity is less direct or clear-cut.

While there is considerable overlap between these four categories in terms of the time since separation of their members, members of the third category have on average been separated longer, whereas the second category contains a subset of individuals who seem to be reaching a 'turning point' in their post-separation repartnering orientations relatively quickly. There is also a degree of variation in the typical time since separation across the three categories containing interviewees who are more positively oriented to repartnering. The next category to be discussed is, of these three categories, the one that contains interviewees who are (typically) closest to the point of separation.

This fifth category, disproportionately though not exclusively consisting of working-class men (i.e. men in manual occupations), and containing about one in eleven of the interviewees, includes individuals who are looking for a new co-resident relationship, but who are at the same time still carrying 'emotional baggage' from their last relationship. Typically, this relationship has both undermined the interviewee's self-esteem and also constitutes unfinished business that still preoccupies them. Interestingly, the attitudinal data collected from our interviewees via a standardized questionnaire show this category of interviewees to have the most 'traditional' and positive view of marriage and its importance.

In contrast, the sixth category of interviewees contains those who are positively oriented to establishing a co-resident relationship with a new partner, but who are to a large extent free of the burden of the past that is carried by the interviewees in the fifth category. The sixth category accounts for about one in seven of the interviewees. These interviewees rarely make much of a distinction between cohabitation and remarriage, though a few are averse to the latter.

Finally, the seventh and largest category, which includes more than a quarter of the interviewees and predominantly consists of women, contains individuals who favour couple relationships which do not involve living together, at least in the first instance. These interviewees are typically independent individuals who have, to a large extent, come to terms with, if not necessarily resolved, issues from the past. Their relationship histories may have made them cautious about commitment, and led to their placing a high value on compatibility with a prospective partner, but they nevertheless typically have an active approach to repartnering. A few have no interest in having a co-residential relationship in the future, but most see cohabitation or marriage as a possibility in the longer term, only rarely being more strongly oriented towards one of these possibilities than towards the other.

Marital status – that is, whether an interviewee was separated, divorced, widowed or a former cohabitee – seems to have relatively little impact on which category they are in. The same is true for the interviewee's age. However, there is some evidence that both characteristics are linked weakly to a 'natural' time-ordering among the categories. Specifically, divorced and older interviewees are disproportionately found in the categories (particularly the third and sixth) that might be regarded as being more likely to be 'end-points' for shifting repartnering orientations.

To summarize some key features of the typology developed in this chapter, our interviewees' orientations to repartnering seem to be structured around a small number of key dimensions: the level and form of their current engagement with issues arising from their past relationship(s) or partner(s), and the stage reached in any process of disengagement, the strength of their motivation to form a co-residential relationship with a new partner, as opposed to having a non-resident partner or being on their own, and whether they demonstrate, and perhaps favour, an active or a passive approach to repartnering. Our interviewees' positions on these various dimensions are not necessarily fixed, but vary over time in many cases, particularly with reference to the length of time since they last lived with a partner. The interviewees' personal characteristics do not appear to provide a particularly reliable basis for predicting category membership, though some features of the typology seem to be linked to gender. Overall, the repartnering orientations of formerly married people and former cohabitees demonstrate considerable diversity, but also appear in most cases to conform relatively well to one of a limited range of broad orientations.

6
'Risk', Emotions and Choice in the Lives of Formerly Partnered Men and Women

Introduction

Risk has become a key and much publicized concept in modern Western societies (Lupton 1999; Tulloch and Lupton 2003). The risks generated by high modernity are in part the result of dramatic changes in the structuring of our private lives (Giddens 1991; Beck 1992). Traditions that once shaped key aspects of our lives – marriage, the nuclear family and lifetime employment – have now been weakened and challenged and, as we saw in Chapter 3, this has been accompanied by high levels of anxiety and insecurity (Tulloch and Lupton 2003). Moreover, commentators have argued that increasing cohabitation and the liberalization of divorce laws have led to more individualized, ever more risky, no longer for life, intimate couple relationships. Though relationship insecurity might be a small price to pay for some for the right to 'cut one's losses' (Bauman 2000b: 90) by leaving an unsatisfactory relationship, for others the potential costs of such uncertainty are too high. This might be especially so for those who have experienced relationship dissolution. There are unquestionable risks in investing strong feelings in a partner since that person can leave at will. All of our interviewees have suffered such a life-changing event; all have lost (or have left) a partner through relationship dissolution or because of bereavement. Such 'suffering events' punctuate our lives (Wilkinson 2004) and, as Emile Durkheim asserts, modernity has been accompanied by a compassionate temperament that provides us with a greater moral imagination of the suffering of others (Wilkinson 2004). This informs the two-fold focus of this chapter. The suffering events experienced by our interviewees enable them to develop a greater imagination of the suffering of others but they also, as would be expected, encourage the development of a heightened awareness of their own capacity to suffer and provide experiential understanding of the feelings that accompany such suffering. In contrast to experiences that engender the development of a taken-for-granted attitude that things will stay the same, such events spotlight the changes that *might* occur and foreground the myriad risks that we feel trouble our daily lives. Thus people construct their own assessment of risk, based on close scrutiny of everyday occurrences and the behaviour of others (Wynne 1996). Although we might take measures to avoid risks, we know that some are less preventable than others and some seem to be entirely inescapable. To make matters worse, when an unwanted decision is taken by another (e.g. a partner leaving) we feel bereft of control over our lives and our emotions.

Decisions about repartnering after relationship dissolution are taken by individuals who often feel that they have learned something from the past. Since suffering is multidimensional and can affect the rest of our lives (Wilkinson 2004), previous relationship experiences and endurances influence our behaviour and view of the future. So, as we saw in Chapters 3 and 4, experiences of past partnerships can lead to caution and reluctance to enter a new couple relationship (Frazier et al. 1996). Such a 'reflexive approach' (Giddens 1992) enables individuals to develop strategies to avoid putting themselves at risk again or at least to avoid their previous 'mistakes'. Some of our interviewees believe their lives could be irreparably damaged if they were to embark on another couple relationship. On the other hand, one way of recovering from the various negative impacts of divorce (and we can add all forms of intimate couple relationship dissolution) is to enter a new relationship. Others interviewed feel that their past experiences presage a more informed future. Thus, as would be expected, our interviewees differ in their perceptions of the risks (or not) they feel willing to impose on themselves by taking on (or not) a future couple relationship. Still, this is not to suggest that decisions lead to desired outcomes. Some of our interviewees are living in loneliness, social isolation or financial impoverishment – conditions that can make establishing a new relationship seem extremely difficult if not impossible.

Decision-making is central to all our lives. Decisions about intimate couple relationships are affected by wants, needs and perceptions of risks, which are influenced by cultural representations (e.g. in popular culture), by our experiences and by the people around us. The 'imagistic power' (Tulloch and Lupton 2003: 5) of the mass media is highly significant as an information-provider about risks (Beck 1992) and about couple relationships. Societal attitudes to mixed-age or same-sex relationships, for example, have some bearing on our feelings about who would make a desirable partner, and the influence of parents, children, ex-spouses and friends can affect courtship patterns (Rodgers and Conrad 1986). Love and romantic involvement are considered to be the most important motivators for intimate couple relationships (Hochschild 1998; Lewis 2001) and thus especially important in relationship choices is the presence (or absence) of romantic love and sexual attraction (Peggs and Lampard 2000). As we saw in Chapter 3, romantic love can provide individuals with a source of meaning in this fragmented world (Beck and Beck-Gernsheim 1995), but can also jeopardize existing relationships by motivating partnership change or two-timing relationships (Lawson 1988; Jackson 1993). Thus romantic love, at the centre of decisions about entering intimate couple relationships, can feel like a risky endeavour since people may feel afraid to love because such a strong emotion can make them feel vulnerable, especially if they feel they can be easily be replaced by another (Hochschild 1998: 9). As one of our interviewees commented:

> I had to stay very much in control of all my emotions and I think I'd be scared that I couldn't do that anymore if I had to.
>
> (Tim, divorced and in his early forties)

This chapter focuses on the ways in which individuals make decisions about future relationships. We investigate theoretical ideas about the decision-making process by examining our empirical data in the light of theories of choice which emphasize a calculative, rational perspective and also those that emphasize the place of 'irrational' behaviour. Thus the focus is on our interviewees' choices and perceptions of risks relating to future relationships. According to Giddens (1992), the expansion of choice is one of the positive aspects of living in a 'risk society'. However, choice is not necessarily positive since the costs of choice in intimate couple relationships can be high (as can the price of constraints on choice). At the theoretical level this chapter seeks to demonstrate the need to qualify the notions of reflexive decision-making proposed by Giddens by emphasizing the role of habitual action in decision-making, as developed by Bourdieu (1984). We show that material circumstances, cultural capital, perceived freedom, moral attitudes to relationships, the views of others and habitus affect perceptions of risk, choice and emotions in the lives of formerly married and previously cohabiting individuals. We begin with a discussion of theories associated with choice and emotions and decision-making, which frame and contextualize the extracts taken from interviews.

Couple relationships, choice and decision-making

Decision-making is complex indeed. Decisions can be made on the basis of memories of past experiences, present-day events, wants and needs, perceptions of future events, encounters and desires, and the views of others. In addition, as we shall see, habit and custom are significantly influential in decision-making, since such factors frame our attitudes to the options we feel are available and our perceptions of the decisions we feel we have to make. Thus, in this chapter, we frame our interviewees' perceptions of and decisions about future relationships within their past experiences and previous decisions that they have made. It is not only decisions that are important but also individuals' perceptions of the decision-making process and their involvement in it. Thus, this chapter addresses a range of questions associated with decision-making. For example, how does increasing knowledge about the ability of the individual to make decisions influence our interviewees' perceptions of future decision-making? How have our interviewees distanced themselves from 'bad' decisions, and how do they explain what they do and use those explanation frames to justify or explain their decisions about the future?

Decisions, whether connected to couple relationships or not, clearly have intention. Barbalet argues that the '[p]urposiveness of action requires the actor's acquisition of an intention in relation to a goal or end, what Weber calls a norm' (2001: 51). Of course, inaction also has consequences and, perhaps, subconscious intentionality. Thus, a person might remain in an unsatisfactory relationship with perhaps the subconscious intention of maintaining a normalized identity or because of a commitment to, say, marriage as an institution. This begs questions about the nature of action, the nature of intention, and so on. It is not our objective to discuss these here, since such questions are beyond the scope of this book. However, we acknowledge that it is very difficult to determine intention through reference to our empirical data. In the course of an interview a person might construct explanations of actions and inactions and present them as intentions. Thus the 'realness' of an intention is open to question since it is not verifiable.

The purpose of decisions can be categorized broadly as those associated with the desire to alter a life situation (a change decision) and those associated with retaining the situation as it is (a status quo decision). This categorization, of course, masks a whole host of complexities. For example, in making decisions about couple relationships a change decision (e.g. a decision to embark on a new relationship after divorce) might have the intention of returning to the status quo (e.g. providing a dependent child with two live-in parent figures). However, this simple categorization serves to illustrate the perceptions of risk and choice that motivated the intentions of and decisions made by our interviewees. Judgements and decisions can be experienced as active in that we choose from an array of possible actions in a particular situation, or experienced as passive, in that they are the outcome of other (or, indeed, of another's) actions or inactions. All involve risk perception since the outcome is unknown and it is only through retrospection, as Frances indicates, that we can evaluate the reliability of our decisions:

> There is this dream, which is about, well, what would it have been like, you know, if one had been able to make the right choices rather than the wrong choices.
>
> (Frances, divorced and in her late forties)

If only we could see into the future. Subsequent to an event we might distance ourselves from decisions that turn out as 'bad' and hold close those that turn out as 'good', but of course we wish that all of our decisions could be good. Orthodox models of rational choice emphasize that action is guided by a *rational* choice between alternative outcomes that are considered in terms of costs and benefits (Coleman 1990). An action is taken only after its 'benefits and costs have been weighed' (Zey 1998: 2) and individuals seek to maximize benefits and minimize costs to produce the optimum outcome in any choice situation (Coleman and Fararo 1992). It is useful here to refer to how our interviewees talk about the factors influencing their previous decisions to embark on their now broken relationships since their responses explicate the advantages and disadvantages of the rational choice approach.

I suppose [I got married] because of the insecurity and I thought he was going to go. I just wanted to make sure he didn't. I know it sounds awful, but just to make sure he didn't go, but now I've found out that it doesn't matter whether you're married or not, if they're going to go, they're going to go, aren't they? I just wanted a big wedding, but I never got a big wedding. I couldn't afford one, but I always wanted to get married. I know I was unfaithful, but if he'd have been unfaithful I would have gone. I know it sounds awful, but I would have gone, but he never, ever went off with another woman, never.

(Maria, separated and in her early thirties)

On the surface this extract seems to confirm rational choice notions of decision-making since, for Maria, marriage meant maximizing the benefits (security, wanting to get married, wanting a big wedding) and minimizing the costs (her partner leaving her, not getting married, not having a big wedding). The success of a decision, however, can by no means be certain. It seems that her attempt to reap the benefits was upset in the short term (no large wedding – compromise) and the long term (her partner left – 'failure'). Drawing on Weber, Bourdieu shows that 'the pure model of rational action cannot be regarded as an anthropological description of practice . . . because real agents only very exceptionally possess the complete information, and the skill to appreciate it, that rational action would presuppose' (1990: 63). So decisions are problematic since we can never perceive the whole picture, we have no control over the actions of others, we cannot see into the future and we will not know the outcomes of a decision until the outcomes are upon us.

Retrospection can lead us to scrutinize the motivations informing the decision as well as the decision itself. Maria's declaration that her reasons for marrying were 'awful' suggests that she now sees her reasons for marrying as cold and 'unemotional'. In contemporary Western societies it is considered at least strange and at worst mercenary if people do not cite love as their primary reason for intending to marry (Lewis 2001: 8). As we saw in Chapter 3, although the regulative tradition of marriage has weakened considerably, the meaning-constitutive tradition of the central role of romantic love remains important (Gross 2005). Maria's offered concern about her reasons might also be linked to the impact that her 'unemotional' intentions might have on her identity (that is, her perceptions of how the interviewer will view her motivations and thus her). (We turn to issues of self and identity in Chapter 7.) To be loved is an important aspect of identity and it seems important for Maria to emphasize that her partner loved her and that it was her fault (she had an extramarital relationship) that he left. This might also be a way of distancing herself from her 'bad' decision to marry; her decision to marry *him* was good in the sense that he loved her; it was *she* who caused the relationship to dissolve.

Anxiety and security are central features of Maria's response and are important aspects of decision-making. Barbalet helpfully clarifies that anxiety is 'a fearful anticipation of future events' whereas security 'is a feeling of comfort in the present' (2001: 89). In Chapter 4 we saw that many of our interviewees are very anxious about future relationships, and this is discussed further below. Our interviewees raised the 'security' and 'commitment' of marriage as a reason for deciding to marry in the first place:

> I suppose we'd reached the stage in our relationship where we needed to go somewhere, from my ex-wife's point of view more than me I think. I would have carried on, I wasn't particularly anxious to get married . . . I think she probably felt that she needed a clear commitment, I suppose, and knowledge of a sense of security about where she was going with her future . . . I think she wanted a decision more than I did.
>
> (Adam, divorced and in his early forties)

Marriage can look like a 'trap that needs to be avoided at all costs' (Bauman 2003: 90), but it can also provide a sense of security. If, following Lewis (2001; see Chapter 3), we consider commitment to be multifaceted and complex, we can see, in Adam's response, that commitment to marriage as an institution (that is, to marry) can prompt a feeling of commitment from another (s/he loves me), thus generating a feeling of security. Rational choice theory focuses on the process by which we make decisions to optimize our position. The way in which individuals view their own decisions complicates this rather simple view of decision-making. Adam's memory of making his decision takes on a rather altruistic slant; he asserts that the decision to marry was for his partner's security, not his own. Rational choice theorists (e.g. Mansbridge 1992) are critical of approaches that place self-interest and altruism in polar positions, since in practice, they argue, seemingly altruistic behaviour is based in selfishness and thus coincides with self-interest (Zey 1992: 20). Perhaps it can be argued that, for Adam, such a discourse is one way of distancing himself from his 'bad' decision. Thus, after re-evaluation, it is possible to fit things together almost as if events were inevitable and perhaps beyond his control.

Time constraints and human limitations often prevent optimizing (Zey 1992: 19) and in the course of making decisions individuals must often consider alternatives sequentially (Simon 1955). Consequently, individuals often *satifice* (choose the first satisfactory alternative) rather than optimize (Simon and Associates 1992: 43). Satificing is clearly more helpful in explaining how individuals choose their partners since it would be impossible to meet *all* potential partners before making a decision.

> You're in a dilemma, aren't you? You need to go out with people for a certain length of time before you find out if they're compatible or have all the attributes that you're looking for. You have to take relationships one at a time unfortunately and it's very difficult to have three or four on the go at the same time which would be the ideal solution, and then you could say right, well, there's Jane and June and Sheila and, and we'll choose. You just can't do it because the social scene doesn't permit you to and it probably wouldn't be fair on any of them anyway. So one is thrown into a social pot where you have to make off-the-cuff decisions which could turn out disastrously which could be what my next decision is going to be. But one has to make decisions . . . when you're dating five women at the time just to find out who's the best and go off with the best one. It just wouldn't work and what about the women? Why don't they do it with the men?
>
> (Giles, divorced and in his mid-fifties)

In relationship decisions optimizing by choosing a partner from a 'pot' of concurrent relationships seems to Giles to be 'ideal', yet morally and socially unacceptable. Though Giles argues that such an approach would be more successful in leading to long-term commitment and security, what he feels he *ought* to do is an overriding concern. In addition, it is unlikely that many women would be persuaded to trust a man who takes such an approach. (Commitment and trust as issues of risk are expanded upon in the following chapter.)

On a theoretical level the notion of satificing retains utility as the goal of choices (Zafirovski 1999) and disregards the role of emotional factors in decision-making since emotions are seen as irrational (Elias 1978a, 1978b). One of our major concerns in this chapter is the nature and significance of emotionally based judgements, and collective understandings of the role of emotion in couple relationships. In contrast to past times, modern couple relationships have become more associated with mutual sexual attraction (Giddens 1992: 38) and emotional satisfaction (Giddens 1991: 88; see Chapter 3) and, as mentioned, emotions are central to relationship decisions:

I don't think you can dictate, you can't dictate emotions. How you decide to act because of them is another matter.

(Giles, divorced and in his mid-fifties)

So, for Giles, emotions are irrational forces that might be the basis of action, but do not dictate how we act.

Such a view reverberates with the theoretical literature. Elster argues that emotions tend to 'overwhelm the rational mental processes' (1985: 379). However, this overemphasis on self-control discounts the possibility of a causal role for emotions in human conduct (Scheff 1992: 101–2). Scheff contends that many of our most important decisions (e.g. choosing a partner) are made on impulse, taking into consideration few, if any, of the possible options, and considering few or none of the consequences. Thus emotions and rationality are not fundamentally opposed (Williams 1998); they are causal agents in the decision-making process (Elias 1978a; Scheff 1992; Williams 1998; Peggs and Lampard 2000). Thus decision-making is difficult if not impossible without emotions because emotions provide the basis for driving us in one direction or another (Williams 1998). In this way emotions are essential to the 'effective deployment' of reason (Williams 1998). So when leaving one couple relationship for another our choice might be based on falling out of love with one person and falling in love with another. Bazerman (1986) notes that people often make 'judgement mistakes' and that such errors are frequently seen as outside rational decision-making:

Nothing lives up to [my ex-partner]. I don't think anything ever could. It sounds stupid to say nothing can live up to something that absolutely destroyed you, but it really was a fantastic relationship ... That's what hurts so much is the shock when you think, or you've been led to believe, that somebody loves you so much, even to the point where it irritates you sometimes. It irritates you because you're not sure that you love them as much as they love you, although I did.

(Emma, a former cohabitee in her early thirties)

Such 'mistakes' are manifest in many of the extracts and, of course, emotions can wreak havoc on rational decision-making (e.g. our intense feelings might lead us into an unsuitable relationship); however, the absence of emotion can be equally devastating (Williams 1998). So emotions are fundamental to reason and are central to the decision-making process (Williams 1998).

Emotions are clearly important in intimate relationship decisions since decision-making in couple relationships is infused with emotion. Williams and Bendelow argue that 'Even to the present day, emotions are seen to be the very antithesis of the detached scientific mind and its quest for "objectivity", "truth" and "wisdom"' (1998: xvi). However, only certain types of decisions are acknowledged to take place without emotions, and, as we have seen, marriage is considered to be one of those decisions that should be taken with emotion – that is, love – as its centre (Lewis 2001). Such an 'emotion convention' (Hochschild 1998) is clear in the following extract:

> I suppose I divorced for what I see is the only reason why people should divorce. I realized I no longer loved him and that to me is why people should divorce. Any other problems can be worked out. If it's another problem within a marriage to me you can possibly work at it and work it out, but if love isn't there, you can't replace that.
>
> (Jean, separated and in her early fifties)

Jean's motivation for divorce (and, she suggests, the only plausible motivation) was falling out of love. For Beck and Beck-Gernsheim love 'is losing its mythology and is turning into a rational system' (1995: 141) because it is used as a motivation for relationship dissolution as well as for relationship formation. However, Jean echoes Giles' views since she sees the emotion 'love' as irrational which, 'unlike other problems', is out of our control and thus cannot be worked out. Since, in Western societies, romantic love is viewed as central to intimate couple relationships it is understandable that Jean sees the absence of love as a core reason for ending her couple relationship. It might be argued that to *stay* married for any other reason would be seen as a sign of a rational, calculating attitude. However, Jean is recounting to the interviewer her motivations for a decision made some years previously. Mills ([1940] 1967, cited in Barbalet 2001: 66) suggests that motives are part of the linguistic apparatus that individuals use as self-justification. Thus the uncontrollable lack of love signals, for Jean, the aptness of her decision to divorce, which, if we concur with Mills, can also be taken as a justification rather than a motivation for the action she took more than a decade earlier.

Making a choice can be very difficult and beset with uncertainty (Melucci 1996). This is compounded when individuals are expected to accept responsibility for the choices they make. As we saw in Chapter 3, Bauman remarks that individuals are wary of the burdens that might ensue from intimate couple relationships since in such partnerships 'the responsibility for failure falls primarily on the individual's shoulders' (2000b: 8). Our responsibility for a 'bad' decision is especially pertinent when we know that we have avoided something that disconfirms the decision we have made:

> But I didn't listen to anybody, I just had to prove it anyway. You're your own person at the end of the day and you make your own decisions, but now I look back on it I wish I never married her, but there you go, that's life.
>
> (Martin, separated and in his mid-twenties)

In the matter of personal finance Aldridge remarks that avoidance strategies include 'avoidance of potentially disconfirming information' (1998: 5). Martin's comments show that such a strategy seems equally fitting for decisions about couple relationships. Clearly, relationship decisions are influenced by interactions with significant others and the suggestions that they put forward.

Rational choice theorists focus on decisions made at the micro-individual level. Though seemingly made at the individual level, decisions about relationships are made in a wider context. As we can see in the next extract, decisions are most frequently made by couples in the context of larger social collectives (Zey 1992: 22).

I blame myself and I blame her and I also sort of realize that it's what happens and some parts are out of control like being out of work and her losing her job are out of our control. We have control of certain aspects, but there's parts where you don't have control over and that's the way of life unfortunately.

(Joe, separated and in his late twenties)

Within couples or larger groups individuals can make independent decisions; however, these decisions are compounded by, or can be the result of, much wider decisions and much wider constraints. As Joe reveals, decisions that seemed to be in his and his ex-partner's control (associated with whether to stay together or split up) are nested within and are in response to decisions imposed by others (losing a job). However, his lack of control over the wider context does not forestall the sense of responsibility and blame that followed his relationship dissolution. Flam (2002) suggests that when individuals are thinking about their painful experiences they move between different explanations, and such explanations are often associated with blame. She proposes that '[i]ndividuals and groups switch between self-blame and other blame frames' (2002: 109). For our interviewees, blame is a key artefact of the dissolution of previous relationships. Most attributed blame outside themselves, to others and to situations.

Although the decision about whether or not to divorce can be mutual, this is not to suggest that there is an equal distribution of power within a couple relationship. Political variables relating to power and domination (Zafirovski 1999) are, for example, gendered. In this respect patriarchal relations ensure that some women remain in appalling relationships, involving, for example, domestic violence, because they face constraints in achieving support to achieve safety (Wilcox 2006). So inequalities in power are more complex than the rational choice notion of the gap between an individual's benefits and the benefits for another (Munch 1992: 138).

Yes I did [instigate the divorce], yes, I did yes because there was a certain amount of violence . . . it started off against me but then when my elder daughter got to about thirteen, well actually she was younger than that, when my elder daughter got to about, well, nine or ten, he just used to go barmy at her, completely barmy, and she was really quite damaged by all that . . . the irony, the irony was that I thought if I leave the children will be here on their own, the house will be empty, he won't make any sort of provision for the children so I might as well kick him out and I couldn't think of any other way round it so I thought, well, we'll starve, you know, I knew we'd starve but I couldn't think – I just couldn't think of a way out of it.

(Sarah, divorced and in her mid-forties)

Such power relations affect decision-making in all sorts of ways:

I'd had probably an unfulfilling marriage in a way, in a lot of ways, but I deferred . . . I don't think [my husband] would think I deferred to him as far as decisions were concerned, but I just deferred to his greater knowledge and wit and intellectualism all the time and never saw myself as my own person. In fact the only time I did I suppose was either at my own job or at choir.

(Carol, divorced and in her mid-forties)

Power relations compromise notions of rational choice; decision-making is complex and relationships are always outside the narrower conditions of rationality since choices and consequent costs and rewards depend on decisions of two or more individuals (Willer 1992). In terms of co-resident intimate couples, the longer that they have lived together the more they will be cut off from alternatives objectively and/or subjectively (Munch 1992: 142). So the decision to stay together might be costly to both partners. In addition, altruistic ideals affect notions of rational choice. Rational choice theorists fail to acknowledge that decisions can be founded in considerations of the welfare of those for whom we care (for Sarah, her children) as well as in our own utility (Zey 1992). So, a given option has implications not only for the self and for the self through others, but also for the well-being of others.

By means of extracts about decisions made by our interviewees about previous relationships, we hope we have shown the complexities of the decision-making process. Though rational choice theories have pointed to some concepts relating to decision-making that are of use when thinking about relationship decisions, decision-making is far more complex than strong rational choice theorists would have us believe. A range of issues and factors complicate notions of 'optimizing' behaviour, and it is with this in mind that we turn to issues of risk, trust and choice in our interviewees' perspectives on taking on future relationships.

Risk, choice and future relationships

As we have seen thus far, risk is perceived as an important feature of relationship decisions, since relationships and the contexts in which they exist are subject to changes. Tulloch and Lupton (2003) contend that in the absence of fixed norms to guide us through our lives, individuals are forced to produce their own biographies and invent new certainties, which incorporate a 'crushing responsibility to make the right life choices' (2003: 4). Intimate couple relationships can be one place in which we try to establish a semblance of certainty. However, Tulloch and Lupton argue that the growing range of complex choices (e.g. about gender roles in couple relationships, whether to marry or cohabit, whether to have children) creates new risks (e.g. relationship and family break-up) 'as people seek to juggle the desire for a self-directed and autonomous life with the need for stable relationships' (2003: 4). All of our interviewees have suffered the end of at least one co-resident couple relationship and some have experienced successive and complex endings to previous couple relationships. In contrast to experiences that encourage the development of a taken-for-granted attitude that things will remain the same, such events bring into focus the changes that *can* occur and the risks that *might* ensue. In consequence, the experiences of some of our interviewees have engendered a heightened awareness of the risks that they see as inherent in couple relationships. This concurs with Shaw's study (1991), discussed previously, that women whose previous marriages had broken down after adultery were wary of entering another marriage.

All our interviewees believed that their previous relationship experiences had affected their view of future relationships. Some felt that embarking on a future relationship would be too risky:

> So that's love and I don't think I could ever seriously love anybody again. I don't think I want to if that's what it entails. I can sort of love people and love to be with them and love certain things about them, but I just feel loving somebody with all of my heart and wanting to spend the rest of my life with them, I don't think I ever want to be in that position again. I don't want to pay for the emotion because I do love. It just drains the effort. You put so much effort into loving something and then it just falls apart. I just feel drained. I just feel like 20 years older than I should be. I'm not prepared to make the effort and when I consciously try to with a relationship, it just fails, either because the whole heart is not in it. I just don't feel as though I've got anything left. I'm just happy to plod. They either like it or lump it. I don't mean that nastily, I just mean I'm not, I'm just happy to continue with life and not to really look for love

or go out of my way to make somebody love me because I don't know whether I'm capable of it. Probably not. I mean I wouldn't want to be in that position again. I don't want to be that vulnerable. I never knew I was vulnerable in any way at all. I always thought I was very, very hard. I would never take the risk of being like that again. Of actually wanting to take my life for somebody else who didn't give a damn really because you want to take your life because you want to make a statement about what you did to me and I don't think they really care.

(Emma, a former cohabitee in her early thirties)

Love, so often represented as uniquely personal, follows culturally prescribed patterns (Barthes 1990) and in this extract we can hear the discourses of romantic love, based in the meaning-constitutive tradition (Gross 2005), expressed in novels, songs, films and poems (Jackson 1993). There are unquestionable risks in investing strong feelings in a partner since they can leave at any time, as Emma discovered. For Emma, being in love induces a feeling of a lack of control and, as a result, vulnerability. Love is an emotion where we 'really let go' (Hochschild 1998) but, as Hochschild reiterates, 'you're not really safe if you do so' (1998: 8). Emma's reference to different types of love is key, since she views 'loving somebody with all of my heart and wanting to spend the rest of my life with them' as the most risky emotional scenario. Thus such intimate relationships grounded in love are risky because 'if you know that your partner may opt out at any moment, with or without your agreement . . . investing your feelings in the current relationship is always a risky step' (Bauman 2003: 90). Power and status are central. Kemper (2002) connects Weber's (1946) distinction between the 'status' and 'power' dimensions of social interaction to emotions in group settings. He shows that power incorporates actions intended to secure conformity with one's desires and interests over those of others, whereas status makes possible the gratification of other people (2002: 54). For Kemper, 'The ultimate status-accord is what we recognize as love' (2002: 55). Emma's status as a lover was taken away and her partner had the power to do this. The impact of this is so great that Emma felt it to be unbearable and it led to suicidal feelings. In Kemper's (2002) terminology, for Emma, love means 'loss of power relative to the other' and, in consequence, it is not worth taking the risk of this happening in the future.

The 'modern paradox of love', Hochschild explains, is a situation in which we 'aim high' but trust little since high divorce rates (and the experience of divorce) warn us against trusting too much (1998: 8).

I think it leaves a scar there. There are scars still left and how that comes out I don't know. Perhaps this is why I'm unsure about what I want because I had a lot of years with one man and I was so betrayed by him, how can I ever trust again? I really don't know what I want, I really don't know what I want.

(Sheila, separated and in her late forties)

It, it, it finished, it finished us really as trust. That's the way I felt. Trust had gone completely.

(Frank, divorced and in his mid-forties)

Investing love in another requires trust (Seligman 1997; Bauman 2003) and our interviewees' experiences brought to the foreground the risks associated with trusting and investing emotionally in one person. The management of choice and risk is often based on trust (Giddens 1991). In couple relationships this is vital, not least because, as we have seen, people invest strong emotions in intimate couple relationships. However, the 'pure relationship' does not foster trust (Beck and Beck-Gernsheim 1995; Bauman 2003), not only because the other might leave at any time, but also because trust creates dependency, a now derogatory condition, on another (Bauman 2003: 90). In addition, as we saw in Chapter 3, this dependency, owing to the pure relationship, need not be reciprocated, thus '*you* are bound, but *your* partner is free to go, and no kind of bond that may keep you in place is enough to make sure that they won't' (Bauman 2003: 90, original emphasis). Demolished trust gives rise to the feeling that the risk of investing love in another is so great that it is inconceivable. However, such pessimistic feelings can dissipate with the reparative qualities often associated with time:

I think if you're married or you're living with somebody, then you know you've got to [trust]. You're trusting that person with your life really, from the emotional stance – and I just don't feel that I could trust anybody. I mean, maybe in time that will get better and I won't feel like that but I don't know, you know, I can't see into the future. That's how I feel at the moment.

(Samantha, separated and in her early forties)

I'm not sure I would ever trust anybody enough to actually get married. I'm not sure. It would have to be peculiar. I would have to know them very well and they would have to be mature and they would have to want to be married because I wouldn't ever do it ... basically unless the other party concerned really felt strongly about it because to me marriage is so difficult to get out of that you've tied yourself to somebody else and you've got to pay them that amount of money to get shot of them and if it hasn't worked you know I just want to pack my bags and go.

(Sarah, divorced and in her mid-forties)

It is interesting that Sarah's experience contradicts the suggestion that divorce has made leaving marriage easy (for some commentators, *too* easy; see Chapter 3). One of the values of the 'pure relationship' is that one can 'cut one's losses' (Bauman 2000b: 90). However, though cutting one's losses is easier in terms of the relaxing of legal restrictions, leaving a marriage has attendant risks associated with the loss of somewhere to live and financial hardship, making divorce very difficult in Sarah's experience and opinion. Thus, the risks attached to being stuck in an unacceptable marriage, coupled with the lack of trust generated by relationship dissolution and attended by the difficulties associated with divorce, can destroy any hope for future marriage. And marriage, it seems, represents more of a risk than other forms of couple relationship:

It's deciding whether you want to marry them, whether you want to spend the rest of your life with that person, what you're committing yourself to. OK, we all know you can get out of it later on, but you can't enter it with that attitude.

(Jean, separated and in her early fifties)

In contrast to the ideas of Bauman (2003), Jean does not feel that it is acceptable to marry for consumerist reasons. She, like most of our interviewees, explained that to marry is a serious decision that should not be taken lightly. Changing societal attitudes and policy changes have alleviated the risks involved in being trapped in an unwanted couple relationship. Paradoxically, the relative ease of divorce and ending a relationship can lead to a feeling of insecurity since a future partner could leave without difficulty, but more liberal divorce laws have also smoothed the way for leaving an unsatisfactory marriage, thus enabling 'bad' decisions to be made good. However, negative consequences can emerge from ending an unsatisfactory couple relationship and these can affect views about having future partnerships:

That's a deep failure, to not hold it together. So rather than letting me off the hook it kind of fixes the idea that I'm not really capable of a loving relationship.

(Fiona, a former cohabitee in her late twenties)

The risks of repartnering are accentuated by a perception of an individual 'biography of failure' (Furstenberg and Spanier 1984: 55), a feeling of being unable to hold together an intimate partnership. Thus *any* future partnership might be regarded as a risky activity (Furstenberg and Spanier 1984: 56).

Security is an important part of this analysis of couple relationships since it is associated with risk, trust and stability. Thus far our discussion of security has mainly focused on security of emotional expression and avoiding hurt. As Berezin notes, emotions 'relate concretely to those secure spaces, that is the home, the neighbourhood, the nation state [and, we can add, intimate couple relationships] where emotions of all sorts are expressed' (2002: 49). As we have seen, people who have experienced relationship dissolution can find that the secure place of emotional expression has been demolished and consequently they are reluctant to take the risk of expressing strong emotions, such as love, again. Thus for some, the end of a couple relationship not only signals the end of relationship stability and security, but also, perhaps, the end of security of emotional expression. However, security and trust relate to many issues. As Sarah points out (above), financial security and security of housing are very important, and these can be put at risk when relationships dissolve. This is confirmed by other interviewees:

I don't think I'd take a financial risk of being left with a mortgage I couldn't afford again . . . You can still be in love and have a relationship. You don't have to share a mortgage. I know it's really, really sad actually, that we should be able to, shouldn't we, but once bitten . . . A horrible situation, getting names off your mortgages or whatever. I just want what's mine to be mine. When you're left in the lurch financially, I'm a bit selfish about what's mine really I suppose . . . when [my husband] left, I was right in it. Oh God, how am I going to pay for this? And then when I brought myself back up and got on top of everything financially, I soon started to feel better about myself. Right, all this is mine now, I can start again and I don't want to let go of that. The house is mine now and everything is mine.

(Emma, a former cohabitee in her early thirties)

If we both keep our houses on and perhaps move into one and rent the other one out [that] wouldn't be a bad idea because then you've still got security at the end of it if it did fall through or whatever . . . you've got the trauma of a relationship ending which would be bad enough if it ever did, and of course then you've got the trauma of losing your home that you've already had to fight hard for to fight hard for again.

(Alison, divorced and in her mid-thirties)

I would never marry again unless it was on my death bed, because again, if you're not married, your partner doesn't automatically get the inheritance and got no rights to your pension, whereas if you're married they automatically have both of those.

(Edward, divorced and in his mid-forties)

I have a house, [and] I've no intention of losing it to somebody else. I have a son [name] and I've no particular wish to get him tied in with somebody else. If I were to risk the material things I feel I have, there isn't much, but the house is a bit of a tip really but nevertheless if I were to risk the material things that I feel I have, there would need to be a good reason for that and that good reason hasn't turned up and equally if there was somebody else. It would need to be something along those lines.

(Duncan, separated and in his mid-thirties)

The well-being of children, financial security and material welfare are clearly important considerations when planning a future relationship. The effect of divorce on the financial position of women in particular and the welfare of children have been subject to research (Chapter 3), however, the risk perceptions of separated, divorced, widowed and formerly cohabiting individuals about finances and material well-being in future relationships need further exploration. Experiences aside, given that individuals have more choice than in the past in how they organize their intimate relationships (Beck 1992), their perceptions of the possible risks associated with particular types of couple relationship (e.g. marriage as opposed to cohabitation) are likely to be multifarious.

The idea of risk is linked with thoughts of controlling the future and making it safe (Giddens 1998). There are risks associated with couple relationships since, as we have noted, one or both partners can leave at any time. To be sure, the majority of women and men who enter marriage think that it is a life-long arrangement (Wu and Schimmele 2005); however, fewer and fewer marriages last for life. Since couple relationships are 'a gamble against the future', Giddens suggests that 'thinking in terms of risk and risk assessment is a more or less ever-present exercise' (1991: 123).

I've had a couple of meaningless affairs which have done me the world of good and changed my attitude but there again could I cope with a serious relationship? I don't know. I'm very, very wary.

(Ray, divorced and in his early fifties)

I made a conscious decision not to [have another relationship], I'm wary I think, you know my life is structured in a way that doesn't allow that to happen [and] I actually quite like being single.

(Colin, a former cohabitee in his mid-thirties)

Scott et al. show that the negotiation of risk entails strategies for managing actual risks and dangers and also strategies for the 'rationalisation of fear and anxiety' (1998: 700). One of the ways of inducing a feeling of control in situations of increasing risks is to plan our lives. However, our plans can be frustrated:

I had a life plan until he bloody well left.

(Davina, divorced and in her early fifties)

Nevertheless, there is a tendency to planning and rationalization in the conduct of life (Beck-Gernsheim 1996: 139), which can enable us to feel that we have some control over our lives. Historical processes mean that people have been released from traditional ties, systems of belief and social relationships (Beck-Gernsheim 1996: 140), which provide greater freedom and choice regarding couple relationships, but come with attendant pressures. The standards of what constitutes an acceptable and satisfying marriage have risen (Furstenberg and Spanier 1984; Spanier and Thompson 1987) and individuals' expectations of the quality of intimate couple relationships are very high. The risk of *not* finding an 'ideal' partner is perhaps ever-present, and for those who have experienced relationship dissolution the risk may seem even more acute. For Colin, avoidance, in the form of structuring his life in order to avoid the possibility of a future couple relationship, is one way of maintaining control. Thus, Colin's 'hodological map' (Sartre 1963: 10) charts the course by which he can fulfil his objective (staying single) by identifying obstacles in the way of and routes to his goal (structuring his life).

Contemporary debates on individualism and commitment show that self-fulfilment and individual happiness countermand commitments made in couple relationships (Chapter 3). Thus it seems that marriage or cohabitation is perceived as a risky and unsafe business, especially for those who have been the injured parties, rather than the perpetrators, of separation or divorce. So for such injured interviewees a sense of security might be difficult to gain:

> I'd be interested to know what reaction you get from people who actually initiate the divorce and how they feel about going into future relationships, but I would imagine that people who are victims of divorce – I would think most people would feel pretty cautious about remarrying, I would guess.
>
> (Adam, divorced and in his early forties)

In addition to commitment and security, choice is a very important consideration in risk and repartnering. For Giddens (1998) one of the positive aspects of the 'risk society' (Beck 1992) we are said to live in is the expansion of choice. In contrast to the ideas of Giddens, too much choice can be unbearable and the options that being single again can bring can seem overwhelming:

> It's hard . . . it's hard thinking and having the whole world at your feet, whether you can go off and live somewhere else. You've just got to think about it, and it's really difficult to think 'Oh, I can go off and do things' and that's scary. What decision shall we take and no one to, say, really [discuss] . . . it with . . . it is quite scary having to face things on your own.
>
> (Amanda, a former cohabitee in her late twenties)

If indeed we do live in a risk society, how do we make decisions when confronted with what Giddens calls 'panoramas of choice' (1991: 139)? Rather like rational choice theory (discussed above), for Giddens the key is 'reflexivity', which involves the continual weighing up of different positions in the light of new information. Reflexivity thus undermines the certainty of knowledge (1991: 20). Consequently, individuals employ a 'calculative attitude to the open possibilities of action' (1991: 28).

It boils down to what I was saying earlier, because you're that little bit wiser . . . although you are wiser, that can work against you because you can see what can happen at the end of it, so it makes you look whereas before at sort of 18 or 19, you just go with the flow of everything and sort of go day by day, whereas if something like what happened to me happens to you, you're more reluctant because you think 'I can't relax because I'm constantly on the lookout for the signs of something bad going to happen' and it is.

(Kevin, a former cohabitee in his mid-twenties)

Bourdieu (1984) does not think that the conscious and deliberate intentions of calculating (reflexive) individuals wholly explain how we make choices (Aldridge 1998). His notion of habitus points to the pre-conscious, non-reflexive ways in which people act. Thus, habitus is 'embodied history, internalized as a second nature and so forgotten as history . . . [it is] spontaneity without consciousness or will' (Bourdieu 1990: 56).

I think I probably couldn't imagine being on my own. It just seemed normal to be married and there was something wrong with you if you weren't, but you see, all my friends were getting married. It wasn't so much getting married. Perhaps it was partly that, but also the fact of having a home and having a family, being part of something which I hadn't felt part of for a long time.

(Carol, divorced and in her mid-forties)

For Bourdieu, individuals acquire their habitus as part of their personal development within a social field, that is, within a 'structured system of social positions [which] includes lifestyle, education and politics' (Jenkins 1992: 84–5). So ultimately, for Bourdieu, it is the less than conscious dispositions of habitus that produce actions (Jenkins 1992: 77), and not the calculations of the rational actor as Giddens (like rational choice theorists) argues. As we saw in Chapter 3, Gross (2005) shows that, though today fewer sanctions are wielded against those who depart from the practices of lifelong marriage, the image of this form of couple relationship continues to function as a 'hegemonic ideal', and, we can include, at the pre-conscious, non-reflexive level of habitus. This seems clear in Carol's response.

Like those interviewed in Tulloch and Lupton's (2003) research, our interviewees are involved in risk assessment and risk management strategies as they attempt to measure and regulate the potential risks from future couple relationships. Though perceiving there to be risks, some of our interviewees are not against entering a new relationship and some are actively looking for a couple relationship:

> I wouldn't be totally resistant to marrying again, but I think I'd want to be sure about it. I don't think I'd want to go through the same thing again, although the averages suggest that it's not good.
>
> (Adam, divorced and in his early forties)

> Sometimes I think someone must think I'd be worth taking on, but then I think, 'Well, is anybody worth taking on? Is there anybody out there that I'd want to take on?' because quite honestly they very often fall very short of my expectations of men. They're a great let down often, I expect too much . . . I just don't want the hurt, I've had enough of it, but then the opportunity's not arisen because no one's come along.
>
> (Carol, divorced and in her mid-forties).

We constantly make decisions in the face of a number of options with potentially disastrous outcomes (Tulloch and Lupton 2003: 6). The potential risks inherent in any relationship lie, in part, in the individuals involved. Past experiences indicate that even when a seemingly 'ideal' person is found, relationship dissolution may still occur. As we saw in Chapter 3, men and women in liquid modernity are in a state of perpetual anxiety, with lives that are infused with the risk of making bad choices, even though choice is the bedrock of individual freedom (Bauman 2000a).

> Well I suppose the whole thrust of it basically is I'm separated now. I would like another relationship, but what I do seems to put me in the situation where that's not likely. I fear not having another relationship before I die I suppose. I fear being a lonely old man, but I'm evidently not prepared to go about doing what would be necessary to make that not happen or give me a fair chance of what I would need to do to break out of what I'm doing now.
>
> (Duncan, separated and in his mid-thirties)

The risks associated with being alone are manifold, though, of course, not all people who live alone are lonely. However, Shaw (1991) found that prominent among reasons given by the women she interviewed for considering remarriage (and our research suggests repartnering) were pressure from others to remarry, being alone, being lonely, needing someone to discuss things with, wanting someone else to make the decisions, wishing for someone to laugh with, habit, a need for stability and the desire for physical (though not necessarily sexual) contact. Duncan reveals that the pain of loneliness and social isolation are felt by men as well. However, such conditions can make a new relationship seem beyond reach.

If a decision to embark on a couple relationship is accompanied by a lack of opportunity to have such a relationship there is no real option:

> I don't go anywhere where I can meet anybody. No. I go to work and there's nobody there at all.
>
> (Carol, divorced and in her mid-forties)

> Meeting people is always very difficult. So meeting them, well, just in general, yes. I'm self-employed, I work by myself so I hardly see anybody.
>
> (Edward, divorced and in his mid-forties)

> I have friends round here or I am invited to friends' houses, but it's all a very closed circle. I don't have the opportunity financially or the time to sort of go out and meet other people.
>
> (Samantha, separated and in her early forties)

Thus a range of factors, not least opportunity and financial constraints, complicates aspirations and decisions. However, Bourdieu (1990) argues, individuals do not consciously tailor their aspirations to an exact evaluation of their chances of success, though the most improbable practices are excluded. For example, none of our interviewees said they had aspirations to embark on a couple relationship with a celebrity, even though this might have been their secret wish. Such aspirations are usually seen as dreams and not as reasonable targets. Decisions made, of course, affect future options about seemingly reasonable targets; for example, remaining in an unwanted relationship perhaps restricts alternative couple relationship options. Thus change decisions and status quo decisions are influenced by perceptions of risk and affect the risks and choices to which we expose ourselves in the future.

Understandably, those among our interviewees who do want to embark on another relationship do not want to risk being hurt again. A high proportion spoke about the risks involved in having relationships with people met by chance, in pubs or clubs, since such people were often felt to be at best unsuitable, and at worst a danger:

> I mean I do go out regular. I go to nightclubs, which is something I never thought I'd do, but after about sort of five or six weeks going to a nightclub, you tend to realize, how can I put it, the sort of situation that is there. To be quite honest, the blokes go there for, like, one night stands and to get totally drunk, right? The women, although I wouldn't say as many do, but you do get the types there and it's not the sort of place

where I feel that I'm going to meet someone who I could start a serious relationship [with].

(Kevin, a former cohabitee in his mid-twenties)

Meeting by chance – the way most of our interviewees had met their first partner – has apparent risks attached. One way of minimizing the risk of finding the 'wrong' person could be to advertise for, or respond to adverts placed by, the 'right' person:

We [friend and I] discussed the best way of getting a man and we decided [that] to advertise was the best way. The people who turn up at singles clubs are people that have nowhere else to go. They're at their wits' end and they need to go somewhere, so they go somewhere like the singles clubs. We call it 'baggage' and they bring baggage with them that most of it is insurmountable. You can't have a relationship and you have to talk about the same thing over and over and over again. Professional men wouldn't be seen dead in a singles club, no way. They won't go to a dating agency because again there's such a stigma, but they might possibly advertise because again, in business, if you want something you go to a supplier . . . So I'm going on the 1st of May to draw up an advert and put it in the [local newspaper] . . . . So why am I advertising? . . . I need somebody who's an equal, who's had an equal upbringing because I am strong and the longer I'm on my own I'm afraid the stronger I'm becoming. I still need somebody in my life.

(Davina, divorced and in her early fifties)

Jagger suggests that 'no longer deemed solely the province of the "sad" or lonely, self advertising has become a well-established and socially acceptable procedure' (2005: 90). Self-advertising, along with dating agencies and more recent Internet procedures, can make meeting others easier and can allay some of the risks associated with chance meetings. This is because information, though perhaps at times fallible, can be gleaned about the person *before* a face-to-face meeting. For example, in response to the questions about why she first advertised for a partner, Jean said:

There was one . . . he was lovely, a lovely looking guy . . . He'd got a good job, he'd never been married or so he said . . . I was always just relieved if they were not scruffy or filthy. I was just relieved that I'm not going to be embarrassed to be seen out with them sort of thing.

(Jean, separated and in her early fifties)

Jean's response reveals a number of risks associated with setting up such a meeting. Advertising perhaps provides only limited opportunities for evaluating the person before attending what can be a relatively long meeting (e.g.

an evening). However, other risk-associated concerns, such as trust ('he'd never been married or so he said'), are no different from those associated with meeting someone by chance. Though it might not be possible to evaluate a person in advance, for Jean contacting someone via an advertisement reduces the risks associated with a lack of knowledge about individuals whom she could meet by chance.

> You know more about them than if I went out and went to a dance and just met someone who could be absolutely anyone. These, at least I'd rung them. I'd rung them at home and the chances were they weren't married. It's a bit dodgy ringing somebody who has advertised and answering a letter and you giving them your phone number to ring, and I felt safer. Usually I'd had a good conversation with them on the phone firstly. What I didn't like is meeting someone who just wanted to spend the evening moaning about the past relationships or their ex-wives because they would all be hard done by, but that's how they come across.
>
> (Jean, separated and in her early fifties)

Risk and trust are closely and dialectally allied; the less we feel at risk from a person the more we feel we can trust them; those we trust less are likely to seem more risky to us. Cvetkovich and Löfstedt argue that 'we trust those who are judged to share with us the values we deem appropriate in a particular risk management domain' (1999: 7). Replying to adverts might be one way of filtering out inappropriate people; however, replying to adverts has attendant risks, not least because we cannot know whether we can trust people to tell the truth about themselves:

> The ones you see in the papers and things, I always think 'well it's easy to say these things'; I mean I could say all these things about myself, saying I'm wonderful, pretty and energetic and everything else, but really at the end of the day I'm not and it would be such a lie and you've got to be prepared that you could meet somebody that is totally not what you're expecting and how do you get out of that situation once you're there? That is the hardest thing . . . I don't know whether I could take the risk and the other thing is you've got to give them some form of contact and telephone number or address . . . I daren't risk it. If I knew there was a guarantee, if I could see the person or could be guaranteed that it was going to be OK before I gave any information, but there are no guarantees because the whole point is – it's supposed to be a blind date and you just don't know.
>
> (Michelle, divorced and in her mid-twenties)

Thus the management of choice and risk is usually based on trust (Giddens 1991). As we have seen, investing love in another person requires trust and our interviewees' past experiences brought into the foreground the risk of trusting and investing emotionally in one person. What Michelle highlights is that trust is vital at all stages of relationship formation and any lack of guarantees about the veracity of routine information, especially for someone who has suffered relationship dissolution, makes liaisons with potential partners seem risky and problematic. It is interesting to note that such risks are associated in particular with ways of promoting relationships that are not based on chance; the identity of those who employ such tactics is suspect. Issues concerning perceptions of the effects of such dating methods on identity are explored in Chapter 7.

Perceptions of risk can restrict the opportunities for relationship formation to which we are willing to expose ourselves. All the women who referred to risks associated with sexual and physical abuse pointed out ways of trying to minimize them:

> I always made sure I was in my own car and bear in mind I'd got their phone numbers and things like this. I always let someone know where I was going and [if I] don't come home, you know. No, so I was always on mutual territory.
>
> (Jean, separated and in her early fifties)

Risk theorists such as Beck have been criticized for failing to take account of social divisions, such as gender, when exploring differences in risk knowledges and strategies for the management of risk (Tulloch and Lupton 2003: 60). In response, Lash (1993, 2000) calls for considerations of the ways in which people respond emotively and aesthetically to risk as members of sub-groups rather than as atomized individuals (Tulloch and Lupton 2003: 60). Although most men do not rape women, the fact that some do keeps women in a state of fear and dependence (Brownmiller 1986). Thus, the threat of male violence controls women's behaviour in public and in private (Hanmer and Maynard 1987).

The risk issues associated with couple relationships raised by our interviewees are not confined to risks that they feel themselves to be exposed to, or to which they feel they might be potentially exposed. On becoming single they felt, and continue to feel, that other people's perceptions of them have changed (see Chapter 7) and some, especially among the women interviewed, perceived others as now seeing them as a threat to their own couple relationships.

> Dangerous to other women maybe. Definitely in some ways you feel people are staying away because of the fact that you're on your own.
>
> (Carol, divorced and in her mid-forties)
>
> I lost touch with my friends mainly because I'd become a single person and I became a threat to their relationship, as stupid as it would be,

because I would never dream of doing anything, but they couldn't help it and I could see it. I could see that they, you know . . . or as much as they wanted to be friends, it was going to be difficult. Their husbands who were as friendly as the women were, were very distant. It's just very difficult. I'm finding it very difficult to try and find groups to join in because of the fact that when you're in a two, you don't seem to be as much of a threat as on your own. It's really strange, but it seems to be that way.

(Michelle, divorced and in her mid-twenties)

One of my closest friends, actually it was her husband I knew first prior to getting to know her and we've formed a very good friendship now and we're very, very close and we're quite open and honest with each other and she did initially see me and she was quite unpleasant to me when I first knew her, but this is what it was. She saw me as a threat and she realizes now how amusing that is, but fortunately we got to know each other, otherwise she would possibly still see me as a threat. Yes, yes, and I can understand why people do.

(Jean, separated and in her early fifties)

'Individuals experience social life somewhere in between predictable comfort and routine (stability) and the discomfort that contingent events (instability) pose' (Berezin 2002: 36). Stability is an important aspect of everyday life and, as Barbalet (2001) reminds us, change itself is a potential source of fear. We often take our lives for granted until changes are forced on us and the changes that occur in the lives of others, we may feel, also threaten our own stability. Such changes, like the dissolution of the couple relationships of friends or neighbours, have the potential to alter our everyday existence and also make apparent the threats that can disrupt the taken-for-granted constancy of our lives. Thus it is not only the dissolution of our own relationships that shapes our feelings of stability; the dissolution of another's relationship reminds us of the fragility and potential instability of our own. Moreover, a person who is single again is perceived to be searching for a new partner and is consequently a threat to our own partnership. Referring to Hebb (1946), Barbalet suggests that we can fear something that might not threaten in any way and thus another individual (in our case, a newly single person) can be 'implicated in another's fear because of what they are likely to do. The past behaviour of an agent may lead to another's fear of them, certainly. But this is not directly because of what the agent had done, but because what they had done leads to an anticipation of what they might do' (Barbalet 2001: 155). We note that it was only women interviewees who expressed such concerns. The compassionate temperament (which provides us with a greater moral imagination of the suffering of others) that has accompanied modernity (Durkheim, cited in Wilkinson 2004) is in evidence here. All the women interviewed have suffered the end of a relationship and, for many of them, relationship dissolution followed their male partner having an adulterous relationship. In consequence these women seem to be highly aware of, and have a sensitive approach to, any possible negative impact that their new identity as a single woman may have on the sense of security held by the women around them.

Risk, emotions and choice and future repartnering

In this chapter we have addressed a range of questions and issues associated with decision-making about future couple relationships. For those who have suffered the end of a relationship, decisions about potential partnerships are influenced by past relationship experiences. As expected, anger, grief and pain spotlight the risks associated with investing love in another, especially in the context of co-resident partnerships. In contrast to experiences that encourage the development of a taken-for-granted attitude that things will remain the same, such experiences bring into focus the changes that *can* occur and the risks that *might* ensue as a result. There is always the risk that a partner will leave and, in addition to the hurt, anguish and humiliation that this might cause, there are the risks to others and to the security of one's home and material well-being. The purposes of decisions can be categorized broadly as those associated with the desire to alter a situation and those associated with keeping a situation as it is. Although this categorization obscures a host of complexities, it serves to illustrate the perceptions of risk and choice that motivate the decisions and intentions of our interviewees. Decisions invariably involve perceptions of risks since they are always based in choice and it is only in retrospect that we can evaluate the quality of our decisions. 'Bad' previous relationships heighten awareness of risk, and the attendant disillusionment can destroy feelings of trust in others, especially when strong emotions, such as love, are involved. When guarantees are not possible – and guarantees in couple relationships are surely always impossible – some will avoid couple relationships altogether.

Thus anxiety about a 'bad' future relationship induces some to choose to retain their situation of secure aloneness. Others may wish for the security of a couple relationship and not want to risk being alone for the rest of their lives. Still, searching for a couple relationship can feel like a risky endeavour. Women in particular feel at risk from sexual abuse and sexual violence and replying to dating advertisements can be one way of reducing the feelings of risk involved, though some view such methods as increasing the risk of meeting someone inappropriate or even dangerous. The risks associated with another relationship are felt to be ever present and thus, even if a potential partner is found, the risks to well-being are at least thought about. However, this is not to say that relationship dissolution engenders a rational approach to decision-making. For decision-making is far more complex than strong rational choice theorists suggest. The women and men we interviewed present a complex picture of relationship decision-making. Although many referred to their weighing-up of economic considerations in decisions about joining or leaving a couple relationship, such considerations were by no means the only, or the most important ones. A range of issues and factors, including altruistic actions, decisions made by others and outside events, complicate notions of 'optimizing' decision-making behaviour. Especially important in relationship choices is the presence (or absence) of romantic love and sexual attraction.

As noted in Chapter 3, legal changes mean that intimate couple relationships are arguably increasingly based on commitment to another (a choice) rather than restrictions on leaving (a constraint). Retaining freedom of choice is an important aspect of contemporary relationship formation, and cohabitation is one way of securing against the risks associated with marriage. Our interviewees' comments reflect a shift to less repressive and more egalitarian 'pure relationships' (Giddens 1991, 1992), but such individualized relationships for many are insecure and thus risky. This can lead to a sense of being burdened by worry, doubt and insecurity. Nevertheless, although the 'regulative tradition' of lifelong marriage has declined, 'meaning-constitutive traditions' based on lifelong marriage and romantic love provide many interviewees with an image of an ideal relationship (Gross 2005), and love and romantic involvement are still considered to be the most important motivators for having an intimate couple relationship. Thus emotions are fundamental to our interviewees' choices and are important to their views about whether to have a future couple relationship and underpin partner choice.

Experiences of relationship dissolution engendered in our interviewees a heightened sense of the risks associated with couple relationships and an awareness of the distress of others. Some of the women demonstrated compassion regarding any possible negative impact that their new identity as a woman without a partner might have on the feelings of security of the women around them. We turn to issues of identity in Chapter 7.

7
Identity and Intimacy in the Lives of Formerly Partnered Men and Women

Introduction

In this chapter we use our interview data to examine the ways in which formerly partnered men and women view themselves and their lives. The focus is on identity. Our aim is not to debate the concept of identity, which itself has been subject to a 'searching critique' (Hall 1996: 1), but rather to explore the concept of identity in relation to perceptions of changing identity, and changes in lifestyle, through couple relationship transitions. Transitions are integral to the life course and with these transitions, such as changes associated with relationship dissolution, come modifications of, and receptions of changes to, identity and lifestyle. Though some of the issues raised are not peculiar to identity and intimate couple relationship dissolution, since issues such as gender, ageing, sexuality and intimacy, beauty, parenthood and singledom are raised, these issues and the interaction between them seem to coalesce at what Giddens (1992) calls such 'fateful moments'. Thus the following discussion is eclectic in essence, drawing out many, but by no means all, of the important points that unite in concepts of identity. Consequently, this discussion is not complete and is not intended to be. Rather, we are interested in how the men and women we interviewed discuss their identities and lifestyles in relation to the changes that have occurred in their lives and how their everyday lives had changed in consequence.

The combined conceptualizations of identity and lifestyle are central to this chapter. Identity is shaped within systems of social relations and thus the focus of this chapter, like the others, is on change and interaction. Performativity is vital since, though our identities may be experienced as essential to us, in fact, following Butler (1999), identity is best conceptualized as something that we *do* rather than something that we *are*. In addition, though we experience our selves as unitary, in fact identity is fragmented, not least because how we see ourselves might differ, indeed is likely to differ, from how others see us. Moreover, changes throughout our lives, like relationship dissolution and relationship formation, affect identity, our perceptions of how others see us (as we saw in Chapter 6), and how others *do* see us. In this regard we offer discussion of the notion of the 'other' and Foucault's conceptualization of 'the gaze', since it is the distinction between others and ourselves, and how we see others and how we perceive others to see us, that provides us with a sense of belonging or exclusion. Furthermore, distinctions over time, between ourselves yesterday and ourselves today, are important aspects of identity, since we must cope with identity upset and transformation at times like relationship dissolution. It is in this respect that we also explore the concept of lifestyle since 'lifestyle choice is increasingly important in the constitution of identity and daily activity' (Giddens 1991: 5). Lifestyle, identity and behaviour are constrained by context (Litva, Peggs and Moon 2001), and lifestyle changes accompany relationship dissolution (e.g. changes in where and with whom we live). By the use of the concept of lifestyle we can explore more 'superficial' changes that impact on an individual's sense of his or her self.

Identity and the self

Identity is formed within social and cultural contexts and thus cannot be defined simply in terms of individual properties (Taylor 1989). For Bourdieu (1984) the three main factors within the social and cultural contexts that underpin the process of identity formation are social location, habitus and taste. Social location is a starting point since it refers to the external 'class-based material circumstances which contextualise people's daily lives' (Shilling 1993: 129). Habitus is formed within the context of social location and, as we saw in Chapter 6, refers to the internalization, as natural, of the ideas and attitudes of an individual's social peers (Frank 1991). Taste pertains to the ways in which individuals adopt lifestyles rooted in the social location, that is, the material constraints of their circumstances (Bourdieu 1984). However, individuals should not be seen as passive entities that merely absorb external influences. As individuals we contribute to and promote the social influences that affect us. Since we are constantly 'on stage' (Goffman 1969) we seek to mirror desired identities and life-styles. Thus identity is associated with yearning and belonging.

In terms of belonging, identity includes notions of similarity, difference and exclusion. As individuals, we simultaneously mark out our sense of similarity with some and our sense of difference from others; thus our identities are 'more the product of the marking of difference and exclusion, than they are the sign of identical, naturally-constituted unity' (Hall 1996: 4). In this respect Derrida (1991) shows that the foundation of identity, which we should see as a power relation, is the exclusion of 'the other'. Thus we can speak of our *identities* since our identity is never finalized (Jenkins

2004: 5) and is multifarious. So identity is a process of 'permanent hybrid-izations and nomadization' (Mouffe 1994, cited in Lloyd 2005: 162) since at any one time in life and throughout life an individual identifies with a number of social positions (Lloyd 2005: 162). Thus we can see identity as a 'practical accomplishment... [which] can be understood using a unified model of the dialectical interplay of processes of internal and external defin-ition' (Jenkins 2004: 23) and it is through such 'repertoires of identification' (Jenkins 2004: 7) that we achieve our everyday lives.

The part played by human agency in identification is thus crucial, and here Giddens' notion of the self as a reflexive project points to the ways in which identity is constituted by a reflexive ordering of self-narratives (Adkins 2001: 35). Giddens argues that the self is revised and negotiated though a 'narrative of self-identity' (1991: 185) because 'self-identity has to be created and more or less continually re-ordered against the back-drop of shifting experiences of day-to-day life and the fragmenting tend-encies of modern institutions' (1991: 186). Perhaps at critical life-changing moments (e.g. relationship dissolution), self-reflexivity becomes obvious and unavoidable:

> Well, it's made me look at myself, which I probably didn't do before. I never sort of thought, 'What sort of person am I?' But I do now... I suppose that I feel that in some way I must have done something wrong or, or not done something I should have done, or he wouldn't have gone.
> (Samantha, separated and in her early forties)

As we will see in the next section, stability is an important aspect of identity (Giddens 1991; Berezin 2002; Jenkins 2004). Though it is by no means the case that all those interviewed identify themselves as having some form of deficit that led to the dissolution of their previous relationship, Samantha shows the powerful influence that her partner leaving had on her sense of her self, with the result that she no longer takes her 'self' for granted.

Relationship dissolution and identity

In Chapter 6 we saw how relationship dissolution and the lifestyle changes associated with such 'suffering events' (Wilkinson 2004) adversely affect the sense of security of many of the men and women interviewed. As we will see, this extends to perceptions of identity, since relationship dissolution can seriously affect notions of who we are. This is because change often threatens the security of selfhood (Jenkins 2004: 62) since individual ontolo-gical security commonly relies on routine and habit (Giddens 1990: 92–100).

We often take for granted our lives until change is forced on us, and change can throw us into a state of confusion and despair:

> My biggest problem was my loss of self-esteem because I was, at the time, I was blaming myself a lot.
>
> (Eric, divorced and in his mid-thirties)

> Well the thing was I knew... I did used to feel sort of down and yes, I think let down, I felt very let down and disappointed in him because of what had happened and all the things that he'd said, you know, I really believed and I tend to think about that. I think disappointed and let down is what I felt. I mean sometimes I used to feel so low and if I used to sometimes go and look in the mirror, I used to look at myself and I used to feel like shit inside, but sometimes I didn't used to look that bad and you think, well, 'I don't look that bad you know, but I feel like shit inside'.
>
> (Maureen, separated, subsequently a cohabitee, and in her early fifties)

> My self-esteem went down in the two relationships I've had – that's what happened, maybe because they finished the relationship as well, that's quite powerful I think, you know, so my self-esteem definitely went down. Yes, it's weird – I mean in some ways it went down and in some ways it released some energy and I remember doing lots of work on both occasions and there was something there which enabled me to do things that previously I hadn't been able to do, so yes I think my self-esteem was pretty low... just, just, big worries I think, worrying about, you know, something that you were lacking basically, lacking something, I don't know what, but something like that, mainly because they finished the relationship. I feel I've got over that now, but it took a long time.
>
> (Simon, a former cohabitee in his mid-thirties)

As we saw in Chapter 6, Giddens notes how the self is 'for everyone today a reflexive project – a more or less continuous interrogation of past, present and future' (1992: 30) and, in the context of intimate couple relationships, he notes how a romance is seen as a way of controlling the future, as well as a form of psychological security (Giddens 1992: 41). The failure of a romantic attachment, especially if it is accompanied by a feeling of rejection, has important implications for self-identity. Rejection implies a perception of deficiency in the person who has been rejected, which can have serious consequences for feelings of self-esteem, especially if, as Eric indicates, if it is accompanied by self-blame. Consecutive rejections may compound the feeling. Though change can be damaging, Simon's comment shows that the changes associated with relationship dissolution can also be liberating since they provide space in which a sense of self can be developed. As we saw in Chapter 3, self-identity is crucial to pure relationships and Bauman emphasizes that though 'changing identity may be a private affair . . . it always includes cutting of certain bonds and cancelling certain obligations' (2000b: 90). However, in all forms of couple relationship tension exists between independence and relatedness (Lewis 2001) and for men and women, events such as divorce can initiate the start of a new phase in life (Smart 2005). Mainly, though not exclusively, female interviewees suggest that relationship dissolution signals a clawing back of self-identity:

> In my marriage I lost my identity, I was [my husband's] wife.
>
> (Davina, divorced and in her early fifties)

> I realize that's what he'd done to me throughout our marriage . . . I wasn't me anymore.
>
> (Nicola, divorced and in her early fifties)

> You see I always relied on [my ex-husband] for my opinions and thoughts because he seemed to have such, not so much sensible views, but he always had a view on nearly anything and I used to think, 'Oh yes, he's got that really well, I'd better go along with that one, that's the right thing to have', never thinking that anybody might just value my opinion and my own very personal one.
>
> (Carol, divorced and in her mid-forties)

> I don't think that when you're married you are yourself. I mean I'm completely different now, even [my ex-husband] says I'm completely different now to when I was married because you're forever – well you're adjusting yourself to fit in with somebody else and you can't be your real self.
>
> (Brenda, divorced and in her early forties)

> [I was] trying to find myself again because I'd lost my identity. I was just his wife . . . I went and bought all the clothes I wanted to wear and I had my hair tinted and everything my husband didn't want me to do I did because that was the true me so [I] started to rebuild my identity.
>
> (Louise, divorced and in her late thirties)

> It was like trying to reassert my identity because I didn't really have any, only his shadow and it's really hard because people didn't believe I could do anything either.
>
> (Amanda, a former cohabitee in her late twenties)

These comments echo those in Smart and Neale's (1999) research. They also found that, for women, divorce heralded a feeling of returning to their 'old selves'. In his discussion of domination, Weber (1978) shows how conformity is an expression of the exercise of power. It is not surprising that the gendered dynamics of power in heterosexual couple relationships, where power is usually located in the (most often male) higher earner (Saul 2003: 15), resulted in some of our women interviewees feeling unable to assert their 'authentic' identity in a co-resident heterosexual couple relationship. Lewis found that married women often asserted a desire for a separate identity, many in respect of their roles as paid workers, with some expressing the need to develop interests that they did not share with their husbands (2001: 142). Thus, it seems that for some of the women in our study it took relationship dissolution for them to feel able to assert their 'authentic' identity, an identity not squashed by a powerful other. Such notions of identity authenticity (Yngvesson and Mahoney 2000) were also expressed by two of the men interviewed:

> I had a lack of confidence. I was going up and down and I'd been rejected ... and I did feel very down and poorly for a while, but yes, I met somebody who made me feel like a man, made me feel good again and made me feel wanted and all those things came up to the fore again.
>
> (Doug, separated and in his late forties)

> All the time I was married to her I felt as if I was trying to be something ... I was going through an identity crisis all the time I was with her. I was trying to be somebody she wanted me to be. What really bugged me and I told the counsellor right from the beginning and it probably is only that, I've had eight years of her, her mum and her sister saying I'm not a man and this brought me down. OK, I have been suffering while I've been on my own with my self-esteem, but I'm coping with that now because I'm finding out about myself and is there anything out there to tell me what a man is?
>
> (Eric, divorced and in his mid-thirties)

Using sex/gender as her focus, Butler argues that gender is 'performative', that is 'what we take to be an internal essence of gender is manufactured through a sustained set of acts, posited through the gendered stylisation of the body' (1999: xv). So Butler contends that 'gender is not an expression of what one *is*; it is what one *does*' (Lloyd 2005: 25). Thus, for Butler, gender identity is always in process, it needs to be reiterated daily and thus is never achieved permanently (Lloyd 2005: 26). In consequence, Lloyd notes, '*all* gender identity is imitative in the sense of its being reiterative' (2005: 26) and it is through discourse that this is achieved and constrained. So, 'every time we state our sex as female on a form, visit a gynaecologist or obstetrician, go to a hairdressers rather than a barber, or buy sanitary products' (Lloyd 2005: 26) we are reiterated as female. So, Lloyd (2005) continues, we are repeating the acts and gestures that gender us as embodied subjects. Thinking about the comments made by those interviewed, perhaps male dominance in the home does not repress *female gender* identity, rather it is women's *self-identity* that is suppressed; submissiveness and suppression of self might, for some women, be perceived as central to what one does as a *wife*, but not to what one does as a *person*. In consequence escape from wifedom is an important symbol of self-identity for many women. Thus male domination in the home challenges self-identity but not female identity for women; however, the relationship between masculinity and gender dynamics in the home suggest that for men to be denied the dominant role in the home challenges both masculine identity and *what one does as a husband*. Of course, masculinities are diverse (Lesko 2000; Pease 2000) and crises in masculinities have been identified. Though Eric is uncertain about *what it is to be a man* he feels that the dissolution of his relationship has given him the space to develop *his individual identity*. The importance of space to develop a sense of self is also referred to by some of the women interviewed:

I think you've got to have a break to get to know who you are, because we're all changing.

(Alison, divorced and in her mid-thirties)

I think it's most important to be by myself at the moment. Whether or not I will feel differently in a year or two years, but at the moment that's how I feel because it's only been six months now.

(Maureen, separated, subsequently a cohabitee, and in her early fifties)

It was very hard because it was like reverting back to a single, independent person. I didn't have a counsellor at all. I'd never been anywhere on my own, never been to the pictures on my own, never went out for meals on my own . . . I, myself, knew it was right for me to try and get something on my own and for them to see me on my own, people to see me in my own right.

(Amanda, a former cohabitee in her late twenties)

Many more individuals now enter marriage and couple relationships after living alone, rather than in households with others, therefore they have had some experience of managing a household, and of managing being alone, prior to partnership formation and are equipped to do so again if the relationship fails (Stein 1981):

Well I think the fact is that when you've lived on your own for a long time you do a lot of things that you never thought you were capable of. You become very independent and looking back that side of me may not ever have come out when I was married.

(Heather, widowed and in her early forties)

As we saw in Chapter 3, for women, relationship dissolution can lead to an 'independent life' (Maclean 1991). Contrary to the ideas of Beck and Beck-Gernsheim (1995), families have not necessarily become individualized with both partners engaged in full-time work, and thus economically independent of each other (Lewis 2001: 60). Independence is often associated with *economic* independence and freedom from domestic responsibilities, and for widowed women, freedom from caring for a partner (Lopata 1996; Davidson 2001; van den Hoonaard 2001).

A lifestyle of living and managing alone, even if not chosen, can have an extremely positive effect on the sense of self. Dependence is fast becoming a derogatory term (Bauman 2003); thus to be independent has become a source of pride. Though for Bauman dependence 'is what moral responsibility for the other is all about' (2003: 90), for Heather, and others we interviewed, independence does not appear to be about a lack of moral responsibility. Rather, it seems to centre on self-reliance, self-capability and self-discovery. In consequence, worries about a loss of found independence are reasons for not wishing to enter a co-resident intimate couple relationship:

> I'm reluctant to give up that independence quite honestly.
>
> (Cheryl, separated and in her mid-forties)

Responses from the men and women interviewed, like those above, exhibit, in Furedi's words, 'the powerful influence of therapeutic culture' (2004: 15) which 'presents itself as the harbinger of a new era of individual choice, autonomy, self-knowledge and self-awareness' (2004: 106). Therapeutic language has become part of 'our cultural imagination' (Furedi 2004: 1) and fundamental to how we present our understanding of our selves:

> I've got naturally low self-esteem, which is not particularly helpful. I get emotional because I wasn't loved properly as a child, but I sort of cry quite easily and I am capable of being quite self-pitying, although quite irrational. I've some reason to be sorry for myself I think, but nevertheless it's not a particularly useful thing
>
> (Eva, divorced and in her mid-fifties)

Though the interviewees certainly talk about the changes in their lives in therapeutic terms, far from feeling like 'victims of circumstance' (Furedi 2004: 114), many felt that relationship dissolution had made available an important period of living on their own, which in turn enabled them to gain independence and a sense of self that they felt was either squashed or missing when they were in their previous intimate couple relationship. Accordingly, interviewees who do want a future relationship express concerns about the challenges to their sense of self that a new intimate relationship with another might bring:

> At the end of the day it would have to be someone who would be my best friend . . . and they accept me for the person that I am. They don't want to change me too much. I would want to change, not for them to want to change me. You can't change anybody else. I would never dream of changing another person.
>
> (Alison, divorced and in her mid-thirties)

> I want a man that's as strong as I am, that stands on his own, is confident and capable of standing on his own because I want to be confident and capable of standing on my own, but I have a lot of loving and caring and I want to give it to somebody who will give it to me back and you can only do that if you come to terms with who you are.
>
> (Davina, divorced and in her early fifties)

> I probably wouldn't get involved with someone who would make me give things up. It would be a person who would go along with what my views are on doing things. I mean simple things. I don't like the heat too much, therefore I wouldn't want to go to the South of France in July if you like.
>
> (Arthur, divorced and in his early sixties)

Recently found independence can be precious. Furedi laments that '[i]nstead of acting as a source of support and strength, human relationships are represented as diminishing the power of the self' (2004: 126). Rather than lamentable, the increasing power of the sense of self that accompanies relationship dissolution is certainly something that is valuable to many of the men and women interviewed in this study. However, though relationship dissolution is a common occurrence, such dissolutions can attack the core of identity.

Couple relationships and identity

The institution of marriage (and cohabitation, since this is a way of 'doing being a married couple'; Jenkins 2004: 137) is 'generative' (Barth, cited in Jenkins 2004: 139) of identification. Though, following Merton's (1957) work on status, the 'status' of being married can be done in a variety of ways, 'depending upon the individual occupant(s), contextual constraints and possibilities, and the demands of significant others' (Jenkins 2004: 140), here we are interested in how the men and women interviewed saw the outward expression of being in a couple relationship as central to their identities. Relationship formation and the type of relationship engaged in say something about who we are, and, for some of the interviewees, being in a couple relationship, especially a heterosexual couple relationship, is seen as necessary to a 'complete' identity, both for their sense of themselves and for being accepted in wider society:

> There is such a strong social pressure on people, and when you're young, and I think the problems that people feel even if they don't articulate them to themselves about having a sexual partner and feeling who that give you a kind of identity, maybe feeling loved or liked by somebody else and that becomes a package.
>
> (Carl, separated and in his early fifties)

Although we feel that love is a very private emotion, Sarsby shows that love is a social phenomenon because '[c]ustom and socialization dictate the way in which love [is experienced] . . . they also dictate the situations which provoke such emotions, and for how long and how intensely they are experienced.' (1983: 1). Thus a heterosexual couple relationship is an expression of love to others outside the relationship. However, romantic love is not understood as a field open to all equally. Sarsby argues that in Western society, 'falling in love is for the most part a prestigious activity, ideally happening to the young, and especially the rich and beautiful, rather than the old, or the physically and mentally disadvantaged' (1983: 4). Thus being loved and wanted by another is an important part of identity, since it not only functions as an insignia of our worth to others but also functions as a sign of the esteemed position we hold in society:

> We all think we need somebody else to make us whole, that's what we're taught. You're not whole unless you've got a man. That was my upbringing and you're not a person unless you've got a husband and a home. You're nothing if you haven't got those two things . . .
>
> (Davina, divorced and in her early fifties)

> I think it was what we working-class girls in the '50s did. We got a man and they became the life.
>
> (Sandra, divorced and in her early fifties)

'Identity is about not being split, about being complete' (Yngvesson and Mahoney 2000: 87) and for these women completeness involves being in a couple relationship with a man. This returns us to habitus, which, for Bourdieu, is acquired by individuals as part of their personal development within a social field, that is within a 'structured system of social positions [which] includes lifestyle, education and politics' (Jenkins 1992: 84–5). Women's social location, which is determined by, for example, familial and financial constraints, the expectation that women's primary role is located in the home and changes in the labour market, affects the options that they have. Women's (and men's) notions of their roles operate at the pre-conscious level of the habitus, pointing to non-reflexive choices (Peggs 2000). So ultimately, for Bourdieu, it is the less than conscious dispositions of habitus that produce actions (Jenkins 1992: 77). For Davina and Sandra, there is a once central, perhaps previously unquestioned, disposition to needing a man to make life and thus identity complete. Male interviewees also referred to the habitual assumption that a partner is necessary for a feeling of being 'complete' and, like some of the women interviewed, some questioned this in the light of their relationship experiences:

> Somebody said to me... do you need to have a partner in order to be a person and weren't you a person before you met [your ex-partner]? It was very good. I mean amongst the gems that come out you get these little trigger points and you thought, 'No, he's bloody right... You're not dependent upon the other person to be you.' What it does is bring out more of you.
>
> (Derek, separated and in his early fifties)

As already noted, although fewer sanctions are wielded today against those who depart from the practices of lifelong marriage, the image of this form of couple relationship continues to function as a 'hegemonic ideal' in many couples (Gross 2005) and, we can add, at the pre-conscious, non-reflexive level of habitus, which is likely to be challenged only at very critical moments. The dissolution of a relationship can have at once positive and negative effects on an individual's pre-conscious perception of what it is to *be* their self and how they should *do* their self. But, thinking back to those who felt their identity was crushed in their previous couple relationship, in their attempts to be whole through relationship formation, they felt they had lost themselves completely. Thus the ending of a partnership forces attention onto 'authentic' identity and the (re) discovery of the 'true' self.

In her thoughts on emotion and political sociology, Berezin (2002) points to issues of stability and instability that are applicable not only at the macro level but also at this micro individual level. She suggests that '[i]ndividuals experience social life somewhere between predictable comfort and routine (stability) and the discomfort that contingent events (instability) pose' (2002: 36). So, stability is an important aspect of everyday life and becoming single after relationship dissolution can be a very difficult transition:

> It was very hard because it was like reverting back to [being] a single independent person.
>
> (Amanda, a former cohabitee in her late twenties)

Living as a single person after relationship dissolution affects not only one's perception of one's own identity but also perceptions of how others see one (as we saw in Chapter 6, vis-à-vis women's perceptions of being viewed as a risk to their friends' or other women's couple relationships). Interviewees speak of the pressures placed on them to find a partner, especially as others seem to make erroneous assumptions about their needs or found their situations difficult to handle:

> Sometimes other people, like my brother, find it embarrassing when I go to something like a wedding, you know, they feel like I have to have a partner.
>
> (Catherine, a former cohabitee in her late twenties)

> I, myself, knew it was right for me to try and get something on my own and for them to see me on my own, people to see me in my own right. Everyone seemed to think that I should have a boyfriend and it's constantly there.
>
> (Amanda, a former cohabitee in her late twenties)

Obligation to the draw of a partnership, in some cases through the demands of a 'significant other' (Jenkins 2004: 140), reflects the wish to 'mirror' the surroundings in which the normative expectations are couple (usually heterosexual) relationships. 'The normal stands indifferently for what is typical, the unenthusiastic objective average' (Hacking 1990: 169) and, although relationship dissolution is a common enough occurrence, in the event it affects how other people identify 'me' and 'this has some bearing on what they perceive my – and, indeed, often *their* - interests to be' (Jenkins 2004: 178). Though the stigma attached to divorce has eroded (Lewis 2001: 20), still common understandings give rise to shared expectations (Sugden 1998) about the obligation to be in a couple relationship:

> You go to a dinner party and you say you're coming on your own . . . It's a nightmare. Yes, there is a social stigma.
>
> (Davina, divorced and in her early fifties)

> It is hard. A lot of social events are geared towards a couple. It's geared towards a couple coming round, have a meal with a couple.
>
> (Ken, divorced and in his early fifties)

> I want to be the norm as if you're not. There is a definition of what's normal, as though people are full of ideas that it's not normal to be on your own. There must be a reason why you're on your own because like you're unsociable or something like this.
>
> (Eric, divorced and in his mid-thirties)

> It's very difficult to continue to go out with people in couples because you feel the oddball and there's so many other things that come into

that, like when you've got a husband on your arm, they go and buy the drinks and that . . . So in the end you start backing off.

(Sheila, separated and in her late forties)

I'm still invited to all the things that we would have been invited to as a couple. I just don't feel the same when I go, I'm no longer part of [it], I don't feel as if I'm any longer part of that group. I am a different person to what I was.

(Samantha, separated and in her early forties)

It's like a bereavement, they sometimes avoid you and they don't talk to you.

(Ellen, divorced and in her early fifties)

The focus of these responses is on identity and difference. The perception of being stigmatized can lead to social isolation and a feeling of being outside the norm, in a range of situations. Thus the effects of a change in lifestyle cause problems for a sense of belonging through a perceived stigmatized identity: a sense that one does not belong. The analogy of bereavement is worthy of note since Elias (1985) talks about how the stigma of death has led to avoidance not only of the dying, but also the bereaved. It seems that such stigma has attached itself to divorce, with similar consequences:

It's very difficult, very difficult, and it's not just difficult from the point of view of perhaps accepting invitations to parties. . . . it's difficult when you're just walking round Tesco's.

(Tony, divorced and in his mid-forties)

I mean I just feel, I feel as though there's something wrong with me that I'm not in a relationship. When I go shopping I see people walking about with a partner and I feel like a leper, even though the fact [is] they're probably very unhappy.

(Arthur, divorced and in his early sixties)

Relationship dissolution affects our perceptions of how others see us, how we see others and how we see ourselves. As noted earlier, it is the distinction between others and ourselves, and how we see others and how we perceive others to see us, that provide us with a sense of belonging or exclusion, and determines whether we feel that we have a legitimate, unified identity. In Foucault's (1977) terms, we are 'gazed' upon and we 'gaze' upon others, often in envy about what they have, and perhaps how they integrate with others in their everyday life in ways which we feel we do not. It is interesting that these men should mention shopping as a site of feeling outside, as the other. None of the women interviewed refers to this. Since shopping, like the majority of domestic consumption practices, is mainly carried out by women (Slater 1997), men shopping alone feel that they are displaying their aloneness, whereas women, whether single or not, often shop on their own. Goffman points out that one of the problems of *performance* is 'information control', where the quest is to ensure that 'the audience must not acquire destructive information about the situation that is being defined for them' (1969: 123). In shopping, an event historically characterized as feminine (Slater 1997), for these men being alone means that their 'secret' is out and this 'threatens their performance' (Goffman 1969: 123)

In their work on identity narratives and child adoption, Yngvesson and Mahoney maintain that a 'complete' family is perceived to be one that includes a father, mother and child, who are all ' "like" one another' (2000: 87). Though lone parenthood is less stigmatized than it used to be (Lewis 2001), the normative family still is a parent of each sex with children. Thus being with children enhances the feeling of exclusion for now single men and women:

> Well, at the beginning I felt very much, when I split up from my husband, I felt very much that I stuck out like a sore thumb . . . Also, going out with the children, when the children were younger, I found it so obvious that everybody else was in couples and there was me with my children. It was not necessarily the case. I'm sure there were lots of other single parents with children, but that's how I perceived it.
>
> (Rosa, divorced and in her late forties)

> . . . it's easier for society to deal with a couple. It's quite clear that people have stayed away from me since all this has happened . . . I'm aware that in most situations in life couples or two parents plus children is easier than one plus children and I've subscribed to that in the past myself I suppose. I'm the other side of it now.
>
> (Carol, divorced and in her mid-forties)

As we saw in Chapter 3, in her study in Canada Power (2005) found that lone mothers are constructed as 'Other', as 'welfare bums' or as 'flawed consumers' who do not have the financial resources to participate in the consumer market. Such identity-markers have serious negative consequences for lone mothers' identity. For lone fathers the identity-markers may be different but just as damaging:

> Being a single parent and that, as I said, it's much easier . . . although I had initial problems with mums at the school and nursery . . . they have sort of a parents' room, it was pretty well exclusively the mums in there and they were quite hostile to me. It was quite strange.
>
> (Tim, divorced and in his early forties)

Now what's wrong with a guy living on his own? I'm not Michael Ryan, I'm not like the Hamilton bloke, I'm not a sexual paedophile or anything like this. I'm just a guy living on my own. I haven't got to live the normal straightforward life.

(Eric, divorced and in his mid-thirties)

Since the 1980s there has been an increasing focus in the media on the risk to children from paedophiles (Macdonald 2003). Discursive constructions of place and space as 'dangerous' or 'safe' (Macdonald 2003) and of 'stranger danger' (Furedi 2002) have led to a permanent state of anxiety about the safety of children (Furedi 2002). The widely publicized acts of a minority of men have amplified the threat and have arguably led to a 'spoiled identity' (Joffe 1999) for all men, especially lone men or lone fathers.

Perceptions that others see one as a threat are not confined to men. As we saw in Chapter 6, some of the women are perceived to be searching for a new partner and consequently feel that they are seen as a threat to the established partnerships of others. The women speak of the effects this has on their perceptions of their selves:

You know I don't think men get the same pressure, maybe when they're a bit older but you know there's always that difference between the wild bachelor and the old spinster. In my parish there are a lot of families who are really conventional and some of the wives don't speak to me, you know they think, 'Oh, who's a single woman, you know what they're like with [a] string of men', or 'They're just after our husbands', and so there's a pressure from women and there seems to be more pressure for women than men to marry.

(Catherine, a former cohabitee in her late twenties)

Quite hostile and overt jealousy. It comes out like a battering ram with these women. So I've come across that. I came across that when I was younger, but I think what's happening now is that I've had one or two offers of help because I took a load of stuff to the tip . . . So the women don't like that. They don't like to see a competent woman and they don't like to have their husbands being helpful . . . I think and I always behave entirely appropriately too. I would never make a pass at somebody else's bloke.

(Eva, divorced and in her mid-fifties)

I think married people perceive you suddenly as a threat, whereas before it was OK for you to just turn up. Suddenly, [it's] 'Hang on a minute, what's she coming round for?' So you do feel that people perceive [you] as a threat . . . well I suppose it's difficult because it's my perception of what I think other people are feeling, but they've got their husband and you're coming in and somehow getting between them. I relate very well to men and because it was a continuance of a friendship I was probably relating to them in exactly the same way as I was before, but suddenly because I didn't have a husband [it's] 'Well hang on a minute, isn't she being a bit over-friendly towards Fred?' or whoever, and I think that's how I view the threat bit.

(Rosa, divorced and in her late forties)

It's funny because some of the women, I don't know whether they see you as a threat, but you stop being invited. Some of the husbands, which I must admit did surprise me, actually see you as an easy target.

(Emily, divorced and in her late forties)

These women perceive being single as providing them with an unwelcome and distinct status, to women as unattached and looking for a man, and to men as available for their sexual advances. One woman also experienced anxieties from friends' husbands about the 'threat' they felt she posed to their couple relationship:

I also found other friends were very wary. They're married and their husbands will not let them go out with me in case I lead them astray. One friend actually said '[my partner] won't let me go out with you because you're single. He's afraid I might meet people.'

(Brenda, divorced and in her early forties)

So some women and men view women who are no longer partnered as a threat to the stability of their own couple relationship. Apart from the distress that this causes to the women involved, this challenges how some of the women judge their capability to attract a new partner. The negative views that these women express about their attractiveness are tied to their perceptions of their bodies. This is discussed in the following section.

Relationship dissolution, relationship formation, identity and sexual attractiveness

Relationship formation is dependent on the desire for a relationship, predilection to others and opportunity (Goldscheider and Waite 1986). Though by no means all the men and women interviewed say they want a future couple relationship, those who do reflect on the possibilities in terms of their perceptions of their attractiveness to others and their age. Even given the use of cosmetic surgery, for most, ageing is written on the body with increasing permanence and thus, as Turner (1995) contends, ageing compels individuals to be reflexive since the self is always subject to change through ageing. We begin by exploring issues concerning bodily attractiveness to others. Here we focus on female interviewees since none of the men interviewed mentioned the possibility that their ability to attract a partner would be affected by their 'unattractive' or ageing bodies. It is, of course, possible that many of the men are as concerned about their 'looks and embodied performances' as many of the male self-advertisers seem to be in Jagger's study (2005: 101). Alternatively, the men in our study might have given little, if any, thought to their embodied abilities to attract others, since, as Jagger reminds us, for younger men youth signifies 'virility, sexuality and physical strength' and for older men 'masculine identity remains realizable as cultural capital' (2005: 93). Nevertheless, none of the men interviewed raised these issues.

Having a 'sexual status' (Lee 2003: 95) is important and feminine identity means, among other things, 'being looked at and identified as objects of male desire' (Connell 1987). Morgan notes that '[w]omen have traditionally regarded (and have been taught to regard) their bodies, particularly if they are young, as beautiful and fertile, *as a locus of power* . . . ' (2003: 170, original emphasis). By no means all the women interviewed expressed the need to feel attractive to men:

> I don't need to feel I'm attractive to men to feel good.
> (Catherine, a former cohabitee in her late twenties)

However, many did comment on their perceptions of their abilities to attract a (male) partner:

> I've always been overweight, all my life and I followed the best diet you could ever get, a broken heart, so I lost three and a half stone in about six weeks because I just stopped eating, not consciously, I just didn't have an appetite at all which is unbelievable because I can always be on a consistent diet and be a persistent cheater all my life as far as food is concerned and I lost this weight which was miraculous and I think that helped me to live, I suppose because it made me feel – I still felt trapped, terrible, but that was the only positive thing that happened, that I suddenly lost all this weight and I guess people started to look at me more because I'd lost the weight.
> (Emma, a former cohabitee in her early thirties)

The loss of weight that followed the dissolution of her relationship is something Emma feels positive about. Some of the women who feel overweight explained why it is important for them to lose weight. Being thinner makes them feel more attractive and, they explain, when they *feel* they are attractive it gives them confidence to be noticed by others. Hence feeling attractive to others enables these women to feel happy, valued and good about themselves, which is crucial at any time and certainly after the dissolution of a relationship. Their focus is on etching social expectations of thinness on their physical bodies. 'Body regimes' are a particularly potent element in the process of identity formation (Featherstone 1991) and the pursuit of an idealized body weight or shape becomes attached to concern about diet (Bordo 1990). Bodily control and body management are usually needed if we are to acquire a desired body image. Where body management failed, relationship dissolution has succeeded and the consequence of Emma's 'broken heart' is the 'ability to live'. The entrapment and insecurity felt by women who perceive themselves to be overweight *and* rejected leads to negative perceptions of how others see them and how they see themselves:

> I think it's because I don't really respect myself. It's partly because I've put all my weight back on again, it's made me very insecure and you feel unlovable. The only time my mum was ever proud of me was when I lost six stone – it was, 'Oh, this is my daughter, she's just lost six stone', and that was my identity with my mum and that was the only thing she was ever really proud of . . . It's very strange – it also comes across in the media. I mean if you've forever got images of slim women – every film, it's always a skinny woman. It can be a fat man, but it's always a skinny woman and you feel that you're not entitled, you've got no right to be sexual or for other people to find you attractive because you're fat . . . I feel that no one wants to love you while you're fat and so I need the security of marriage to get round it . . . when you're fat you feel you're not entitled to have sexual feelings . . . At least there's other men that find me attractive whether I'm fat or not and sometimes I feel like that and I think well, because I forget that I've got fat again because I still feel thin sometimes and I forget and I think that to a lot of men it doesn't matter and they say . . . [that they find you attractive] for who you are, but then other times I'm very, very aware of it and I think, 'Oh no, they just laugh at me' or whatever.
>
> (Brenda, divorced and in her early forties)

Bodies can be seen as physical capital (Bourdieu 1984) since we can distinguish between those that assume responsibility and treat themselves as projects and those that do not. Shilling (1993) notes that bodies can be malleable projects since they can be moulded by individuals who are expected to assume responsibility for the way they look, and can be transformed by lifestyle choices. A 'good' body secures lifestyle rewards, which result from an enhanced appearance (Hepworth and Featherstone 1982). In the case of these women the reward is outward attractiveness to others and self-respect and self-esteem. However, Brenda has internalized a 'fragmented body image' (Balsamo 1998) where her 'flawed', 'overweight' body needs 'fixing'. Brenda's negative view of her body has resulted in her feeling unloved and, she declares, she needs 'the security of marriage to get round it'.

The 'gaze' of men accentuates this 'tyranny of slenderness' (Chernin 1983). As Bartky (quoted in Lloyd 1996: 91) suggests, the 'panoptical male consumer resides within the consciousness of most women', thus most women discipline their physical bodies with the male gaze in mind. The pressure can lead to anxiety in a world where individuals are increasingly preoccupied with promoting a particular self (Smart and Neale 1999). The body is a 'visible carrier of self-identity' (Giddens 1992: 31) and through the media we are encouraged to scrutinize physical appearance and make age classifications. Slenderness and youthfulness are much desired (Warde 1997). These women want their 'mirroring bodies' to reflect what is around them (Frank 1991), and media images of what it means to be a beautiful woman have been internalized. As Chapkiss writes '[t]he body beautiful is women's responsibility and authority. She will be valued and rewarded on the basis of how close she comes to embodying the ideal' (1986: 14). Many of the women interviewed are well aware that they are constantly judged by their appearance. Relationship dissolution has led them to reflect on their appearance and they have, to different degrees, inscribed social values on their bodies. Having a body that meets some of the social criteria for beauty enables them to feel good about themselves. However, those who feel they do not measure up to such standards feel bad about themselves. In this context, a major issue associated with beauty, attractiveness and attracting a partner is ageing.

In Western societies, age, like gender, is central to our understanding of who we are. We live in a culture that 'idealizes youth and the youthful body' (Jagger 2005: 95), thus couple relationships that break down after 'youth' has dwindled bring ageing into focus. Ageing compels individuals to be reflexive (Turner 1995), as does the dissolution of a couple relationship. Such critical issues and changes interact with each other, transforming perceptions of the self. Only a small minority of our female interviewees see ageing as positive:

> I mean when I was a teenager, I'd go out with anybody really and it was just testing out who you liked, who you didn't like. Now, you see, you know what you don't want much more than you would have done then.
>
> (Heather, widowed and in her early forties)

For many their feelings about getting older coupled with their feelings of being rejected by their previous partner have had a very negative effect on their self-perceptions:

> I look at myself, a middle aged, used, rejected woman ... I feel that, that he's sort of had the best years of my life ...
>
> (Samantha, separated and in her early forties)

Oh, it was very simple. He traded me in for a younger model is the simple answer to that one . . . I think to some extent it is the kind of male menopause, it's a horrible phrase, but I think he suddenly felt that there he was, forty-odd and hadn't really 'lived'. Obviously, seeing a younger, much younger, very attractive lady, he thought there was a chance to go and live I suppose. It's a scenario that you come across time and time again, so that's the simple answer to that.

(Isla, divorced and in her early fifties)

The tendency of men to seek younger women can lead to a devaluation of the self for older women, who, as a result, feel less valuable and decidedly rejected. However, discourses about mid-life crises can help explain such rejection:

I'd just passed forty and my wife sort of sees it that I had a breakdown, I got to forty and I had a breakdown sort of thing. I think that, I'm not saying it's totally untrue, but I think . . . when you're younger you still feel that there's a lot left for you. I think I got to the age of forty where I was thinking in ten years' time the kids will go and how are we going to sit and look at each other across the dinner table? . . . I'm forty now, I've lost it – She's [previous partner] [in her late twenties] and [has] got all the chances.

(Ian, separated and in his early forties)

I feel middle-aged. Probably a couple of years ago, a couple of years ago I was two years younger, a couple of years ago I would have felt quite young, but I don't now, I feel middle aged now definitely, the lower end of middle aged.

(Samantha, separated and in her early forties)

Middle age (Bytheway 2005) or 'middleescence' (Blaikie 1999) is ill-defined. The concept is fraught with ambiguity since individuals are considered to be out of the previous age category yet not yet into the next (Blaikie 1999: 184). This can give rise to a mid-life crisis in identity. Though it might be, as Lasch suggests, that the 'premature' fears of growing old associated with the mid-life crisis are an irrational panic reflecting the 'emergence of the narcissistic personality' in which the narcissist 'looks to others to validate his [*sic*] sense of self' (Lasch 1991: 210), the 'crisis' of middle age coupled with the 'crisis' of rejection can feel only too real.

Older people with a 'well-preserved' appearance and youthfulness are praised, and those who 'let themselves go' are often criticized. Ageing affects all aspects of identity. Though old age is a social construct and not solely a biological process, individuals experience *as real* the consequences of getting older. These are not just physical but also emotional and structural, and the meanings we give to these processes and evaluations of ageing reflect the beliefs and values found in our particular culture during a particular period of time (Blaikie 1999). Age is an extremely important aspect of our identity, in the way we see ourselves and in our perceptions of how others see us. Such perceptions move far beyond looks, into the realms of feelings of worth and self-worth. As we saw in Chapter 4, a key factor and source of diversity in relation to repartnering is age. In a society in which ageing is viewed as negative it is not surprising that those interviewed, in the main, see ageing as negative in general and in terms of their chances in relationships in particular. Thus ageing is a form of self-consciousness (Blaikie 1999: 65):

I've had some . . . well there's one or two mates that have come through the same problem and the first thing they've done when they separated is clubbing it and clubbing it every night. I must admit I don't feel comfortable. I'm probably getting older and that just ain't me. If I don't feel comfortable, why get into something?

(Eric, divorced and in his mid-thirties)

As you get older you've got to be realistic, you're not one of the lads anymore, although you still can be, but that probably ends when you're about thirty-five anyway and yet I'm not an old man, I'm just somewhere in-between and I don't really fit . . . it really doesn't worry me because as I say I know where I'm going and at the end of the day I've got a certain amount of financial independence anyway, so people can think what they like.

(Peter, widowed and in his mid-forties)

I still feel like I did when I was a teenager, but I walk into a pub and like all these people in here, they look like sort of eleven and twelve year olds to me.

(Kevin, a former cohabitee in his mid-twenties)

It's very difficult, I, I feel it's difficult for somebody my age, I mean, you know I don't care what anybody says about this emancipation and whatever. Somebody my age could not walk into a pub on their own without attracting the wrong sort of attention and giving out the wrong sort of vibes, you know I just don't think they could do it. I certainly couldn't. I would not feel comfortable with that sort of thing . . . it's a difficult sort of thing to do on your own, when you're a woman. I think it's probably different if you're a man. It's more acceptable if you're a man to sort of be on your own in a pub or, you know a restaurant . . . where do people my age go where they're not sort of sticking out like a sore thumb or where they're not giving out this message, you know, 'I'm here, come and get me' sort of thing.

(Samantha, separated and in her early forties)

As a form of self-consciousness ageing influences our notions of age-appropriate behaviour (Blaikie 1999: 65). Blaikie notes that '[l]eisure and consumption play an important symbolic role in affirming personal identities' (1999: 175). The interaction of perceptions about ageing identity and gender identity has resulted in interviewees denying themselves opportunities for leisure activities and socializing with others in places that they associate with 'the young'. Their feelings of being marginalized result in their wanting to find places frequented by people similar to themselves who want to do similar things. As we saw in Chapter 3, people who have experienced the dissolution of a previous intimate couple relationship often have difficulties meeting others due to their changed networks and social activities (Kalmijn and Bernasco 2001). As is palpable in the extracts above, the perception of age-appropriate leisure activities is just one of these difficulties; perceptions of age-appropriate behaviour relating to searching for a potential partner, evident in the next extracts, is another:

> Because at twenty-five you are expected to be sort of on the lookout for members of the opposite sex whereas at my age, you're not. Well, I don't think you are, which is silly really you know with the amount of divorces that go on, there are, there must be a lot of people my age who are in that position.
>
> (Samantha, separated and in her early forties)

> I feel I'm too old and that everybody at my age is settled down and sensible and sorted, so the option isn't there like it would have been ten or twelve years ago and now I don't really see anything now.
>
> (Claire, separated and in her mid-thirties)

So, for those seeking a future relationship, assessments of age-appropriate (and, for women, gender-appropriate) leisure activities together with estimations of age-appropriate relationship search behaviour serve to hamper – or at least alter – opportunities for finding a partner.

Specific bodily attributes are associated with ageing, for example loss of or greying hair and loss of skin elasticity. 'Premature' greying hair has an extremely negative effect on who Sandra feels she is:

> Sexually, I have no identity, absolutely nothing and this, white hair, grey hair, was a tremendous source of problem for me and I refused to dye it ... I had a big problem with trying to work out who I was as a woman ... because you see white-haired women in their seventies and eighties and you see – you don't very often see women in their forties with white hair and I was [in my mid-forties]. So I was youngish, I felt youngish, but I didn't look it and I had a real problem with how men saw me. Did they see me as an old woman or not?
>
> (Sandra, divorced and in her early fifties)

Women are accustomed to being judged on their looks (Jagger 2005) and their appearance affects their perceptions of themselves. Though hair and appearance affect men's social position, this is to a much lesser extent (Jackson 1992; Sullivan 2001). For women 'attractiveness serves as an indirect form of power . . . as long as the women's attractiveness lasts . . . [it] typically brings women more marital prospects and friendships, higher salaries, and higher school grades' (Weitz 2003: 133). As we saw above, our 'fragmented body images' (Balsamo 1998) lead us to focus on certain 'flawed' parts of our bodies. Hair is one of these focal points since it plays an important role in assessments of attractiveness (Weitz 2003: 131). Women are often acutely aware of cultural expectations regarding their hair, yet women do not simply acquiesce as they can resist the expectations (Weitz 2003: 147). Sandra feels that her greying hair 'spoils' her identity and indeed leads to a 'false identity' of being older. Yet she has chosen to resist by not dyeing her hair and she later suggests that in having a relationship with a younger man she has relieved her crisis in identity:

> I had got [a lover] who was a very young man . . . and [I] had a little amazing relationship with him sexually and so I did a lot of good talking with him which helped me no end to get a handle on what I was and who I was and help[ed] to shape my feelings.
>
> (Sandra, divorced and in her early fifties)

As we saw in Chapter 4, the age difference between partners in couples comprised of people who have previously experienced relationship dissolution deviate somewhat from the typical pattern of the male partner being, on average, two or three years older. In her study of self-advertising, Jagger found that only a minority of the women were prepared to advertise for the 'previously "forbidden fruit"' of younger men (2005: 102). However, a large proportion (13) of the women in our study spoke of relationships with younger men, though such relationships were not usually considered to be 'serious'. Although some of the women feel that their experience of this 'forbidden fruit' has been negative, most are very positive and thought it was an important boost to their sense of themselves as attractive. However, though having a relationship with a younger man can be a positive boost to a woman's identity it can also have the opposite effect:

> I wouldn't like . . . a young man. All these stretch marks, but I just wouldn't feel comfortable. I just wouldn't. It all stems back to your self-esteem, doesn't it? If I felt good about myself I probably would.
>
> (Brenda, divorced and in her early forties)

Even though ageing is something that happens to men and women alike (the alternative – early death – is much less palatable), as Jagger (2005) reminds us, ageing remains more problematic for women because their 'marketability' depends on their faithfulness to embodied norms of youthfulness. For Brenda the contrast between his youth and her age emphasizes how far she has strayed from those embodied norms.

Some women perceived there to be far less social acceptance and social recognition of their relationships with younger men than there is for relationships between older men and younger women:

> We'd have weekends away in hotels and so on and I don't think people actually could accept [it] . . . I don't think people ever saw us as a couple because the race bit and the age bit. I mean it's all very well seeing an older man with a younger woman, but I don't think it enter people's minds when we sat at breakfast that we had actually shared the same bed, although you did get looks.
>
> (Sandra, divorced and in her early fifties)

Though the relationships of older female celebrities, such as Gina Lollobrigida and Joan Collins, with younger men have gained much media attention (and, at times, ridicule) traditional perceptions of gendered age differentials in couple relationships largely remain:

> You can get into embarrassing situations then where you get like a sixteen- or seventeen-year-old girl come up to you and say, 'Would you like to buy me a drink?' and you think, you know, it's weird to admit to it, you think, 'I would but I'm too old for you, mentally I'm too old for you'.
>
> (Kevin, a former cohabitee in his mid-twenties)

For older men, the gaze of younger women testifies to their continued attractiveness. However, for Kevin there is an age difference that is beyond bounds but, unlike Brenda, whose concern is her ageing body, Kevin's ambivalence is associated with the intellectual differences that he perceives there to be between younger and older minds. He seems to be talking about 'wisdom', promoted as a consolation for getting older (Lasch 1991), a consolation that is often gendered. Kevin is one of a small minority of the men in our study who spoke of having relationships with younger women. Whether this is because it was not an issue given the 'ordinariness' of it is difficult to determine, but we can perhaps assume that this is the case.

Dating, identity and consumer society

As discussed above, being in a couple relationship, especially a heterosexual couple relationship, is seen by some to be necessary for identity to be complete, for perceptions of self and for acceptance in wider society. Contemporary society privileges couples (Jagger 2005: 89) and so it is no surprise that being single is seen by some as having a negative effect on identity:

> I think people do treat you differently. They see a wedding ring on your finger, they treat you differently. They treat you more as an adult.
>
> (Michelle, divorced and in her mid-twenties)

Though a significant number of single adults wish to meet a partner, 'the notion that "boy meets girl" with relative ease is, perhaps, an enduring aspect of social mythology' (Jagger 2005: 89). As we have seen, those whose previous relationships have broken down often have greater difficulties meeting others due to their changed networks and social activities (Kalmijn and Bernasco 2001). New partners are often found through leisure activities and social networks (Kalmijn and Flap 2001) and for those with dependent children the opportunities to go out may be even more limited (Wallerstein and Blakeslee 1989). Moreover, as we saw above, assessments of age-appropriate (and, for women, gender-appropriate) leisure activities, together with estimations of age-appropriate relationship search activities, serve to hamper (or at least alter) opportunities for finding a partner. Thus the probability of meeting someone by chance as one gets older diminishes since, as our interviewees suggest, opportunities for socializing that are open to younger people seem to close down as one gets older. Indeed, purposely going out and looking for a partner is viewed in negative terms:

> I just wanted love in my life and it wasn't happening and I know now that if you go out and you're looking, people know that you're looking and they think you're just a sad person and it wasn't until I started to be out and to be laughing and sort of not going out for that reason that I think people became attracted to me then. If I wasn't purposely out to pull somebody into finding this person who was going to fall in love with me that very night and make life better again and get back to normal, if I wasn't being like that then people would be attracted to me and talk to me like a normal person and want to be in my company.
>
> (Emma, a former cohabitee in her early thirties)

Our selected way(s) of meeting others – and, indeed, how we choose a partner (within constraints of course) – can be seen as a lifestyle choice, and such choices have implications for our identity. Like Giddens' (1992) example of food, how we meet others and who we end up with as a partner (if we end up with anyone) is a lifestyle choice (1992: 32) that is influenced by, and constructed through, various cultural discourses. With food, 'diet connects physical appearance, self-identity and sexuality in the context of social changes with which individuals struggle to cope' (Giddens 1992: 32). What an individual eats 'becomes a reflexively infused question of dietary selection' (Giddens 1992: 32) and, we suggest, this is the same with partnership decisions. This is evident in the interview extracts, especially in those concerning self-advertising, dating agencies and singles clubs as ways of meeting others. As we saw in Chapter 6, such approaches are perceived by some as *reducing the risk* of meeting an 'unsuitable' partner, but by others as *increasing the risk* of meeting someone inappropriate or even dangerous. As Jagger notes, 'the process of meeting a partner via advertising can be seen as a lifestyle decision' (2005: 90) and though Jagger suggests that it is 'no longer deemed solely the province of the "sad" or lonely, self advertising has become a well-established and socially acceptable procedure' (2005: 90), although we found only limited evidence for this in the comments made by the men and women interviewed. Responding to adverts is treated more blithely – many interviewees read the dating ads and many consider replying:

I've done it. It's in the personal column of a magazine we have – yesterday.
(Dorothy, divorced and in her mid-fifties)

I did meet some girls through [the local newspaper] and I had a strange panic thinking nobody wants me so I answered four different ads.
(Ray, divorced and in his early fifties)

However, one of the stigmatized aspects of identity associated with self-advertising is loneliness. This is evident in the concerns that the interviewees have about replying to adverts:

I mean I can't remember what attracted me to the advert, but it wouldn't be the people who describe themselves as lonely, searching for a soul mate. That would put me right off.
(Heather, widowed and in her early forties)

I do read them. You look at when people say 'lonely', you think, 'Well I don't want a lonely person'.
(Sylvia, divorced and in her late forties)

In consequence self-advertising is seen as acceptable by only a small minority of the men and women interviewed:

I did do this actually in London . . . in London, everyone does this. They've got so many papers and things.
(Maureen, separated, subsequently a cohabitee, and in her early fifties)

Definitely, I'd advertise . . . I would feel no problems at all about it but I would still have a range of defensive postures . . . it might be a reasonable way of meeting people and not committing yourself to anything. The answer therefore is an emphatic yes but whether I will or not, I don't know.

(Arthur, divorced and in his early sixties)

. . . I put it in the envelope, walked up the road and put it in a letterbox and thought, 'Oh shit . . . ' it dropped out of your hand you know. Gulp. And then I thought, 'What the hell, if I get any replies I don't have to answer. If I don't then what the hell it cost me whatever it was.' I'd never done it like that before and I've never done it since and – I don't know. I mean that was the first and only time that I'd ever done anything that I call compulsive.

(Ken, divorced and in his early fifties)

I don't really have a problem with it. I actually think that if that would work then that's OK . . . If it were a way to meet somebody else then I find that perfectly acceptable. It is true however that I wouldn't go around owning up to having done that simply because of the circle that I move in. I wouldn't have a problem with anybody at work. I wouldn't own up to my political circle because that would cast [me] out . . . and that would not be something that I would want.

(Duncan, separated and in his mid-thirties)

Thus, though sometimes acceptable to individuals, revealing self-advertising to significant others can seem intolerable.

Goffman (1969) notes how we engage in measures of 'information control' in such situations, with our mission being to keep 'destructive information' away from the audience. Thus self-advertising is somehow characterized as shameful if revealed to significant others since it threatens the 'performance of a positive identity' (Goffman 1969: 123). But if a couple relationship is sought, but is not forthcoming, why do some interviewees choose to 'play the "waiting game"' (Jagger 2005: 101)?

I want to, but it's something I've not really tried to be honest and thinking about why I wouldn't; subconsciously in your mind it's not the 'normal', is not the right word, nor is 'right', but it's not the usual way of meeting people. Maybe it's that that's in your mind that you think that you don't meet people like this.

(Claire, separated and in her mid-thirties)

Relationship dissolution plunges us into a new set of circumstances, but the way we behave in these new circumstances is based on habit and what is customary; what we do is based on what we know. Habit and custom are stockpiled in habitus and for many of the men and women interviewed meeting potential partners other than by chance is not the 'norm'; it is associated with desperation and linked to being at the lowest point:

> No I don't think so, I wouldn't advertise, me, and I don't think I would ever – I don't think I would, I would have to have a peculiarly ghastly day to get that desperate I think.
>
> (Sarah, divorced and in her mid-forties)
>
> No, the phrase that comes to mind is 'I'm not that desperate'.
>
> (Kieran, divorced and in his late forties)
>
> No I haven't, I've never done that. I mean I've thought about it – I mean I'm trying to be honest, yes I've probably thought about it in bleaker moments but not recently – like when you think there's not much hope or you know you just think, I don't know, nobody loves me, nobody cares and you wonder how you're ever going to meet someone you like . . . I went through a crisis and I remember thinking that I couldn't meet anybody and I actually considered advertising but it's like selecting a human product really.
>
> (Colin, a former cohabitee in his mid-thirties)
>
> I haven't got to the syndrome yet where I'm actually advertising in the papers and like talking to anybody – anybody who will go out with me.
>
> (Rob, a former cohabitee in his mid-thirties)
>
> I always think that's pretty desperate actually. In fact I met somebody, a girl, and she said she's done that . . . and she's a really attractive girl, very attractive and you just would not think that she would have to do anything like that.
>
> (Sharon, divorced and in her late thirties)

The stereotype of the sad and lonely self-advertiser seems to be deep-rooted in many of those interviewed, however it is somewhat antediluvian. A range of people self-advertise and a growing number meet their partners via the Internet (France 2002, cited in Jagger 2005). Sautter et al.'s (2006) study in the US reveals that those who are most likely to be online in general are younger, richer, have more education, are not disabled, are more likely to live in a suburb or a city, and are more likely to be white. Though there are certainly gaps along demographic lines in Internet usage (Sautter et al. 2006), the potential range of self-advertisers in all media is considerable. In newspapers, more men than women self-advertise (Jagger 1998) and male self-advertisers are more likely to be relatively young (Jagger 2005). Coupland (1996) contends that these ways of meeting others in a high modern mass-mediated society are 'relationally efficient' in lives that are highly work-centred and time-pressured.

Identity, intimacy, the self and future couple relationships

In this chapter we have explored the concept of identity in relation to perceptions of changing selves and changes in lifestyle associated with couple relationship transitions. The women and men interviewed discuss their identities and lifestyles relative to the changes that have occurred in their lives and how their everyday lives have changed as a result. Relationship dissolution can seriously affect notions of who we are. Rejection can lead to a feeling of deficiency in the person who has been rejected, which can have serious consequences for self-esteem. The perception of being stigmatized for being single compounded by, for some, being a lone parent can lead to social isolation and a feeling of being 'outside the norm'. Women without partners feel they are seen as a threat to the stability of couple relationships, and lone parents feel that their identities are compromised by their single status. Thus the harmful effects of their changes in lifestyle on their identities include a sense of not belonging and a feeling of having a stigmatized distinctiveness. Envy of how others integrate in everyday situations can follow. Loneliness is an additional stigmatized aspect of being single and alone. Even though all the men and women interviewed are now single again, and some have been so for a long time, their comments on the kinds of people who self-advertise reveal how ingrained in the habitus are the ideas and attitudes prevalent in a society that favours couples. Their views of others in the same position as they are in seem to veer towards popular negative perceptions, and this says something about how they perceive other people view them. How we view ourselves can be at odds with how others view us, and how we view others can be at odds with how they see themselves. This points to the fragmented nature of identity. Our identities are always in process, they are never finished, and are constantly moving in relation to lifestyle changes, changing perceptions and shifting trends. Relationship dissolution has a significant effect on both lifestyle and identity, even though what we see as our 'authentic self' may not have changed (though we may feel that it has been liberated). So, notwithstanding Butler's notion of the 'performative' self, our interviewees experience their identities as *performances*, with a central, 'authentic', inner identity performing the drama. Although, for a minority, a couple relationship is a means of answering a 'lack' of something in the self, for many a positive consequence for identity of relationship dissolution is the finding, or liberation, of that 'authentic' self. Since the self is so important in more individualized couple relationships it is no surprise that feelings of liberation of the self involve cutting bonds with powerful others. Although men and women alike voice this need, more of the women interviewed express this view. This is not unexpected given the gendered dynamics of power within heterosexual couple relationships.

A lifestyle of living alone and managing alone, even if not chosen, can have an extremely positive effect on one's sense of self. Dependence is fast becoming a derogatory term, and being independent has become a source of pride. This can have a positive effect on identity. In consequence, worries about the loss of newfound independence are a reason for not wishing to embark on a co-resident intimate couple relationship. On the other hand, being loved and wanted is an important part of identity since it not only functions as an insignia of our worth to others but also functions as a sign of a valued position in society. Wishing to mirror the norms of society is a norm in itself, and wishing to be in a partnership reflects the desire to 'mirror' the surroundings in which couple (usually heterosexual) relationships are the normative expectation. Although by no means all the men and women interviewed say that they want a new couple relationship, those who do reflect on the possibilities in terms of their perceptions of their bodily attractiveness. Since relationship dissolution often occurred when 'youthfulness had dwindled', it has had a serious effect on the identities of those interviewed (especially the women) as feelings of rejection interacted with their perceptions of their own attractiveness. The body is a carrier of identity (Giddens 1991) and since we may wish to plunge ourselves into searching for a new partner after relationship dissolution, we are led to reflect on our bodily appearance. Although 'body regimes' (Featherstone 1991) are a standard part of the self-reflective lives that most of us live, perhaps at such 'fateful moments' (Giddens 1992) as relationship dissolution, body regimes become an important coping mechanism. Body regimes associated with diet and exercise may help us to cope with the negative effects that relationship dissolution can have, since having a body that meets some of the social criteria for beauty and youthfulness may enable us to feel good about ourselves. However, for those seeking a couple relationship, assessments of age-appropriate (and, for women, gender-appropriate) leisure activities, together with assumptions about age-appropriate relationship search activities, serve to restrict, or at least alter, opportunities for finding a partner.

Coming back to Bauman, our identities are never complete since our sense of ourselves is bound up with the choices that we make (Bauman 2000a), and our identities and lifestyles are affected by social values which lend acceptability and prestige to particular identities associated with appropriate behaviour, suitable body management and beauty, and apposite intimate relationships.

8
The Formerly Partnered and Repartnering in Contemporary Britain

In this book we have examined theoretical and substantive literature relating to intimate couple relationships, the formerly partnered and repartnering, and have explored the lives and future relationship plans of formerly partnered people in contemporary Britain. In this final chapter we draw on material from the preceding chapters to provide, in a more concise form, an account of some of the key themes and issues that have emerged about and from the lived experiences and perspectives on repartnering of formerly partnered people, and consider the implications of insights arising from these for our understanding of couple relationships and repartnering in contemporary Britain. We start with some essential information about the formerly partnered population in Britain and about formerly partnered people's repartnering orientations and behaviour.

The formerly partnered population: characteristics, orientations and behaviour

Our results in Chapter 4 led us to estimate that, in April 1996, there were more than 3.25 million formerly partnered people in their mid-fifties or younger living in private households in Britain.[1] The proportion of the population who are formerly partnered subsequently appears to have grown and the number of people who have *ever* been a formerly partnered person is approximately twice as high.

About half of formerly partnered people under 60 have had a sexual partner (or partners) in the last month, and nearly a third have a regular, non-resident intimate partner. Being formerly partnered is frequently a relatively transitory experience, since more than a third of people who were formerly partnered in April 1996 had repartnered within five years. In fact, the formerly partnered, especially men, form (new) relationships more quickly than single people of the same age. However, not all sub-groups within the formerly partnered population repartner at the same rate or to the same extent, and formerly partnered people's orientations towards repartnering are diverse, with some not wanting a new relationship in the foreseeable future, a substantial minority being ambivalent and/or not actively seeking a new relationship, and those who would like a new relationship having split preferences for resident and non-resident couple relationships (see Chapter 5). Of course, orientations can shift and develop over time in response to events, and some, but by no means all, of those favouring a relationship with a partner who lives elsewhere see such an arrangement as potentially being a first step.

It should be evident that the formerly partnered are not a homogeneous category, and we move on to consider some potential sources of variability within the formerly partnered population, starting with a key distinction that has as yet received a limited amount of research attention: the distinction between the formerly married and former cohabitees.

Former cohabitees

Since between a quarter and a third of formerly partnered people aged under 60 are former cohabitees, and the number of former cohabitees in the population appears to be growing, former cohabitees constitute an important sub-group of the formerly partnered population. Furthermore, the distinction between cohabitation and (legal) marriage has been the focus of a considerable amount of academic research and public debate in recent years. However, neither of these points implies that former cohabitees are necessarily distinctive relative to the formerly married, other than in some important and perhaps predictable ways. Former cohabitees are (on average) markedly younger than the formerly married, for the most part being under 40, and this key difference can in itself explain other superficial (bivariate) differences, which might otherwise be interpreted as reflecting, say, underlying attitudinal differences between the two sub-groups.[2] Former cohabitees are also somewhat more likely to be men than are formerly married people, and (except for older women) less likely to be living with dependent children. In addition, past research has identified differences (but also some similarities in the case of women[3]) between the economic circumstances of formerly married and formerly cohabiting parents; our research suggests a stronger (negative) effect of dependent children on the likelihood of paid work for formerly cohabiting women than for formerly married women.

While former cohabitees have a relatively high repartnering rate, once age has been taken into account it is similar to that for formerly married people. However, the repartnering rate for formerly cohabiting women with dependent children is lower than that for formerly married women with dependent children. Other research has suggested that former cohabitees are less likely to reunite with a former partner.[4] People with past experience of cohabitation, including former cohabitees, are disproportionately unlikely to marry as opposed to cohabiting if they repartner, and former cohabitees are disproportionately likely to enter into new, cohabiting relationships that dissolve within a relatively short period of time, as are (to a lesser extent) other people with past experience of cohabitation. As former cohabitees are generally relatively young, they are most likely to form new relationships with single people, but, once age has been taken into account, they are disproportionately likely to repartner other former cohabitees.

Taking account of age, former cohabitees do not differ from formerly married people in their likelihood of having had a sexual partner in the last month. However, they are markedly less likely to have regular, non-resident partners. Perhaps surprisingly, given their tendency to cohabit with rather than marry a new partner, former cohabitees do not seem to have particularly distinctive partnership orientations. Since this was the case in both our quantitative and qualitative analyses, we should not ignore this result. More generally, the lack of distinctiveness of former cohabitees within our qualitative analyses is striking; occasionally there are possible echoes of the fact that the former cohabitees form a younger group, but otherwise there is very little evidence that they differ from our formerly married interviewees.

To summarize, former cohabitees (unsurprisingly) appear to have a disproportionate affinity with cohabitation and with other cohabitees, and to be somewhat more hesitant than the formerly married to enter (or re-enter) couple relationships, if one includes non-resident ones. However, for the most part, former cohabitees do not seem to differ from other formerly partnered people of a similar age. In Chapter 3, literature hypothesizing a lower level of adherence among cohabiting people to a moral-normative component of commitment (Lewis 2001) to co-resident relationships was referred to. Although it may be the case that a sub-group of former cohabitees exists who are more willing to enter co-residential relationships 'lightly', it is equally plausible that such a sub-group exists among the formerly married. It is also equally plausible that another sub-group of former cohabitees are very cautious about moving in with a partner, and this may also be true of a sub-group of the formerly married. While research suggests that a higher proportion of former cohabitees may be positively oriented to 'pure relationships', we suggest that former cohabitees (like cohabitees) are probably too heterogeneous for one to make legitimate simple generalizations about them. Furthermore, the greater emphasis placed by formerly partnered people in general on commitment to a partner and commitment to a relationship than on legal marriage when discussing future relationships (see Chapter 5), together with the important role played by cohabitation in repartnering among formerly married people, should make one cautious about interpreting cohabitation among the formerly partnered as an indicator of a lack of belief in all forms of commitment. It is also worth remembering that the results of comparisons between cohabitation and marriage are likely to reflect in part the views or behaviour of the minority of people who still have a particular 'moral' or cultural attachment to marriage as an institution.

Age and ageing

It is evident that age is a crucial source of variation between the lives of formerly partnered people. While we wish to avoid ageist stereotypes that suggest that older people have no sexual desires or are physically unattractive and undesirable (for an overview, see Pointon 1997), results presented in Chapter 4 suggest that sexual activity diminishes markedly with rising age (e.g. formerly partnered people under 30 are nearly three times as likely to have had a sexual partner in the last month than are those in their fifties), and the gradient in the repartnering rate is even steeper. Older formerly partnered people may have higher expectations of potential partners, but often perceive the opportunities to repartner as being limited. Furthermore, social and leisure activities which might provide repartnering opportunities can be constrained by perceptions of age-appropriate behaviour. Ageing and 'rejection' by their previous partner can have a mutually reinforcing negative effect on self-identity and self-esteem. Visible ageing and concerns about bodily attractiveness affect the identities and repartnering behaviour of some formerly partnered women, although improving one's sense of physical self-worth via 'body regimes' can have a positive effect on an important aspect of identity (see Chapter 7).

A substantial number of formerly partnered women break with tradition by having (non-resident) relationships with younger men. Furthermore, where formerly married women form new, co-resident relationships with single (never married) men, the men are on average a number of years younger, and in 1 in 10 heterosexual couples involving a formerly partnered person the female partner is five or more years older (see Chapter 4). For formerly partnered women who have non-resident relationships with younger men, doing so can have a positive effect on their sense of self and their feelings about their own physical attractiveness; however, for some, the presence of a younger partner may make them self-consciousness about physical ageing (see Chapter 7).

Legacies of earlier relationships

While past relationship experiences vary in relevance among different individuals, they have negative implications for many formerly partnered people. Unsurprisingly, they may cause disillusionment about relationships, or heighten formerly partnered people's awareness of the risks attached to intimate relationships (see Chapter 7). Alternatively, they may act as a constraint on 'moving on' by tying an individual to the past, whether materially, emotionally, via children or by an ongoing desire for reconciliation (see Chapter 5). Formerly partnered people's attitudes and responses to their past relationship experiences are diverse. Some are acutely aware of the scope for relationships to damage their self-esteem and sense of self, whereas others are concerned about the risks in relation to material circumstances (see Chapters 5 and 6). Some have had a sense of their own ability to have a relationship that 'works' undermined; others are sceptical about the likelihood of finding a partner with whom they can have a satisfactory relationship (see Chapter 6).

Being a widowed person may mean that there are strong ties to the past. However, widows and widowers who view their past relationship and partner positively may find it easier than other formerly married people to visualize a 'good' future relationship, although they may be less inclined to repartner or may envisage a future partner and relationship as being different from (and perhaps not on a par with) the one ended by their partner's death (see Chapter 5).

The extent to which the typology of repartnering orientations developed in Chapter 5 appears linked to the effect of past relationships is striking. In some cases past relationships temporarily or permanently remove any inclination towards repartnering (or lead to a passive approach to repartnering), and in many other cases they shape people's repartnering orientations and behaviour by burdening them with unfinished business, or by inducing caution among the formerly partnered about the implications of forming co-resident relationships, or by acting as a barrier to their entering such a relationship. In only one of the seven categories of the typology are past relationships clearly 'in the past', though a process of disengagement from or management of past relationship issues is evident in other categories. Overall, while past relationships are not of universal salience among the formerly partnered, they typically have some form and degree of importance. Often the end of a relationship has affected a formerly partnered individual's identity, and it is to the concept of identity that we turn next.

Identity/identities

In Chapter 7 we noted that people do not have fixed identities based on individual characteristics. Rather, identity is a process that is formed within social and cultural contexts. As with all people, formerly partnered people's identities are always in a state of flux. However, stability is an important aspect of identity and consequently relationship breakdown can have important implications for an individual's sense of self. While our research seems to support studies finding that the stigma of divorce has declined in contemporary Britain (see Chapters 4 and 5), it also seems to corroborate research reporting that 'being alone' (that is, without a partner) in contemporary society, and perhaps especially being seen as 'lonely', is potentially problematic (see Chapters 4 and 7). For many formerly partnered people, the process of identification as a formerly partnered person may be made difficult by a sense of being 'other' (that is, of not belonging), or of 'stigmatized distinctiveness', or of being a threat. On the other hand, the development, or rediscovery, of an independent, 'authentic' self-identity may consolidate a formerly partnered person's sense of self, thus rendering repartnering (especially co-residential repartnering) unattractive. For example, living alone and managing alone can have an extremely positive effect on an individual's sense of self. Then again, as for most of us, for many formerly partnered people being loved is a source of a (positive) facet of self-identity (which is an ingrained part of their habitus) (see Chapter 7), and ideals of romantic love and lifelong partnership may motivate repartnering behaviour (see Chapter 6). Thus a paradox of contemporary intimate relationships as perceived by many formerly partnered people is that such relationships may offer something positive to their sense of self while at the same time appearing inconsistent with other aspects of identity and lifestyle.

For some formerly partnered people, busy lives resulting from what might be regarded as other aspects of hybridized self-identity (e.g. the presence of dependent children or involvement in paid work; see Chapter 5) constrain the scope for repartnering, and for other formerly partnered people (perhaps especially women) the development of an independent self-identity (perhaps grounded in economic independence) means that there is no pressure, or 'need', to repartner. Thus some formerly partnered people, without rejecting the idea of a future relationship, at least temporarily set the idea of couple relationships (including non-resident ones) aside. However, setting aside intimate couple relationships, or viewing them as too risky to contemplate, is not the same as seeing them as redundant and perceiving the tradition of a lifelong partnership to be an outmoded source of self-identity in contemporary Britain. There is little evidence that anything other than a small minority of formerly partnered people see a life based on friendship, family and work-related networks as being inherently preferable to a life involving an intimate partner, although such a preference may be more prevalent among other groups of people in contemporary Britain (defined in terms of age, region, education, etc.).

'Risk', rationality and emotions

Both the legacies of earlier relationships (see Chapters 5 and 6) and a fear of compromising any positive influences on their current identity or lifestyle heighten formerly partnered people's perceptions of the risks attached to repartnering. In some cases formerly partnered people favour or are engaged in non-resident relationships that may provide the benefits of an intimate relationship without constituting as great a perceived risk as living with a partner. However, while some formerly partnered people may have adopted 'living apart together' relationships as a new ideal (and such relationships conceivably come closer to 'pure relationships' since they may be easier to end at will) in many cases a non-resident relationship seems to represent a compromise that falls short of the kind of relationship that formerly partnered people, influenced by traditional ideals and contemporary high expectations, would prefer.

Engaging in 'compromise' relationships, like other aspects of formerly partnered people's decision-making and behaviour, can be interpreted as demonstrating a degree of rationality within decisions made as part of an individual's 'reflexive project of self' (see the discussion of Giddens' work in Chapter 3). However, while evaluating 'risks' and balancing them against the benefits of a relationship may sometimes be 'rational', such evaluations also take place in the context of various constraints and of emotions (see Chapter 6). 'Pure relationships' that are seen as easier to end, while bringing benefits to a person if they want to leave, may also be perceived 'non-reflexively and pre-consciously' as unappealing or second-best, whereas seemingly lifelong partnerships based on romantic love may seem more satisfactory, even though they may seem to formerly partnered people to be less likely to be attainable. Perceptions of 'commitment' (see Chapters 3, 5 and 6) are clearly of relevance (and the concept is discussed below), although we note that 'commitment' is open to contrasting definitions, and definitions may vary among formerly partnered people, and also between formerly partnered people and academic and social commentators.

Commitment

In Chapter 3 we discussed literature relating to the concept of commitment, and the importance of the idea of commitment to formerly partnered people themselves is evident from our analyses in Chapters 5 and 6. However, notwithstanding other authors' attempts to unpack the term (e.g. Johnson, Lewis), or to define it in a way that is specific to their argument (e.g. Giddens), considerable ambiguity remains in the meaning attached to the term.

It is evident from Chapters 5, 6 and 7 that many formerly partnered people are cautious about entering new relationships that would involve a legal or material commitment, because of the implications of such a formal or *de facto* obligation should 'things go wrong'. It also seems evident that an abstract 'moral' or 'cultural' commitment to marriage as an 'institution' is rare among formerly partnered people; support for the idea of commitment seems to relate to a specific partner and relationship, and perhaps also to a cultural notion of how contemporary (individualised) relationships should be.

If we move on to focus on commitment viewed at the level of a specific (albeit hypothetical) relationship, the meaning of the term retains a normative element. For the formerly partnered people in our study, commitment to carry on with a relationship seems to be an appropriate and necessary implication of 'love', intimacy and respect for one's partner as an individual, and they would prefer to have a partner who subscribed to this idea of commitment (and whose 'love' and respect for them were not so volatile as to be likely to evaporate in the foreseeable future). This notion of commitment, which bears some resemblance to the 'attraction component', but perhaps also includes features of a weak version of the moral-normative component of the broader concept of commitment, as discussed in Chapter 3, sets up what is required of a relationship for 'commitment' to become a reasonable and legitimate expectation.

Traditional relationships, 'pure relationships', culture and agency

The idea of commitment outlined above may be as much or more of an ideal than a normative expectation, since a formerly partnered person may be sceptical about whether they will receive that type of commitment, or even find a relationship in which they would want it to occur. However, it is indicative of the way in which the formerly partnered (like people in general) appear to have adapted traditional ideas about couple relationships rather than wholly abandoning them (see the discussion of Gross's work in Chapter 3). The idea of finding a lifelong relationship may not be squeezed out in the contemporary world in which 'pure relationships' are said to prevail. It appears from our research that 'important' couple relationships are generally seen, at their conception, as being lifelong, whereas 'pure relationships' (although not labelled as such) may be perceived as risky, or as a rather unsatisfactory compromise, or as a stepping stone, or as best suited to an earlier stage of the life course, or as only appropriate for couples without dependent children. However, 'pure relationships' can also be seen as guarding against entrapment. Couple relationships change over time, and it might be suggested that seeing one's relationship as a 'pure relationship' is more acceptable when one wants to leave it, but that one sees it as a lifelong relationship when things are going well or when one wants a partner to stay. Although 'pure relationships' can act as an important source of (positive) self-identity, a reflexive individual who has experienced the end of a number of couple relationships may feel that they have been engaged in a 'destructive project of self' (see the discussion of Giddens' work in Chapter 3).

Many of our formerly partnered interviewees appear to be reflexive in their decision-making and some are actively engaged in the construction of 'biographies of self', in which independence and control over their own lives are important tools for establishing their identity and a secure sense of self. However, even individuals of this sort may on occasions be curiously reluctant to approach their repartnering goals in an active, pragmatic way.

More precisely, cultural stereotypes relating to approaches to repartnering which are based on self-advertisement act as a barrier to some formerly partnered people using such approaches (see Chapters 5 and 7), even though formerly partnered people often comment on the limitations of their social lives and of more conventional mechanisms as a source of partners. In short, some formerly married people feel that they would be labelling themselves as 'lonely and desperate' and would only meet people whom they would see as similarly undesirable.

This is not, however, the only reason for rejecting approaches to repartnering such as self-advertising. Issues of risk (see Chapter 6) and perceived inefficiency (see Chapter 5) also deter some formerly partnered people. Furthermore, notwithstanding the views of Giddens and Bauman regarding the pervasiveness of consumerism in contemporary society (see Chapter 3), some formerly partnered people are resistant to the idea of acting as consumers selecting a form of commodity. Other formerly partnered people are more explicit about favouring a 'natural' approach to finding a partner (see Chapter 5), based on opportunities occurring within their current, day-to-day lives. (Some favour a compromise, consisting of the indirect development of opportunities via changes within their social lives.)

Favouring a seemingly 'natural' approach to finding a partner would seem to be giving more weight to tradition than to rationality, and to indicate a greater degree of comfort with longstanding notions of romantic love than with the idea of 'shopping for a partner'. Perhaps for some, unfamiliar, active approaches seem too risky. Once again, the cultural changes that have occurred regarding intimate relationships do not appear to have completely driven out traditional ideas, although they may have been adopted in a revised format.

Gender

While both formerly partnered women's and men's identities have sometimes been damaged by a past relationship or relationships (see Chapters 5, 6 and 7), women appear more likely to be wary of the perceived risks of a new relationship. In addition, formerly partnered women more frequently value the merits of a non-resident relationship (e.g. independence and space), and are perhaps more sceptical about the likelihood of finding a partner and relationship that would meet their expectations. Arguably, such gender differences reflect, to a substantial extent, the internal inequalities of traditional marriage and different levels of acceptance of, and engagement with, the cultural changes of recent decades (relating to intimate couple relationships). Formerly partnered women are also markedly more likely than men to be living with dependent children, and the presence of young children reduces their chances of repartnering (at least temporarily) for reasons that we have discussed in an earlier paper (see Chapter 4, and Lampard and

Peggs 1999). Turning our attention from relationships to partners, formerly partnered women appear to be more likely to want a different, 'new' type of male partner. Those that do often appear to want a man with a number of characteristics traditionally seen as 'feminine', and one who complements their own independent sense of self (see Chapter 5).

Diversity, heterogeneity and marginality

The impact of characteristics such as age, gender and parental status inevitably leads to a degree of heterogeneity in the repartnering orientations and repartnering behaviour of formerly partnered people. Furthermore, while relationship histories are very frequently of relevance to formerly partnered people's lives, the ways in which they affect them are relatively diverse. However, notwithstanding the diversity of formerly partnered people's characteristics and relationship histories, part of the variety in broad partnership orientations among the formerly partnered is provided by quite small groups of individuals who favour celibate or 'promiscuous' lifestyles, and a larger minority who favour non-resident relationships in the medium term or longer (see Chapter 4). Nearly three-quarters of formerly partnered people would like to be living with a partner in five years' time.

The apparent homogeneity of many formerly partnered people's broad orientations to repartnering is, however, misleading. For a start, opportunities to repartner vary markedly between different formerly partnered people according to their particular circumstances (see Chapters 3, 4 and 5). More specifically, some formerly partnered people feel the prospects of finding a suitable partner to be so limited that it is not worth trying. Others do not want to expose themselves to any risks accompanying repartnering, even if they would prefer to be with a partner, or do not feel that an active approach to repartnering is appropriate.

While our empirical research provides less scope for examining the self in process than studies involving repeated interviews (see Chapter 4), the potentially dynamic nature of identity post-separation is evident, for example, from the typology of repartnering orientations developed in Chapter 5. Variations in the extent and nature of changes in the self after separation constitute an important form of heterogeneity among the formerly partnered. Some formerly partnered people whose selves have been 'damaged' by the end of a relationship go on to recover or develop selves that are acceptable to them.

The constraints on opportunities to repartner experienced by many formerly partnered people highlight one way in which they remain marginal in contemporary Britain: the changes relating to intimate relationships that have taken place do not seem to have been accompanied (yet) by a restructuring of social lives that facilitates couple relationship formation at any stage of the life course. Beyond a certain age society still appears to be primarily 'heterosexual couple-based', and the awkwardness that many formerly partnered people feel about being without a partner no doubt reflects this. Britain does not seem to be, or to incorporate, a 'world of the formerly partnered' (see the discussion of Hunt's work in Chapter 4). Once again, however, a sense of social, cultural or economic marginality is not experienced by all formerly partnered people.

A final note on formerly partnered people's accounts of their lives

We noted in Chapter 2 that in-depth interviews such as those that we carried out can take the form of 'presentations of self', consciously (and pre-consciously) shaped by interviewees. Viewed in these terms, our interviews frequently appear to be stories of a lost or damaged identity, or of an identity in limbo, or of a new or recovered identity. Our research has only begun to examine the complexity of the lives and future relationship plans of formerly partnered people. Notwithstanding recurring themes in formerly partnered people's lives, it is not easy to make credible generalizations about them as a group. Nevertheless, we can conclude that relationship dissolution and its aftermath constitute an extremely distressing experience for many people, including any children involved as well as the adults. However, the possibilities for enrichment - not least through the opportunity to establish or re-establish an 'authentic' sense of self - should not be overlooked.

Notes

Chapter 1

1. In this book we use pseudonyms rather than our interviewees' actual names.

Chapter 2

1. The project title was 'The Remarriage Process: Structural and Individual Perspectives', although the intention was to incorporate former cohabitees in the research, alongside divorced, separated and widowed people. Our use of the term 'repartnering' when discussing the project is intended to emphasize the absence of a restriction to people who have been legally married, and also the absence of a restriction to (legal) remarriage.
2. Kay carried out 60 interviews as planned, and Richard carried out 21.
3. As award holder, and thus having specified the number of interviews in the research proposal to the ESRC, Richard felt obliged to ensure that this sample size was achieved, but this may not have been the most constructive approach.
4. Notwithstanding his research proposal's original specifications, Richard acknowledges that some of the most interesting material was provided by male interviewees and interviewees aged over 45, and is indebted to Kay and others for their contributions to the broadening of the sample's target population.
5. The number of former cohabitees in the sample would appear substantially greater if the category were redefined with reference to an individual's last co-residential relationship, rather than being defined as the category of people who have cohabited but who have never been married. Furthermore, in addition to the six widowed people already mentioned, another formerly legally married interviewee had been widowed before their last co-residential relationship. Such ambiguities illustrate the potential complexity of contemporary relationship histories.
6. Our point of comparison, the 1991 Census, does not allow former cohabitees to be identified.
7. The BSA surveys do not allow former cohabitees to be identified.
8. Pole and Lampard (2001: 41–2) contains a further discussion of sampling and recruitment within our study.
9. More recently, following a consultancy on qualitative research resources, the ESRC commissioned a consultancy on the feasibility of a major qualitative longitudinal study (Holland et al. 2004), and such a study is due to start in 2007.

Chapter 3

1. At the time of writing, the media are reporting government proposals to reform the family justice system to allow children to express their views to the judge or magistrate presiding in a divorce case (Dyer 2006).

217

2. In 'pure' no fault divorce the courts have little interest in the reasons for divorce since these are a private matter between the partners concerned. See Lewis (2001).
3. Though, Bauman adds, 'dependency, now fast becoming a derogatory term, is what moral responsibility for the other is all about' (2003: 90).
4. Lewis's schema is summarized in Smart (2005).

Chapter 4

1. Allan and Crow (2001: 121) note that most divorces in England and Wales in 1991 involved children aged under 16.
2. See Amato (2000) for a review.
3. See the review by Coleman et al. (2000).
4. See Wallerstein and Kelly (1990: 319).
5. US research (McManus and DiPrete 2001; cited in Avellar and Smock 2005) highlights how both support payments from men to their children and ex-spouses and also the diversity of female partners' contributions to pre-separation income can lead to heterogeneous changes for men.
6. A means-tested benefit paid to people without paid employment.
7. For a policy-oriented discussion of the contributions to women's resources after separation of earnings from employment, benefits and maintenance from ex-partners, see Maclean (1991).
8. Flowerdew et al. (1999) analysed the residential mobility of divorced people during the year preceding the 1991 Census.
9. For a discussion drawing on individual experiences of the housing consequences of relationship breakdown, see Bull (1993).
10. Results relating to the contemporary balance of importance of these explanations vary (Cheung 1998, Hope et al. 1999: 386).
11. GHQ is a measure of psychological well-being.
12. For an overview of marital breakdown and health, see McAllister (1995).
13. For discussions of experiences of mediation and of contact with the Child Support Agency, see Smart and Neale (1999) and Bradshaw et al. (1999).
14. Their data came from a random sample of over 1,500 ever divorced people.
15. Some of these former cohabitees may have been married at an earlier stage, and a substantial number had repartnered and separated during the ten-year period. In addition, the difference between them and other formerly married lone parents was somewhat less than the difference between them and lone parents who had not lived with a partner.
16. A more sophisticated analysis using BLPC data demonstrated that currently having two or more dependent children under five significantly reduced lone parents' repartnering rate (Finlayson et al. 2000: 53).
17. Their analysis did not control for social class, hence the two results may echo the same underlying factor(s).
18. The specifics of the analyses of BLPC data also imply that changes in working hours may be pertinent.
19. We acknowledge the problems and prejudices associated with the measurement of 'mental health' and 'intellectual ability'.
20. Halpin and Chan (2003: 493) refer to research in progress on the relationship between remarriage and educational similarity.
21. Most of the differences or effects that are implicitly significant at the 1 per cent level are also significant at the 0.1 per cent level.

22. For discussions of the basics of statistical testing and bivariate analysis, see Pole and Lampard (2001: Chapters 3 and 9).
23. For technical and practical discussions of binary logistic regression and log-linear modelling, see Hutcheson and Sofroniou (1999), and George and Mallery (2002).
24. The 2001–2 GHS surveyed nearly 9,000 households and more than 20,000 individuals within them, and had a response rate of 72 per cent (ONS 2002).
25. See, for example, our earlier analysis using the 1991–2 GHS (Lampard and Peggs 1999).
26. A close examination suggested that separation dates tended to be missing for individuals who had separated some considerable time beforehand and had not repartnered, perhaps reflecting recall problems or the 'fuzzy' nature of separation as a phenomenon. Excluding such individuals might have distorted the composition of the sample, so separation dates were imputed with reference to typical durations from marriage to separation.
27. The estimation process was made more complicated by the fact that the single people who did not complete the section were mainly individuals living in households of three or more adults, about whom proxy informants within the household supplied basic information.
28. Only 0.25 per cent and 2.5 per cent within these shortfalls correspond to individuals for whom specific items of data were missing, with the remainder relating to people who did not complete the Family Information section.
29. The estimated totals are subject to sampling error of up to ±5 per cent.
30. This value is similar to the 36 per cent of formerly legally married people under 60 shown to be male using 1991 Census data in our earlier paper (Lampard and Peggs 1999: 462).
31. Once again, these values needed to be estimated because of missing family-related information, but focusing on 2001–2 served to minimize the effect. It appears that only a minority of the people who had ever been formerly partnered were also currently formerly partnered. However, the number of people who had passed through a formerly partnered stage in their lives is arguably an overestimate, since it includes currently married or cohabiting people with earlier co-resident relationships who moved directly from each co-resident relationship into the next one. In a sense, such people had never actually belonged to the formerly partnered population.
32. The relatively recent introduction of cohabitation histories within the GHS means that different years of the survey could not be used to check this by making a comparison between equivalent data sources at adequately separated time points.
33. Since the proportion of longer separations inevitably increases with age, the use of an upper age limit disproportionately restricts the number of these. However, the period-based, cross-sectional approach to constructing a sample of formerly partnered people used here generates a smaller proportion of shorter separations than would be generated by a cohort-based, life-history approach to looking at people who have ever been formerly partnered.
34. Not including 'white' minority ethnic groups.
35. The shortfall of about 7 per cent relative to our earlier estimate for the GHS 2001–2 sample reflects non-completion of the Family Information section.
36. Excluding students and retired people.
37. Information on work status was available for 1,632 of the 1,641 individuals.
38. Note when interpreting these results that many men and older women have conceived children in the past who no longer live with them, and that some people live with older, adult children, who are no longer classed as dependent.

39. Adequate information was available for 1,631 of the 1,641 individuals in our 2001–2 sample of formerly partnered people.
40. This can be explained via a range of demographic and socio-economic factors: see Lampard (1992: 318).
41. This restriction also minimizes the potential distortion resulting from the absence of many students from the GHS sampling frame.
42. Interestingly, the data in Table 4.3 do not replicate the high rates for men over 40 shown in our earlier paper (Lampard and Peggs 1999: 448). This may reflect the fact that the analysis in this book focuses on repartnering in the *next* five years for a range of separation durations, whereas the relevant table in our earlier paper documents repartnering within the *first* five years after separation. In other words, the disparity may highlight a tendency for men over 40 to have a particularly high repartnering rate immediately after separation, perhaps because they are disproportionately likely to have known their new partner before separation.
43. The models take account of the differences between the age distributions of formerly partnered people and single people.
44. There are insufficient single people aged 40 or more for it to be demonstrated conclusively that the difference in rates increases with rising age.
45. Eighty cases are excluded from Table 4.4 because of missing separation dates.
46. A multivariate analysis using a log-linear model shows that the effects of separation duration and of age do not interact. Another multivariate analysis, again based on a log-linear model, shows that, once age has been taken into account, the difference between the impacts of separation duration on the repartnering rate corresponding to former cohabitees and to formerly married people is not statistically significant.
47. The technique used is binary logistic regression, hence each factor's impact is quantified as a multiplicative effect on the odds of repartnering.
48. Where the separation date was unknown, the number of births by April 1996 was used. The 2001–2 GHS recorded mothers' ages at the births of their children, rather than precise birth dates, introducing a degree of inaccuracy into the analysis.
49. Straightforward comparisons of the effects found in our current and earlier analyses are made difficult by the different statistical models used.
50. Our multivariate analysis does not show a significant difference between the effects of having children for former cohabitees and for formerly married people.
51. The statistical insignificance of the results reflects the relatively small number of widowed people, and the fact that four widowed cohabitees had repartnered.
52. This effect does not vary significantly according to sex or for former cohabitees.
53. There were twelve individuals for whom this age could not be established.
54. This effect corresponds to a small subgroup of individuals only, since just 5 per cent of the GHS sample first married (or cohabited) at age 30 or more.
55. The magnitude of the effect for cohabitation or marriage at an age of under 30 rises to 3.15 as a result of the inclusion of the gender-specific effect, and neither effect is substantially altered when additional factors are included, ending up as 2.98 and 1.93.
56. Incorporating age at first cohabitation or marriage and the factors considered in the next section within the multivariate analysis weakens the effect of the number of past co-resident relationships, although it remains statistically significant ($p < 0.05$), and its impact continues to be of sufficient magnitude to be of substantive interest, with two or more earlier co-resident relationships increasing the odds of repartnering by a factor of 1.44. Clearly, number of past co-resident relationships

and age at first cohabitation or marriage are correlated, and both appear to affect the likelihood of repartnering, but the former seems of less statistical importance.

57. The volume of sampling error would in any case have rendered a finding of the magnitude of our earlier one statistically insignificant.

58. While the sample size is not sufficient for a more disaggregated analysis by ethnic group, the effect appears consistent across minority ethnic groups. However, including the remaining factors considered in this section slightly weakens the effect and renders it statistically insignificant (0.50; $p < 0.08$). Note that 'white' minority ethnic groups were not considered.

59. There is insufficient evidence to say conclusively that the effect varies according to gender, but it may be substantially stronger for men.

60. For an international review, see De Graaf and Kalmijn (2003: 1462).

61. This appears to be the situation here, although the difference is not statistically significant.

62. These effects are only slightly reduced, to 3.12 and 1.64, by the inclusion in the multivariate analysis of the final factor considered in this section.

63. In five cases it could not be established whether past cohabitation had occurred.

64. The Family Information section was not completed by some members of some households, and in 13 additional cases, no data were available about a respondent's partner.

65. For a discussion of this general issue, see Rindfuss and Vandenheuvel (1990).

66. Thirteen couples (<2 per cent) included a partner who had not completed the Family Information section because they were aged 60 or over, and a further 130 (14 per cent) included a partner who had not completed it for another reason. In one couple, one partner failed to answer a key question regarding past cohabitation.

67. The slightly greater number of single first partners than single second partners who partner formerly partnered people may reflect the higher repartnering rate for men.

68. For discussions of odds ratios in general and in this context, see Pole and Lampard (2001: 224) and Kalmijn (1998).

69. The last finding is a consequence of strong evidence of a relationship between the first partner's age and the second partner's marital status, reflecting a disproportionately large group of (formerly married) women in their fifties who married single men (in their thirties).

70. Both values remain statistically significant.

71. Adequate information relating to this was available for 748 out of 749 couples.

72. According to t-tests assuming unequal variances.

73. The age differences between partners in couples involving a former cohabitee and a single or a formerly married person also deviated from the typical pattern of the male partner being, on average, two or three years older, but to a somewhat lesser degree.

74. According to Levene's test for homogeneity of variances.

75. The values for couples where one or both partners had been previously married and for couples where neither partner had been married but one or both had previously cohabited are very similar, 20 per cent and 18 per cent.

76. The hierarchy has levels equivalent to degrees, 'A' levels, 'O' levels/GCSEs, and no such qualifications.

77. The latter figure rises to 35 per cent once the data have been weighted in the analyses that follow to take account of differential selection probabilities resulting from the sample design.

78. Approximately 30 per cent had not had a sexual partner in the last year, including a small number of recently separated individuals who had not had a sexual partner since their separation.
79. Age at first heterosexual intercourse was available for all but twelve respondents.
80. Age at first cohabitation or marriage has a negative (bivariate) relationship with having had a sexual partner in the last month, but this effect is not significant and is rendered close to zero within a multivariate analysis taking both age and age at first heterosexual intercourse into account. (The available data on age at first homosexual encounter were less extensive and less clearly defined than those for the heterosexual measure.)
81. A relationship between the number of children of whom an individual was or had been the biological parent and having had a sexual partner in the last month is rendered statistically insignificant when age is taken into account within a multivariate analysis.
82. However, the effect of agreeing with 'I usually feel that I control what happens to me in life' as opposed to 'I mostly find that things just happen in my life', while positive, is not significant.
83. Women favouring this lifestyle outnumbered men by a ratio of more than three to two ($p < 0.02$), but this relationship becomes weaker, and ceases to be significant, in the multivariate analysis.
84. For some people this may have reflected a regret that an earlier co-resident relationship had not continued.
85. While the relationships identified by this question may not be consistent with some authors' usage of the term 'living apart together', this simply highlights the difficulties inherent in operationalizing such a concept.
86. Relationships of less than three months were excluded. It also cannot be established whether or not some respondents with past relationships that were not co-resident 'for the majority of the relationship' had cohabited.
87. Approximately 8 per cent of formerly partnered people sampled refused to complete the survey (6 respondents), the module (14 respondents) or the question about having a current regular partner (1 respondent).
88. A substantial minority of these individuals (24) had, in the past, lived at the same address as their partner. Two women and one man had same-sex partners.
89. A significant difference, according to a *t*-test not assuming equal variances in the two groups.
90. An appropriate estimate for the number of partnerships of this sort ending per year is the number that have been in existence for less than a year. Here the relevant value is 19, but the existence of a cluster of respondents reporting relationships of exactly a year in length suggests that this would be an underestimate.
91. As noted earlier, some of the respondents with regular non-resident partners had already cohabited with their current partner at some stage; hence moving in together again at a later date might simply constitute residential oscillation within an ongoing relationship. An apparent similarity to couples reuniting after a period of separation is superficial, since that is still repartnering, albeit with an earlier partner, whereas the phenomenon of residential oscillation highlights the conceptual crudeness involved in equating coupledom to co-residence.

Chapter 5

1. Notwithstanding the time that has elapsed since the interviews were conducted, in this chapter and also in Chapters 6 and 7 we follow the convention adopted by

many qualitative researchers of presenting our results using the present tense, with a few exceptions, for example where interviewees were referring to past events.

Chapter 8

1. The results discussed in this conclusion typically relate to formerly partnered people aged under 60.
2. Unless stated otherwise, the results referred to in this section are drawn from Chapter 4.
3. As reported in Chapter 3, Avellar and Smock (2005) found that, in the US, formerly cohabiting men's economic standing declines moderately after separation, whereas formerly cohabiting women's declines much more sharply, leaving a substantial proportion of the latter in poverty. Consequently, they conclude, the end of a couple relationship leaves married and cohabiting women in noticeably similar economic positions.
4. It is also possible that pre-marital cohabitation may be associated with a lower repartnering rate.

References

Abel, R. L. 1973. 'Law books and books about law', *Stanford Law Review* 26: 175–228.

Adams, J. M. and Jones, W. H. 1997. 'Conceptualization of marital commitment: an integrative analysis', *Journal of Personality and Social Psychology* 72.5: 1177–96.

Adkins, L. 2001. 'Risk culture, self-reflexivity and the making of sexual hierarchies', *Body and Society* 7.1: 35–55.

Ahrons, C. R. 1994. *The Good Divorce: Keeping Your Family Together When Your Marriage Comes Apart*. New York: HarperCollins.

Akerloff, G. A. 1998. 'Men without children', *Economic Journal* 108 (March): 287–309.

Alcock, P. 1984. 'Remuneration or remarriage? The Matrimonial and Family Proceedings Act 1984', *Journal of Law and Society* 11.3: 357–65.

Aldridge, A. 1998. '*Habitus* and cultural capital in the field of personal finance', *Sociological Review* 46.1: 1–23.

Allan, G. and Crow, G. 2001. *Families, Households and Society*. Basingstoke: Palgrave.

Amato, P. R. 2000. 'The consequences of divorce for adults and children', *Journal of Marriage and the Family* 62.4: 1269–87.

Amato, P. R. and Booth, A. 1997. *A Generation at Risk, Growing up in Era of Family Upheaval*. Cambridge, MA: Harvard University Press.

Ambrose, P., Harper, J. and Pemberton, R. 1983. *Surviving Divorce: Men beyond Marriage*. Brighton: Harvester Wheatsheaf.

Arber, S., Price, D., Davidson, K. and Perren, K. 2003. 'Re-examining gender and marital status'. In Arber, S., Davidson, K. and Ginn, J. (eds) *Gender and Ageing: Changing Roles and Relationships*, pp. 148–67. Maidenhead: Open University Press.

Arendell, T. 1986. *Mothers and Divorce: Legal, Economic and Social Dilemmas*. London: University of California Press.

Arendell, T. 1995. *Fathers and Divorce*. London: Sage.

Armstrong, J. 2003. *Conditions of Love: The Philosophy of Intimacy*. London: Penguin.

Askham, J. 1984. *Identity and Stability in Marriage*. Cambridge: Cambridge University Press.

Avellar, S. and Smock, P. J. 2005. 'The economic consequences of the dissolution of cohabiting unions', *Journal of Marriage and Family* 67.2: 315–27.

Balsamo, A. 1998. 'On the cutting edge: cosmetic surgery and the technological production of the gendered body'. In Mirzoeff, N. (ed.) *The Visual Culture Reader*, pp. 224–33. London: Routledge.

Barbalet, J. M. 2001. *Emotion, Social Theory and Social Structure: A Macrosociological Approach*. Cambridge: Cambridge University Press.

Barthes, R. 1990. *A Lover's Discourse: Fragments*. London: Penguin.

Batalova, J. A. and Cohen, P. N. 2002. 'Premarital cohabitation and housework: couples in cross-national perspective', *Journal of Marriage and Family* 64.3: 743–55.

Bauman, Z. 1995. *Life in Fragments*. Oxford: Blackwell.

Bauman, Z. 1997. *Postmodernity and its Discontents*. Cambridge: Polity.

Bauman, Z. 1998. *Work, Consumerism and the New Poor*. Buckingham: Open University Press.

Bauman, Z. 2000a. *The Individualized Society*. Cambridge: Polity.
Bauman, Z. 2000b. *Liquid Modernity*. Cambridge: Polity.
Bauman, Z. 2003. *Liquid Love: On the Frailty of Human Bonds*. Cambridge: Polity.
Bazerman, M. 1986. *Judgement in Managerial Decision-Making*. New York: Wiley.
Beck, U. 1992. *Risk Society: Towards a New Modernity*. London: Sage.
Beck, U. and Beck-Gernsheim, E. 1995. *The Normal Chaos of Love*. Cambridge: Polity.
Becker, G. 1981. *A Treatise on the Family*. Cambridge, MA: Harvard University Press.
Becker, G. S., Landis, E. M. and Michael, R. T. 1977. 'An economic analysis of marital instability', *Journal of Political Economy* 85.6: 1141–87.
Beck-Gernsheim, E. 1996. 'Life as a planning project'. In Lash, S., Szerszynski, B. and Wynne, B. (eds) *Risk, Environment and Modernity: Towards a New Ecology*, pp. 139–53. London: Sage.
Bengston, V., Biblarz, T. and Roberts, R. 2002. *How Families Still Matter*. Cambridge: Cambridge University Press.
Benjamin, O. and Sullivan, O. 1999. 'Relational resources, gender consciousness and possibilities of change in marital relationships', *Sociological Review* 47.4: 794–820.
Berezin, M. 2002. 'Secure states: towards a political sociology of emotion'. In Barbalet, J. (ed.) *Emotions and Sociology* (Sociological Review Monograph), pp. 33–52. Oxford: Blackwell.
Berger, P. and Kellner, H. 1964. 'Marriage and the construction of reality'. In Coser, R. L. (ed.) *The Family: Its Structures and Functions*. New York: St. Martin's Press.
Bernard, J. 1976. *The Future of Marriage*. Harmondsworth: Penguin.
Bernhardt, E. and Goldscheider, F. 2002. 'Children and union formation in Sweden', *European Sociological Review* 18.3: 289–99.
Bernhardt, E. M. 2000. 'Repartnering among Swedish men and women: A case study of emerging patterns in the second demographic transition'. Paper contributed to the FFS Flagship conference, Brussels, May.
Berrington, A. 2001. 'Entry into parenthood and the outcome of cohabiting partnerships in Britain', *Journal of Marriage and Family* 63.1: 80–96.
Berrington, A. and Diamond, I. 2000. 'Marriage or cohabitation: a competing risks analysis of first-partnership formation among the 1958 British birth cohort', *Journal of the Royal Statistical Society* (Series A) 163.2: 127–51.
Berthoud, R. and Gershuny, J. (eds) 2000. *Seven Years in the Lives of British Families: Evidence on the Dynamics of Social Change from the British Household Panel Survey*. Bristol: Policy Press.
Birch, M. and Miller, T. 2000. 'Inviting intimacy: the interview as therapeutic opportunity', *International Journal of Social Research Methodology* 3.3: 189–202.
Blaikie, A. 1999. *Ageing and Popular Culture*. Cambridge: Cambridge University Press.
Boden, S. and Williams, S. J. 2002. 'Consumption and emotion: the romantic ethic revisited', *Sociology* 36.3: 493–512.
Booth, A. and Amato, P. R. 1991. 'Divorce and psychological distress', *Journal of Health and Social Behaviour* 32.4: 396–407.
Bordo, S. 1990. 'Reading the slender body'. In Jacobus, M., Fox-Keller, E. and Shuttleworth, S. (eds) *Body/Politics: Women and the Discourses of Science*, pp. 83–112. London: Routledge.
Borell, K. and Ghazanfareeon Karlsson, S. 2003. 'Reconceptualizing intimacy and ageing'. In Arber, S., Davidson, K. and Ginn, J. (eds) *Gender and Ageing: Changing Roles and Relationships*, pp. 47–62. Maidenhead: Open University Press.
Bourdieu, P. 1984. *Distinction: A Social Critique of the Judgement of Taste*. London: Routledge.
Bourdieu, P. 1990. *The Logic of Practice*. Cambridge: Polity.

Bradshaw, J., Stimson, C., Skinner, C. and Williams, J. 1999. *Absent Fathers?* London: Routledge.

Brannen, J. 1992. *Mixing Methods: Qualitative and Quantitative Research.* Aldershot: Avebury.

Brannen, J. and Nilsen, A. 2006. 'From fatherhood to fathering: transmission and change among British fathers in four-generation families', *Sociology* 40.2: 335–52.

Browne, K. 2002. *Introducing Sociology for AS level.* Cambridge: Polity.

Brownmiller, S. 1986. *Against Our Will: Men, Women and Rape.* Harmondsworth: Penguin.

Bryman, A. 1988. *Quantity and Quality in Social Research.* London: Unwin Hyman.

Bryman, A. 2004. *Social Research Methods* (2nd edition). Oxford: Oxford University Press.

Bryman, A. 2006. 'Integrating quantitative and qualitative research: how is it done?' *Qualitative Research* 6.1: 97–113.

Bull, J. 1993. *The Housing Consequences of Relationship Breakdown.* Department of Environment. London: HMSO.

Bumpass, L. 1990. 'What's happening to the family? Interactions between demography and institutional change', *Demography* 27.4: 483–98.

Bumpass, L. L. and Sweet, J. E. 1989. 'National estimates of cohabitation', *Demography* 26.4: 615–25.

Bumpass, L., Sweet, J. and Martin, T. C. 1990. 'Changing patterns of remarriage', *Journal of Marriage and the Family* 52.3: 747–56.

Burch, T. 1990. 'Remarriage of older Canadians', *Research on Aging* 12.4: 546–59.

Burck, C. and Daniel, G. 1995. 'Moving on: gender beliefs in divorce and stepfamily process'. In Burck, C. and Speed, B. (eds) *Gender, Power and Relationships*, pp. 185–201. London: Routledge.

Burgoyne, C.B. and Morison, V. 1997. 'Money in remarriage: keeping things simple – and separate', *Sociological Review* 45: 363–395.

Burgoyne, J. and Clark, D. 1984. *Making a Go of It? A Study of Stepfamilies in Sheffield.* London: Routledge & Kegan Paul.

Butler, J. 1999. *Gender Trouble* (2nd edition). London: Routledge.

Bytheway, B. 2005. 'Age identities and the celebration birthdays', *Ageing and Society* 25.4: 463–77.

Carrington, C. 1999. *No Place Like Home: Relationships and Family Life among Lesbians and Gay Men.* Chicago: Chicago University Press.

Cauhapé, E. 1983. *Fresh Starts: Men and Women after Divorce.* New York: Basic Books.

Chambers, D. 2001. *Representing the Family.* London: Sage.

Chandler, J. 1991. *Women without Husbands: An Exploration of the Margins of Marriage.* London: Macmillan.

Chapkiss, W. 1986. *Beauty Secrets: Women and the Politics of Appearance.* Boston, MA: South End Press.

Cherlin, A. J. 1992. *Marriage, Divorce, Remarriage.* Cambridge, MA: Harvard University Press.

Chernin, K. 1983. *Womansize: The Tyranny of Slenderness.* London: The Women's Press.

Cheung, Y. B. 1998. 'Can marital selection explain the differences in health between married and divorced people? From a longitudinal study of a British birth cohort', *Public Health* 112.2: 113–17.

Chiriboga, D., Catron, L. and Associates 1991. *Divorce: Crisis, Challenge or Relief?* New York: New York University Press.

Churchill, H. 2004. 'Lone motherhood, welfare and paid work: identities and experiences'. Unpublished PhD thesis. Oxford: Oxford Brookes University.

Clarkberg, M., Stolzenberg, R. M. and Waite, L. J. 1995. 'Attitudes, values and entrance into cohabitational versus marital unions', *Social Forces* 74.2: 609–34.

Clarke, S., Diamond, I., Spicer, K. and Chappell, R. 1993. 'The relationship between marital breakdown and childbearing in England and Wales', *Studies on Medical and Population Subjects* 55: 125–36.

Cockett, M. and Tripp, J. 1994. *The Exeter Family Study*. Exeter: Exeter University Press.

Coleman, D. and Salt, J. 1992. *The British Population: Patterns, Trends and Processes*. Oxford: Oxford University Press.

Coleman, J. S. 1990. *Foundations of Social Theory*. Cambridge, MA: Harvard University Press.

Coleman, J. S. and Fararo, T. J. (eds) 1992. *Rational Choice Theory: Advocacy and Critique*. Newbury Park, CA: Sage.

Coleman, M., Ganong, L. and Fine, M. 2000. 'Reinvestigating remarriage: another decade of progress', *Journal of Marriage and the Family* 62.4: 1288–1307.

Colletta, N. D. 1983. 'Stressful lives: the situation of divorced mothers and their children', *Journal of Divorce* 6.3: 19–31.

Collins, R. 1981 'On the microfoundations of macrosociology', *American Journal of Sociology* 86.5: 984–1014.

Collins, S. 1991. 'The transition from lone-parent family to step-family'. In Hardey, M. and Crow, G. (eds) *Lone Parenthood: Coping with Constraints and Making Opportunities*, pp. 156–75. London: Harvester Wheatsheaf.

Connell, R. W. 1987. *Gender and Power*. Stanford, CA: Stanford University Press.

Coupland, J. 1996. 'Dating advertisements: discourses of the commodified self', *Discourse and Society* 7.2: 187–207.

Cresswell, J. W., Trout, S. and Barbuto, J. E. 2002. 'A decade of mixed methods writings: A retrospective'. Available online at: http://www.aom.pace.edu/rmd/2002forum/retrospect.pdf.

Crosbie-Burnett, M. 1989. 'Application of family stress theory to remarriage: a model for assessing and helping stepfamilies' *Family Relations* 38.3: 323–31.

Cvetkovich, G. and Löfstedt, R. E. (eds) 1999. *Social Trust and the Management of Risk*. London: Earthscan.

Dale, A. and Marsh, C. (eds) 1993. *The 1991 Census User's Guide*. London: HMSO.

Davidson, K. 2001. 'Late life widowhood, selfishness and new partnership choices: a gendered perspective', *Ageing and Society* 21.3: 297–317.

Davidson, K. 2002. 'Gender differences in new partnership choices and constraints for older widows and widowers', *Ageing International* 27.4: 43–60.

Davidson, K., Daly, T. and Arber, S. 2003. 'Exploring the social worlds of older men'. In Arber, S., Davidson, K. and Ginn, J. (eds) *Gender and Ageing: Changing Roles and Relationships*, pp. 168–85. Maidenhead: Open University Press.

Day Sclater, S. 1999. *Divorce: A Psychosocial Study*. Aldershot: Ashgate.

de Graaf, P.M. and Kalmijn, M. 2003. 'Alternative routes in the remarriage market: competing-risk analyses of union formation after divorce', *Social Forces* 81.4: 1459–98.

de Jong-Gierveld, J. 2004. 'Remarriage, unmarried cohabitation, living apart together: partner relationships following bereavement or divorce', *Journal of Marriage and Family* 66.1: 236–43.

de Singly, F. 1996. *Modern Marriage and its Loss to Women: A Sociological Look at Marriage in France*. London: Associated University Press.

Dean, G. and Gurak, D. 1978. 'Marital homogamy the second time around', *Journal of Marriage and the Family* 40.3: 559–70.

DeGarmo, D.S. and Kitson, G. C. 1996. 'Identity relevance and disruption as predictors of psychological distress for widowed and divorced women', *Journal of Marriage and the Family* 58.4: 983–97.

Delphy, C. 1984. *Close to Home: A Materialist Analysis of Women's Oppression*. London: Hutchinson.

Delphy, C. and Leonard, D. 1992. *Familiar Exploitation: A New Analysis of Marriage in Contemporary Societies*. Cambridge: Polity.

Derrida, J. 1991. 'Signature event context'. In Kamuf, P. (ed.) *Between the Blinds: A Derrida Reader*, pp. 82–111. Hemel Hempstead: Harvester Wheatsheaf.

Dewilde, C. 2002. 'The financial consequences of relationship dissolution for women in Western Europe'. In Ruspini, E. and Dale, A. (eds) *The Gender Dimension of Social Change: The Contribution of Dynamic Research to the Study of Women's Life Courses*, pp. 81–110. Bristol: Policy Press.

Duncan, G. and Hoffman, D. 1985 'Economic consequences of marital instability'. In Smeeding, T. and David, M. (eds) *Horizontal Equity and Economic Well-Being*, 427–70. Chicago: University of Chicago Press.

Dyer, C. 2006. 'Children to get new voice in divorce cases', *The Guardian*, 9 October.

Elam, D. 1994. *Feminism and Deconstruction: Ms. en Abyme*. London: Routledge.

Elias, N. 1978a. *What is Sociology?* London: Hutchinson.

Elias, N. 1978b. *History of Manners*. New York: Pantheon.

Elias, N. 1985. *The Loneliness of the Dying*. Oxford: Blackwell.

Elliot, A. 2001. *Concepts of the Self*. Cambridge: Polity.

Elster, J. 1985. 'Sadder but wiser? Rationality and the emotions', *Social Science Information* 24.2: 375–406.

Ermisch, J. 1989. 'Divorce, economic antecedents and aftermath'. In Joshi, H. (ed.) *The Changing Population of Britain*. Oxford: Blackwell.

Ermisch, J. 2002. 'Trying again: repartnering after dissolution of a union', *Working Papers of the Institute for Social and Economic Research*, Paper 2002–19. Colchester: University of Essex.

Ermisch, J. and Francesconi, M. 1998. *Cohabitation in Great Britain: Not for Long. But Here to Stay*, Working Paper 98–1. University of Essex: ESRC Research Centre on Micro-social Change.

Featherstone, M. 1991. 'The body in consumer culture'. In Featherstone, M., Hepworth, M. and Turner, B. (eds) *The Body: Social Processes and Cultural Theory*. London: Sage.

Ferri, E., Bynner J. and Wadsworth M. (eds) 2003. *Changing Britain, Changing Lives: Three Generations at the Turn of the Century*. London: Institute of Education.

Field, J., Johnson, A., Wadsworth, J. and Wellings, K. 1995. *National Survey of Sexual Attitudes and Lifestyles, 1990* [computer file]. Colchester, Essex: UK Data Archive [distributor], SN: 3434.

Finlayson, L., Ford, R., Marsh, A., McKay, S. and Mukherjee, A. 2000. *The British Lone Parent Cohort 1991 to 1998*. Department of Social Security Research Paper No. 128. Leeds: Corporate Document Services.

Flam, H. 2002. 'Corporate emotions and emotions in corporations'. In Barbalet, J. (ed.) *Emotions and Sociology* (Sociological Review Monograph), pp. 90–112. Oxford: Blackwell.

Flowerdew, J. and Neale, B. 2003. 'Trying to stay apace: children with multiple challenges in their post-divorce lives', *Childhood: A Global Journal of Child Research* 10.2: 147–62.

Flowerdew, R., Al-Hamad, A. and Hayes, L. 1999. 'The residential mobility of divorced people'. In McRae, S. (ed.) *Changing Britain: Families and Households in the 1990s*, pp. 427–40. Oxford: Oxford University Press.

Ford, R., Marsh, A. and Finlayson, L. 1998. *What Happens to Lone Parents: A Cohort Study, 1991–1995*. Department of Social Security Research Report No. 77. London: The Stationery Office.

Foucault, M. 1977. *Discipline and Punish: The Birth of the Prison*. Harmondsworth: Penguin.

Foucault, M. 1979. *The History of Sexuality (Volume 1: An Introduction)*. Harmondsworth: Penguin.

France, L. 2002. 'Love at first site', *Observer Magazine*, 30 June.

Frank, A. 1991. 'For a sociology of the body: an analytical review'. In Featherstone, M., Hepworth, M. and Turner, B. (eds) *The Body: Social Processes and Cultural Theory*, pp. 36–102. London: Sage.

Frazier, P. Arikian, N., Benson, S., Losoff, A. and Maurer, S. 1996. 'Desire for marriage and life satisfaction among unmarried heterosexual adults', *Journal of Social and Personal Relationships* 13.2: 225–39.

Fukuyama, F. 1999. *The Great Disruption: Human Nature and the Reconstitution of Social Order*. London: Profile Books.

Furedi, F. 2002. *Culture of Fear: Risk-taking and the Morality of Low Expectation* (revised edition). London: Continuum.

Furedi, F. 2004. *Therapy Culture: Cultivating Vulnerability in an Anxious Age*. London: Routledge.

Furstenberg, F. F. and Cherlin, A. J. 1991. *Divided Families: What Happens to Children when Parents Part?* Cambridge, MA: Harvard University Press.

Furstenberg, F. F. and Spanier, G. B. 1984. *Recycling the Family: Remarriage after Divorce*. Beverly Hills, CA: Sage.

George, D. and Mallery, P. 2002. *SPSS for Windows Step-by-Step: A Simple Guide and Reference, 11.0 Update* (4th edition). Harlow: Pearson Education (Allyn & Bacon).

Gershuny, J. and Berthoud, R. 1997. *New Partnerships? Men and Women in the 1990s*. Colchester: ESRC Research Centre on Micro-social Change, University of Essex.

Giddens, A. 1989. *Sociology*. Cambridge: Polity.

Giddens, A. 1990. *The Consequences of Modernity*. Cambridge: Polity.

Giddens, A. 1991. *Modernity and Self-Identity: Self and Society in the Late Modern Age*. Cambridge: Polity.

Giddens, A. 1992. *The Transformation of Intimacy: Sexuality, Love and Eroticism in Modern Societies*. Cambridge: Polity.

Giddens, A. 1998. 'Risk society: the context of British politics'. In Franklin, J. (ed.) *The Politics of Risk Society*, pp. 23–34. Cambridge: Polity.

Gillis, J. 1985. *For Better, For Worse: British Marriages, 1600 to the Present*. Oxford: Oxford University Press.

Gillis, J. 1996. *A World of Their Own Making*. Cambridge. MA: Harvard University Press.

Gillis, J. 2000. 'Marginalisation of fatherhood in Western countries', *Childhood* 17.2: 225–38.

Glaser, B. G. and Strauss, A. L. 1967. *The Discovery of Grounded Theory: Strategies for Qualitative Research*. New York: Aldine.

Glendinning, C. and Millar, J. 1992. *Women and Poverty in Britain: The 1990s*. London: Harvester Wheatsheaf.

Glick, P. C. and Spanier, G. B. 1980. 'Married and unmarried cohabitation in the United States', *Journal of Marriage and the Family* 42.1: 19–30.

Goffman, E. 1969. *The Presentation of Self in Everyday Life*. Harmondsworth: Penguin.

Goldscheider, F. K. 2000. 'Men, children and the future of the family in the third millennium', *Futures* 32.6: 525–38.

Goldscheider, F. K. and Waite, L. J. 1986. 'Sex differences in the entry into marriage', *American Journal of Sociology* 92.1: 91–109.

Goode, W. J. 1956. *After Divorce*. New York: Free Press.

Griffiths, M. 1995. *Feminisms and the Self: The Web of Identity*. London: Routledge.

Gross, N. 2005. 'The detraditionalization of intimacy reconsidered', *Sociological Theory* 23.3: 286–311.

Hacker, D. 2005. 'Motherhood, fatherhood and law: child custody and visitation in Israel', *Social and Legal Studies* 14.3: 409–31.

Hacking, I. 1990. *The Taming of Chance*. Cambridge: Cambridge University Press.

Hakim, C. 1996. *Key Issues in Women's Work: Female Heterogeneity and the Polarisation of Women's Employment*. London: Athlone.

Hall, S. 1996. 'Introduction: who needs identity?' in Hall, S. and du Gay, P. (eds) *Questions of Cultural Identity*, pp. 1–19. London: Sage.

Halpin, B. and Chan, T. W. 2003. 'Educational homogamy in Ireland and Britain: trends and patterns', *British Journal of Sociology* 54.4: 473–95.

Hanmer, J. and Maynard, M. 1987. (eds) *Women, Violence and Social Control*. Basingstoke: Macmillan.

Hart, N. 1976. *When Marriage Ends: A Study in Status Passage*. London: Tavistock.

Haskey, J. 1983. 'Remarriage of the divorced in England and Wales: a contemporary phenomenon', *Journal of Biosocial Science* 15.3: 253–71.

Haskey, J. 1991. 'Lone parenthood and demographic change'. In Hardey, M. and Crow, G. (eds) 1991. *Lone Parenthood: Coping with Constraints and Making Opportunities*, pp. 19–46. Hemel Hempstead: Harvester Wheatsheaf.

Haskey, J. 1993. 'First marriage, divorce and remarriage: birth cohort analyses', *Population Trends* 72: 24–33.

Haskey, J. 1995. 'Trends in marriage and cohabitation: the decline in marriage and the changing pattern of living in partnerships', *Population Trends* 80: 5–15.

Haskey, J. 1999. 'Divorce and remarriage in England and Wales', *Population Trends* 95: 18–22.

Haskey, J. 2001. 'Cohabitation in Great Britain: past, present and future trends – and attitudes', *Population Trends* 103: 4–25.

Haskey, J. 2005. 'Living arrangements in contemporary Britain: having a partner who usually lives elsewhere and Living Apart Together (LAT)', *Population Trends* 122: 35–45.

Hawkins, D. N. and Booth, A. 2005. 'Unhappily ever after: effects of long-term, low-quality marriages on well-being', *Social Forces* 84.1: 451–71.

Hayes, C. L., Anderson, D. and Blau, M. 1993. *Our Turn: The Good News about Women and Divorce*. New York: Pocket Books.

Hebb, D. O. 1946. 'On the nature of fear', *Psychological Review* 53.5: 259–76.

Hepworth, M. and Featherstone, M. 1982. *Surviving Middle Age*. Oxford: Blackwell.

Hetherington, E. M. 1989. 'Coping with marital transition: winners, losers and survivors', *Child Development* 60.1: 1–14.

Hetherington, E. M. and Kelly, J. 2002. *For Better or For Worse: Divorce Reconsidered*. London: W.W. Norton.

Hetherington, E. M., Cox, M. and Cox, R. 1985. 'Long-term effects of divorce and remarriage on the adjustment of children', *Journal of the American Academy of Child Psychiatry* 24.5: 518–30.

Hobson, B. (ed.) 2002. *Making Men into Fathers*. Cambridge: Cambridge University Press.

Hochschild, A. 1983. *The Managed Heart: The Commercialization of Human Feeling*. Berkeley, CA: University of California Press.

Hochschild, A. 1998. 'The sociology of emotions as a way of seeing'. In Bendelow, G. and Williams, S. J. (eds) *Emotions in Social Life: Critical Themes and Contemporary Issues*, pp. 3–15. London: Routledge.

Hochschild, A. 2003. *The Commercialisation of Intimate Life: Notes from Home and Work*. Berkeley, CA: University of California Press.

Hockey, J. and James, A. 1993. *Growing Up and Growing Old: Ageing and Dependency in the Life Course*. London: Sage.

Holden, K. C. and Smock, P. J. 1991. 'The economic costs of marital disruption: why do women bear a disproportionate cost?', *Annual Review of Sociology* 17: 15–78.

Holland, J., Thomson, R. and Henderson, S. 2004. 'Feasibility study for a possible qualitative longitudinal study: discussion paper'. Paper produced for the Economic and Social Research Council.

Holmans, A. E. 2000. *Divorce, Remarriage and Housing: The Effects of Divorce, Remarriage, Separation and the Formation of New Couple Households on the Number of Separate Households and Housing Demand and Conditions*. London: Department of the Environment, Transport and the Regions.

Holstein, J. A. and Gubrium, J. F. 1997. 'Active interviewing'. In Silverman, D. (ed.) *Qualitative Research: Theory, Method and Practice*, pp. 113–29. London: Sage.

Hope, S., Rodgers, B. and Power, C. 1999. 'Marital status transitions and psychological distress: longitudinal evidence from a national population sample'. *Psychological Medicine* 29: 381–9.

Huby, M. and Dix, G. 1992. 'Merging methods: integrating quantitative and qualitative approaches to survey design, analysis and interpretation'. In Westlake, A., Banks, R., Payne, C. and Orchard, T. (eds) *Survey and Statistical Computing*, pp. 179–87. London: North-Holland.

Hughes, J. 2000. 'Repartnering after divorce', *Family Matters* 55: 16–21.

Hunt, M. 1966. *The World of the Formerly Married*. New York: McGraw-Hill.

Hutchens, R. 1979. 'Welfare, remarriage and marital search', *American Economic Review* 69.3: 369–79.

Hutcheson, G. and Sofroniou, N. 1999. *The Multivariate Social Scientist*. London: Sage.

Jackson, L. A. 1992. *Physical Appearance and Gender: Sociobiological and Sociocultural Perspectives*. Albany, NY: SUNY Press.

Jackson, S. 1993. 'Even sociologists fall in love: an exploration in the sociology of emotions', *Sociology* 27.2: 201–20.

Jackson, S. 1998. *Britain's Population: Demographic Issues in Contemporary Society*. London: Routledge.

Jagger, E. 1998. 'Marketing the self, buying an other: Dating in a post-modern, consumer society', *Sociology* 32.4: 795–814.

Jagger, E. 2005. 'Is thirty the new sixty? Dating, age and gender in postmodern consumer society', *Sociology* 39.1: 89–106.

Jamieson, L. 1998. *Intimacy: Personal Relationships in Modern Societies*. Cambridge: Cambridge University Press.

Jamieson, L. 1999. 'Intimacy transformed? A critical look at the "pure relationship"', *Sociology* 33.3: 477–94.

Jarvis, S. and Jenkins, S. P. 1999. 'Marital splits and income changes: evidence from the British Household Panel Survey', *Population Studies* 53.2: 237–54.

Jefferies, J., Berrington, A. and Diamond, I. 2000. 'Childbearing following marital dissolution in Britain', *European Journal of Population* 16.3: 193–210.

Jenkins, R. 1992. *Pierre Bourdieu*. London: Routledge.

Jenkins, R. 2004. *Social Identity* (2nd edition). London: Routledge.

Joffe, H. 1999. *Risk and 'the Other'*. Cambridge: Cambridge University Press.

Johnson, A., Wadsworth, J., Wellings, K. and Field, J. with Bradshaw, S. 1994. *Sexual Attitudes and Lifestyles*. Oxford: Blackwell Scientific Publications.

Johnson, C. and Troll, L. 1996. 'Family structure and the timing of transitions from 70–100 years of age', *Journal of Marriage and the Family* 58.1: 178–87.

Johnson, M. P. 1991. 'Commitment to personal relationships'. In Jones, W. H. and Perlman, D. (eds) *Advances in Personal Relationships: A Research Annual*, pp. 117–43. London: Jessica Kingsley.

Jones, S. and Carvel, J. 2005. 'Marriage à la mode: Lifetime commitment back in fashion'. *The Guardian*, 5 February.

Joshi, H., Dale, A., Ward, C. and Davies, H. 1995. *Dependence and Independence in the Finances of Women aged 33*. London: Family Policy Studies Centre.

Jowell, R. Witherspoon, S. and Brook, L. (eds) 1987. *British Social Attitudes: the 1987 Report*. Aldershot: Gower.

Jowell, R., Witherspoon, S. and Brook, L. (eds) 1990. *British Social Attitudes: the 7th Report*. Aldershot: Gower.

Kahn, S. S. 1990. *The Ex-Wife Syndrome: Cutting the Cord and Breaking Free after the Marriage Ends*. London: Ebury Press.

Kalmijn, M. 1998. 'Intermarriage and homogamy: causes, patterns, trends', *Annual Review of Sociology* 24: 395–421.

Kalmijn, M. and Bernasco, W. 2001. 'Joint and separated lifestyles in couple relationships', *Journal of Marriage and Family* 63.3: 639–54.

Kalmijn, M. and Flap, H. 2001. 'Assortative meeting and mating: unintended consequences of organized settings for partnership choices', *Social Forces* 79.4: 1289–1312.

Kalmijn, M. and van Groenou, M. B. 2005. 'Differential effects of divorce on social integration', *Journal of Social and Personal Relationships* 22.4: 455–76.

Karney, B. R. and Bradbury, T. N. 1995. 'The longitudinal course of marital quality and stability: a review of theory, method and research', *Psychological Bulletin* 118.1: 3–34.

Kemper, T. D. 2002. 'Predicting emotions in groups: some lessons from September 11'. In Barbalet, J. (ed.) *Emotions and Sociology* (Sociological Review Monograph), pp. 53–68. Oxford: Blackwell.

Kielty, S. 2005. 'Mothers are non-resident parents too: a consideration of mothers' perspectives on non-residential parenthood', *Journal of Social Welfare and Family Law* 27.1: 1–16.

Kiernan, K. and Estaugh, V. 1993. *Cohabitation, Extramarital Childbearing and Social Policy*. London: Family Policy Studies Centre.

Kiernan, K. and Mueller, G. 1999. 'Who divorces?' In McRae, S. (ed.) *Changing Britain: Families and Households in the 1990s*, pp. 377–403. Oxford: Oxford University Press.

Kiernan, K., Land, H. and Lewis, J. 1998. *Lone Mother Families in Twentieth-Century Britain*. Oxford: Oxford University Press.

Kim, H. K. and McKenry, P. C. 2000. 'Relationship transition as seen in the National Survey of Families and Households', *Journal of Divorce and Remarriage* 34.2: 163–8.

King, V. and Scott, M. E. 2005. 'A comparison of cohabiting relationships among older and younger adults', *Journal of Marriage and Family* 67.2: 271–85.

Klett-Davies, M. 2005. 'The diversity of state benefit-dependent lone mothers: the use of type categories as an analytical tool', *Sociological Research Online* 10.1.

Lampard, R. 1992. 'An empirical study of marriage and social stratification'. DPhil thesis. Oxford: University of Oxford.

Lampard, R. 1993. 'Availability of marriage partners in England and Wales: a comparison of three measures', *Journal of Biosocial Science* 25.3: 333–50.

Lampard, R. 1994. 'An examination of the relationship between marital dissolution and unemployment'. In Gallie, D., Marsh, C. and Vogler, C. (eds) *Social Change and the Experience of Unemployment*, pp. 264–98. Oxford: Oxford University Press.

Lampard, R. 1996. 'Marital dissolution and formation: combining quantitative and qualitative approaches'. In Dale, A. (ed.) *Exploiting National Survey and Census Data: Longitudinal and Partnership Analyses*. Centre for Census and Survey Research Occasional Paper No. 10, pp. 127–33. University of Manchester: CCSR.

Lampard, R. 1997. 'Endogamy among the divorced in Britain'. Paper presented at the British Society for Population Studies annual conference, University of Exeter, September.

Lampard, R. and Peggs, K. 1999. 'Repartnering: the relevance of parenthood and gender to cohabitation and remarriage among the formerly married', *British Journal of Sociology* 50.3: 443–65.

Lasch, C. 1991. *The Culture of Narcissism: American Life in an Age of Diminishing Expectations*. London: W.W. Norton.

Lash, S. 1993. 'Reflexive modernisation: the aesthetic dimension', *Theory, Culture and Society* 10.1: 1–23.

Lash, S. 2000. 'Risk culture'. In Adam, B., Beck, U. and Van Loon, J. (eds) *The Risk Society and Beyond*, pp. 47–62. London: Sage.

Lawson, A. 1988. *Adultery: An Analysis of Love and Betrayal*. Oxford: Blackwell.

Lee, J. 2003. 'Menarche and the heterosexualization of the female body'. In Weitz, R. (ed.) *The Politics of Women's Bodies: Sexuality, Appearance and Behavior* (2nd edition), pp. 82–99. Oxford: Oxford University Press.

Lesko, N. (ed.) 2000. *Masculinities at School*. London: Sage.

Lesthaeghe, R. 1995. 'The second demographic transition in Western countries: an interpretation'. In Mason, K. O. and Jensen, A.-M. (eds) *Gender and Family Change in Industrialized Countries*, pp. 17–62. Oxford: Clarendon Press.

Levin, I. 2004. 'Living apart together: a new family form', *Current Sociology* 52.2: 223–40.

Lewis, C., Papacosta, A. and Warin, J. 2002. *Cohabitation, Separation and Fatherhood*. York: Joseph Rowntree Foundation.

Lewis, J. 1992. *Women in Britain since 1945*. Oxford: Blackwell.

Lewis, J. 2001. *The End of Marriage? Individualism and Intimate Relations*. Cheltenham: Edward Elgar.

Lewis, J. and Maclean, M. 1997. 'Recent developments in family policy in the UK: the case of the 1996 Family Law Act'. In May, M., Brunsdon, E. and Craig, G. (eds) *Social Policy Review 9*, pp. 69–86. London: Social Policy Association.

Lewis, J., Clark, D. and Morgan, D. H .J. 1992. *'Whom God hath Joined Together': The Work of Marriage Guidance*. London: Routledge.

Lincoln, Y. S. and Guba, E. G. 1985. *Naturalistic Inquiry*. London: Sage.

Litva, A., Peggs, K. and Moon, G. 2001. 'The beauty of health: locating young women's health and appearance'. In Dyck, I., Davis Lewis, N. and McLafferty, S. (eds) *Geographies of Women's Health*, pp. 248–64. London: Routledge.

Lloyd, M. 1996. 'Feminism, aerobics and the politics of the body', *Body and Society* 2.2: 79–98.

Lloyd, M. 2005. *Beyond Identity Politics: Feminism, Power and Politics*. London: Sage.

Lopata, H. Z. 1980. 'The widowed family member'. In Datan, N. and Lohmann, N. (eds) *Transitions of Aging*, pp. 93–118. New York: Academic Press.

Lopata, H. Z. 1996. *Current Widowhood: Myths and Realities*. Thousand Oaks, CA: Sage.

Lupton, D. 1999. *Risk and Sociocultural Theory: New Directions and Perspectives*. Cambridge: Cambridge University Press.

Lutz, C. 1986. 'Emotion, thought and estrangement: emotion as a cultural category', *Cultural Anthropology* 1.3: 287–309.

Lye, D. N. and Waldron, I. 1997. 'Attitudes toward cohabitation, family and gender roles: relationships to values and political ideology', *Sociological Perspectives* 40.2: 199–225.

Macdonald, M. 2003. *Exploring Media Discourse*. London: Arnold.

Maclean, M. 1991. *Surviving Divorce: Women's Resources after Separation*. London: Macmillan.

Maclean, M. and Eekelaar, J. 1983. *Children and Divorce*. Oxford: SSRC/Centre for Socio-Legal Studies.

Maclean, M. and Eekelaar, J. 1997. *The Parental Obligation*. Oxford: Hart.

Manning, W. D. and Smock, P. J. 2005. 'Measuring and modeling cohabitation: new perspectives from qualitative data', *Journal of Marriage and Family* 67.4: 989–1002.

Mansbridge, J. 1992. 'On the relation of altruism and self-interest'. In Zey, M. (ed.) *Decision Making: Alternatives to Rational Choice Models*, pp. 112–28. Newbury Park, CA: Sage.

Manting, D. 1996. 'The changing meaning of cohabitation and marriage', *European Sociological Review* 12.1: 53–65.

Marsh, A. and Vegeris, S. 2004. *The British Lone Parent Cohort and their Children 1991 to 2001*. Department of Work and Pensions Research Report No. 209. Leeds: Corporate Document Services.

Mason, J. 1996. *Qualitative Researching*. London: Sage.

Mastekaasa, A. 1995. 'The subjective well-being of the previously married: the importance of unmarried cohabitation and time since widowhood or divorce', *Social Forces* 73.2: 665–92.

Mauthner, N. S. and Doucet, A. 2003. 'Reflexive accounts and accounts of reflexivity in qualitative data analysis', *Sociology* 37.3: 413–31.

McAllister, F. (ed.) 1995. *Marital Breakdown and the Health of the Nation* (2nd edition). London: One Plus One.

McKeever, M. and Wolfinger, N. H. 2001. 'Re-examining the economic costs of marital disruption for women', *Social Science Quarterly* 82.1: 202–17.

McRae, S. (ed.) 1999. *Changing Britain: Families and Households in the 1990s*. Oxford: Oxford University Press.

Melucci, A. 1996. *The Playing Self: Person and Meaning in the Planetary Society*. Cambridge: Cambridge University Press.

Merton, R. 1957. *Social Theory and Social Structure* (2nd edition). Glencoe, IL: Free Press.

Montgomery, M. J., Anderson, E. R., Hetherington, E. M. and Clingempeel, W. G. 1992. 'Patterns of courtship for remarriage: implications for child adjustment and parent–child relationships', *Journal of Marriage and the Family* 54.3: 686–98.

Morgan, D. H. J. 1985. *The Family, Politics and Social Theory*. London: Routledge & Kegan Paul.

Morgan, K. P. 2003. 'Women and the knife: cosmetic surgery and the colonization of women's bodies'. In Weitz, R. (ed.) *The Politics of Women's Bodies: Sexuality, Appearance and Behavior* (2nd edition), pp. 164–83. Oxford: Oxford University Press.

Mott, F. L. and Moore, S. F. 1983. 'The tempo of remarriage among young American women', *Journal of Marriage and the Family* 45.2: 427–35.

Munch, R. 1992. 'Rational choice theory: a critical assessment of its explanatory power'. In Coleman, J. S. and Fararo, T. J. (eds) *Rational Choice Theory: Advocacy and Critique*, pp. 137–60. Newbury Park, CA: Sage.

Murphy, M. and Wang, D. 1999. 'Forecasting British families into the twenty-first century'. In McRae, S. (ed.) *Changing Britain: Families and Households in the 1990s*, pp. 100–37. Oxford: Oxford University Press.

Nakonezny, P. A., Shull, R. D. and Rogers, J. L. 1995. 'The effect of no-fault divorce law on the divorce rate across 50 states and its relation to income, education and religiosity', *Journal of Marriage and the Family* 57.2: 477–88.

National Statistics Online. 2005. 'Fourth successive increase in UK [divorces]', http://www.statistics.gov.uk/CCI/nugget.asp?ID=170.

Neale, B. and Smart, C. 2002. 'Caring, earning and changing: parenthood and employment after divorce'. In Carling, A., Duncan, S. and Edwards, R. (eds) *Analysing Families: Morality and Rationality in Policy and Practice*, pp. 183–98. London: Routledge.

Newcomb, M. D. 1987. 'Cohabitation and marriage: a quest for independence and relatedness', *Applied Social Psychology Annual* 7: 128–56.

Ní Bhrolcháin, M. 1988. 'Changing partners: a longitudinal study of remarriage', *Population Trends* 53: 27–34.

Ní Bhrolcháin, M. 2005. 'The age difference at marriage in England and Wales: a century of patterns and trends', *Population Trends* 120: 7–14.

Nock, S. L. 1995. 'A comparison of marriages and cohabiting relationships', *Journal of Family Issues* 16.1: 53–76.

O'Brien, M. 1987. 'Patterns of kinship and friendship among lone fathers'. In Lewis, C. and O'Brien, M. (eds) *Reassessing Fatherhood: New Observations on Fathers and the Modern Family*, pp. 225–45. London: Sage.

O'Brien, M. and Shemilt, I. 2003. *Working Fathers: Earning and Caring*. London: Equal Opportunities Commission.

Okin, S. M. 1989. *Justice, Gender and the Family*. New York: Basic Books.

ONS [Office for National Statistics] 2002. *Living in Britain: Results from the 2001 General Household Survey*. London: The Stationery Office.

ONS [Office for National Statistics] 2003a. 'In brief', *Population Trends* 113: 2–5.

ONS [Office for National Statistics, Social Survey Division] 2003b. *ONS Omnibus Survey, April 2002* [computer file]. Colchester: UK Data Archive [distributor], SN: 4702.

ONS [Office for National Statistics] 2005. *Focus on Families: Summary Report*. London: Office for National Statistics.

ONS [Office for National Statistics] 2006a. 'First marriages: age and sex (England and Wales)', *Population Trends* 124: 53.

ONS [Office for National Statistics, Social Survey Division]. 2006b. *General Household Survey, 2001–2002* [computer file] (4th edition). Colchester: UK Data Archive [distributor], SN: 4646.

ONS [Office for National Statistics] 2006c. 'Remarriages: age, sex, and previous marital status (England and Wales)', *Population Trends* 124: 54.

Oppenheimer, V. K. 1988. 'A theory of marriage timing', *American Journal of Sociology* 94.3: 563–91.

Payne, J. and Range, M. 1998. *Lone Parents' Lives: An Analysis of Partnership, Fertility, Employment and Housing Histories in the 1958 British Birth Cohort*. Department of Social Security Research Report No. 78. London: Stationery Office.

Pease, B. 2000. *Recreating Men: Postmodern Masculinity Politics*. London: Sage.

Peggs, K. 1995. 'Women and pensions'. PhD thesis. University of Surrey.

Peggs, K. 2000. 'Which pension? Women, risk and pension choice', *Sociological Review* 48.3: 249–364.

Peggs, K. and Lampard, R. 2000. '(Ir)rational choice: a multidimensional approach to choice and constraint in decisions about marriage, divorce and remarriage'. In Archer, M. S. and Tritter, J. Q. (eds) *Rational Choice Theory: Resisting Colonisation*, pp. 93–110. London: Routledge.

Perry, A., Douglas, G., Murch, M., Bader, K. and Borkowski, M. 2000. *How Parents Cope Financially on Marriage Breakdown*. London: Family Policy Studies Centre.

Pevalin, D. J. and Ermisch, J. 2004. 'Cohabiting unions, repartnering and mental health', *Psychological Medicine* 34.8: 1553–59.

Phillips, R. 1988. *Putting Asunder: A History of Divorce in Western Society*. Cambridge: Cambridge University Press.

Pointon, S. 1997. 'Myths and negative stereotypes about sexuality in older people', *Generations Review* 7: 6–8.

Pole, C. J. and Lampard, R. 2001. *Practical Social Investigation: Qualitative and Quantitative Methods in Social Research*. Harlow: Prentice Hall (Pearson Education).

Power, E. M. 2005. 'The unfreedom of being other: Canadian lone mothers' experiences of poverty and "life on the cheque" ', *Sociology* 39.4: 643–60.

Rajulton, F. and Burch, T. K. 1992. *A Behavioural Analysis of Remarriage: Motivation and Market Influences*. Discussion Paper 92–8, Population Studies Center, University of Western Ontario.

Raley, R. K. and Bratter, J. 2004. 'Not even if you were the last person on earth! How marital search constraints affect the likelihood of marriage', *Journal of Family Issues* 25.2: 167–81.

Ribbens, J. 1994. *Mothers and Their Children: A Feminist Sociology of Childrearing*. Thousand Oaks, CA: Sage.

Ribbens McCarthy, J., Edwards, R. and Gillies, V. 2000. 'Moral tales of the child and the adult: narratives of contemporary family lives under changing circumstances', *Sociology* 34.4: 785–803.

Rich, A. 1980. 'Compulsory heterosexuality and lesbian existence', *Signs: Journal of Women in Culture and Society* 5.4: 631–60.

Richards, L. N. 1989. 'The precarious survival and hard-won satisfactions of white single-parent families', *Family Relations* 38.4: 396–403.

Riessman, C. K. 1990. *Divorce Talk: Women and Men Make Sense of Personal Relationships*. London: Rutgers University Press.

Riessman, C. K. 1993. *Narrative Analysis*. London: Sage.

Riessman, C. K. 2004. 'Narrative analysis' and 'Narrative interviewing'. In Lewis-Beck, M. S., Bryman, A. and Liao, T. F. (eds) *The Sage Encyclopedia of Social Science Research Methods*, pp. 705–10. London: Sage.

Rindfuss, R. R. and Vandenheuvel, A. 1990. 'Cohabitation: a precursor to marriage or an alternative to being single?' *Population and Development Review* 16.4: 703–26.

Riseman, B. J. 1998. *Gender Vertigo: American Families in Transition*. New Haven, CT: Yale University Press.

Rodger, J. 1996. *Family Life and Social Control: A Sociological Perspective*. Basingstoke: Macmillan.

Rodgers, R. H. and Conrad, L. M. 1986. 'Courtship for remarriage: influences on family reorganization after divorce', *Journal of Marriage and the Family* 48.4: 767–75.

Rose, D. and Pevalin, D. 2003. *A Researcher's Guide to the National Statistics Socio-economic Classification*. London: Sage.

Rowlingson, K. and McKay, S. 1998. *The Growth of Lone Parenthood: Diversity and Dynamics*. London: Policy Studies Institute.

Sakraida, T. J. 2005. 'Common themes in the divorce transition experience of midlife women', *Journal of Divorce and Remarriage* 43.1-2: 69–88.

Sarsby, J. 1983. *Romantic Love and Society: Its Place in the Modern World*. Harmondsworth: Penguin.

Sartre, J. 1963. *Sketch for a Theory of Emotions*. London: Methuen.

Saul, J. M. 2003. *Feminism: Issues and Arguments*. Oxford: Oxford University Press.

Sautter, J., Tippett, R. and Morgan, S. P. 2006. 'Check out my profile: demographic characteristics of the internet dating population'. Paper presented at the 69th Annual Meeting of the Southern Sociological Society, New Orleans, 22–25 March.

Scheff, T. J. 1992. 'Rationality and emotion: homage to Norbert Elias'. In Coleman, J. S. and Fararo, T. J. (eds) *Rational Choice Theory: Advocacy and Critique*, pp. 101–19. Newbury Park, CA: Sage.

Schneller, D. P. and Arditti, J. A. 2004. 'After the breakup: interpreting divorce and rethinking intimacy', *Journal of Divorce and Remarriage* 42.1/2: 1–37.

Scott, J. 1999. 'Family change: revolution or backlash in attitudes?' In McRae, S. (ed.) *Changing Britain: Families and Households in the 1990s*, pp. 68–99. Oxford: Oxford University Press.

Scott, S., Jackson, S. and Backett-Milburn, K. 1998. 'Swings and roundabouts: risk anxiety and the everyday worlds of children', *Sociology* 32.4: 689–705.

Seligman, A. B. 1997. *The Problem of Trust*, Princeton, NJ: Princeton University Press.

Shaw, C. and Haskey, J. 1999. 'New estimates and projections of the population cohabiting in England and Wales', *Population Trends* 95: 7–17.

Shaw, S. 1991. 'The conflicting experiences of lone parenthood'. In Hardey, M. and Crow, G. (eds) *Lone Parenthood: Coping with Constraints and Making Opportunities*, pp. 143–55. London: Harvester Wheatsheaf.

Shaw, S. 1994. 'Women and lone parenthood: an account of the experiences and feelings of divorced and separated lone mothers'. Unpublished PhD thesis. Sheffield: University of Sheffield.

Shilling, C. 1993. *The Body and Social Theory*. London: Sage.

Simon, H. A. 1955. 'A behavioural model of rational choice', *Quarterly Journal of Economics* 69: 99–118.

Simon, H. A. and Associates. 1992. 'Decision-making and problem-solving'. In Zey, M. (ed.) *Decision-Making: Alternatives to Rational Choice Models*, pp. 32–53. Newbury Park, CA: Sage.

Simon, R.W. 2002. 'Revisiting the relationships among gender, marital status, and mental health', *American Journal of Sociology* 107.4: 1065–96.

Simpson, B. 1998. *Changing Families: An Ethnographic Approach to Divorce and Separation*. Oxford: Berg.

Simpson, B. 1999. 'Nuclear fallout: divorce, kinship and the insecurities of contemporary family life'. In Vail, J., Wheelock, J. and Hill, M. (eds) *Insecure Times: Living with Insecurity in Modern Society*, pp. 119–34. London: Routledge.

Slater, D. 1997. *Consumer Culture and Modernity*. Cambridge: Polity.

Smart, C. 2005. 'Textures of family life: further thoughts on change and commitment', *Journal of Social Policy* 34.4: 541–56.

Smart, C. 2006. 'Children's narratives of post-divorce family life: from individual experience to an ethical disposition', *Sociological Review* 54.1: 155–70.

Smart, C. and Neale, B. 1999. *Family Fragments?* Cambridge: Polity.

Smart, C. and Stevens, P. 2000. *Cohabitation Breakdown*. London: Family Policy Studies Centre.

Smart, C., Neale, B. and Wade, A. 2001. *The Changing Experience of Childhood: Families and Divorce*. Cambridge: Polity.

Smith, K. R., Zick, C. D. and Duncan. G. J. 1991. 'Remarriage patterns among recent widows and widowers', *Demography* 28.3: 361–74.

Smock, P. J. 2000. 'Cohabitation in the United States: an appraisal of research themes, findings, and implications', *Annual Review of Sociology* 26: 1–20.

Spanier, G. and Thompson, L. 1987. *Parting: the Aftermath of Separation and Divorce* (updated edition). Beverly Hills, CA: Sage.

Spanier, G. B. and Furstenberg, F. F. 1982. 'Remarriage after divorce: a longitudinal analysis of well-being', *Journal of Marriage and the Family* 44.3: 709–20.

Stacey, J. 1996. *In the Name of the Family*. Boston, MA: Beacon Press.

Stacey, J. 1998. *Brave New Families: Stories of Domestic Upheaval in Late-Twentieth-Century America*. Berkeley, CA: University of California Press.

Stein, P. J. (ed.) 1981. *Single Life: Unmarried Adults in Social Context*. New York: St. Martin's Press.

Stewart, S. D., Manning, W. D. and Smock, P. J. 2003. 'Union formation among men in the US: does having prior children matter?' *Journal of Marriage and Family* 65.1: 90–104.

Stone, L. 1990. *Road to Divorce: England 1530–1987*. Oxford: Oxford University Press.

Strohschein, L., McDonough, P., Monette, G., and Shao, Q. 2005. 'Marital transition and mental health: are there gender differences in the short-term effects of marital status change?' *Social Science and Medicine* 61.11: 2293–2303.

Sugden, R. 1998. 'Conventions'. In Newman, P. (ed.) *The New Palgrave Dictionary of Economics and Law* (Volume 1). London: Macmillan.

Sullivan, D. A. 2001. *Cosmetic Surgery: The Cutting Edge of Commercial Medicine in America*. New Brunswick, NJ: Rutgers University Press.

Sullivan, O. 2000. 'The division of domestic labour: twenty years of change?' *Sociology* 34.3: 437–56.

Sutphin, S. T. 2006. 'Explaining the effect of physical attractiveness versus race in socially acceptable romantic relationships in the South'. Paper presented at the 69th Annual Meeting of the Southern Sociological Society, New Orleans, 22–25 March.

Sweeney, M. M. 1997. 'Remarriage of women and men after divorce: the roles of socio-economic prospects', *Journal of Family Issues* 18.5: 479–502.

Taylor, C. 1989. *Sources of the Self: The Making of the Modern Identity*. Cambridge, MA: Harvard University Press.

Thomas, C. 1997. 'The baby and the bathwater: disabled women and motherhood in social context', *Sociology of Health and Illness* 19.5: 622–43.

Thompson, S. 1989. 'Search for tomorrow: on feminism and the reconstruction of teen romance'. In Vance, C. S. (ed.) *Pleasure and Danger: Exploring Female Sexuality*, pp. 350–84. London: Pandora.

Thomson, R., Bell, R., Holland, J., Henderson, S., McGrellis, S. and Sharpe, S. 2002. 'Critical moments: choice, change and opportunity in young people's narratives of transition', *Sociology* 36.2: 335–54.

Thuen, F. 2000. 'Psychiatric symptoms and perceived need for psychiatric care after divorce', *Journal of Divorce and Remarriage* 34.1: 61–76.

Tulloch, J. and Lupton, D. 2003. *Risk and Everyday Life*. London: Sage.

Turner, B. S. 1995. 'Ageing and identity'. In Featherstone, M. and Wernick, A. (eds) *Images of Ageing*, pp. 245–60. London: Routledge.

Uunk, W. 2004. 'The economic consequences of divorce for women in the European Union: the impact of welfare state arrangements', *European Journal of Population* 20.3: 251–85.

van den Hoonaard, D. K. 2001. *The Widowed Self: The Older Woman's Journey though Widowhood*. Waterloo, Ontario: Wilfrid Laurier University Press.

Vaughan, D. 1987. *Uncoupling: How and Why Relationships Come Apart*. London: Methuen.

Voas, D. and Crockett, A. 2005. 'Religion in Britain: neither believing nor belonging', *Sociology* 39.1: 11–28.

Wade, T. J. and Pevalin, D. J. 2004. 'Marital transitions and mental health', *Journal of Health and Social Behavior* 45.2: 155–70.

Waites, M. 2003. 'Equality at last? Homosexuality, heterosexuality and the age of consent in the United Kingdom', *Sociology* 37.4: 637–55.

Walker, J. 2001. *Information Meetings and Associated Provisions within the Family Law Act 1996: Key Findings from the Research*. London: Lord Chancellor's Department.

Waller, M. R. and McLanahan, S. S. 2005. '"His" and "her" marriage expectations: determinants and consequences', *Journal of Marriage and Family* 67.1: 53–67.

Wallerstein, J. and Blakeslee, S. 1989. *Second Chances: Men, Women and Children a Decade after Divorce*. London: Bantam.

Wallerstein, J. and Kelly, J. 1980. *Surviving the Breakup: How Children and Parents Cope with Divorce*. London: Grant Macintyre.

Wang, H. Y. and Amato, P. R. 2000. 'Predictors of divorce adjustment: stressors, resources, and definitions', *Journal of Marriage and the Family* 62.3: 655–68.

Warde, A. 1997. *Consumption, Food and Taste: Culinary Antinomies and Commodity Culture*. London: Sage.

Watson, N., McKie, L., Hughes, B., Hopkins, D. and Gregory, S. 2004. '(Inter) Dependence, needs and care: the potential for disability and feminist theorists to develop an emancipatory model', *Sociology* 38.2: 331–50.

Weber, M. [1910] 1978. *Economy and Society*. Berkeley, CA: University of California.

Weber, M. 1946. *From Max Weber: Essays in Sociology*. New York: Oxford University Press.

Weitz, R. 2003. 'Women and their hair: seeking power through resistance and accommodation'. In Weitz, R. (ed.) *The Politics of Women's Bodies: Sexuality, Appearance and Behavior* (2nd edition), pp. 135–51. Oxford: Oxford University Press.

Weitzman, L. J. 1985. *The Divorce Revolution*. New York: Free Press.

White, L. K. and Booth, A. 1985. 'The quality and stability of remarriage: the role of children', *American Sociological Review* 50.5: 689–98.

Wilcox, P. 2000. 'Lone motherhood: the impact on living standards of leaving a violent relationship', *Social Policy and Administration* 34.2: 176–90.

Wilcox, P. 2006. *Surviving Domestic Violence: Gender, Power and Agency*. London: Palgrave.

Wilkinson, I. 2004. *Suffering: A Sociological Introduction*. Cambridge: Polity Press.

Willer, D. 1992. 'The principles of rational choice and the problem of a satisfactory theory'. In Coleman, J. S. and Fararo, T. J. (eds) *Rational Choice Theory: Advocacy and Critique*, pp. 49–78. Newbury Park, CA: Sage.

Williams, S. J. 1998. 'Modernity and the emotions: corporeal reflections on the irrational', *Sociology* 32.4: 747–69.

Williams, S. J. and Bendelow, G. 1998. 'Introduction: emotions and social life: mapping the sociological terrain'. In Bendelow, G. and Williams, S.J. (eds) *Emotions in Social Life: Critical Themes and Contemporary Issues*, pp. xv–xxx. London: Routledge.

Willitts, M., Benzeval, M. and Stansfeld, S. 2004. 'Partnership history and mental health over time', *Journal of Epidemiology and Community Health* 58.1: 53–8.

Windebank, J. 2001. 'Dual-earner couples in Britain and France: gender divisions of domestic labour and parenting work in different welfare states', *Work, Employment and Society* 15.2: 269–90.

Wright, G. C. and Stetson, D. M. 1978. 'The impact of no-fault divorce law reform on divorce in American states', *Journal of Marriage and the Family* 40.3: 575–80.

Wu, Z. and Balakrishnan, T. R. 1994. 'Cohabitation after marital disruption in Canada', *Journal of Marriage and the Family* 56.3: 723–34.

Wu, Z. and Schimmele, C. M. 2005. 'Repartnering after first union disruption', *Journal of Marriage and Family* 67.1: 27–36.

Wynne, B. 1996. 'May the sheep safely graze? A reflexive view of the expert/lay knowledge divide'. In Lash, S., Szerszynski, B. and Wynne, B. (eds) *Risk, Environment and Modernity: Towards and New Ecology*, pp. 44–83. London: Sage.

Xu, X., Hudspeth, C. D. and Bartowski, J. P. 2006. 'The role of cohabitation in remarriage', *Journal of Marriage and Family* 68.2: 261–74.

Yngvesson, B. and Mahoney, M. A. 2000 ' "As one should, ought and wants to be". Belonging and authenticity narratives', *Theory, Culture and Society* 7.6: 77–110.

Yodanis, C. 2005. 'Divorce culture and marital gender equality: a cross-national study', *Gender and Society* 19.5: 644–59.

Zafirovski, M. 1999. 'What is really rational choice? Beyond the utilitarian concept of rationality', *Current Sociology* 47.1: 47–113.

Zey, M. 1992. 'Criticisms of rational choice models'. In Zey, M. (ed.) *Decision Making: Alternatives to Rational Choice Models*, pp. 9–31. Newbury Park, CA: Sage.

Zey, M. 1998. *Rational Choice Theory and Organizational Theory: A Critique*. Thousand Oaks, CA: Sage.

Zick, C. D. and Smith, K. R. 1988. 'Recent widowhood, remarriage and changes in economic well-being', *Journal of Marriage and the Family* 50.1: 233–44.

Zick, C. D. and Smith, K. R. 1991. 'Marital transitions, poverty, and gender differences in mortality', *Journal of Marriage and the Family* 53.2: 327–36.

Name Index

Subject Index